SHAME AND GLORY

OF THE INTELLECTUALS

By PETER VIERECK

Shame and Glory of the Intellectuals: Babbitt Jr. vs. the Rediscovery of Values. Published by Beacon Press, Boston, 1953.

The First Morning: New Poems. Published by Charles Scribner's Sons, N. Y., 1952.

Strike Through the Mask: New Lyrical Poems. Published by Charles Scribner's Sons, N. Y., 1950.

Terror and Decorum. Published by Charles Scribner's Sons, N. Y., 1948. A book of lyrics and philosophical poems, 1940-48. Pulitzer Prize, 1949.

Conservatism Revisited: The Revolt Against Revolt. Published by Charles Scribner's Sons, N. Y., 1949. British edition by John Lehmann, Ltd., London, 1950.

Who Killed the Universe? A satirical novelette published in *New Directions Ten,* New Directions Press, N. Y., 1948.

Metapolitics: From the Romantics to Hitler. A historical and psychological analysis of modern Germany. Published by Alfred A. Knopf, N. Y., 1941. Swedish edition, 1942, Italian edition, 1948.

Never Forget This: The Nazi Mind Yesterday and Today. To be published by Beacon Press, 1953 (title tentative).

SHAME AND GLORY
OF THE INTELLECTUALS

Babbitt Jr. vs. the Rediscovery of Values

by

PETER VIERECK

THE BEACON PRESS · BOSTON

Copyright 1953

THE BEACON PRESS

Published February, 1953
Second Printing, April, 1953

Library of Congress Catalog Card Number: 52-13751
Printed in U.S.A.

THIS BOOK IS DEDICATED TO

WINSTON CHURCHILL

whose career as great liberal social reformer in the 1900's, as opponent of an appeasing and commercialized Chamberlain-conservatism in the 1930's, and as unabashed "warmonger" of the 1940's against both Nazism and Communism has made him the inspiration and world-symbol of the independent new conservatism now being born out of the agony of the 1950's.

*   *   *   *

Telegram of April, 1944, to the British ambassador in Greece: "You speak of living on the lid of a volcano. Wherever else do you expect to live in times like these?"

—WINSTON CHURCHILL

Contents

Acknowledgments

Nearly all of the basic chapters were written only for this book; they have never before appeared in print (except for brief extracts). Others have appeared in the following periodicals, to which acknowledgment is herewith gratefully made:

American Historical Review
American Mercury
American Quarterly
Antioch Review
Arizona Quarterly
Atlantic Monthly
Bulletin of the Institute of Social Studies
The Catholic World
Commentary
Commonweal
Confluence
Current History
Dalhousie Review (Canada)
Fortune
Freedom and Union (Washington, D.C.)
Georgia Review
Harper's Magazine
Harvard Alumni Bulletin
Hopkins Review
Journal of the History of Ideas

National Labor Journal (Canada)
The New Leader
New York Herald Tribune
The New York Times Book Review
The News-Herald (Marion, Indiana)
Political Science Quarterly
The Progressive (Madison, Wis.)
Public Affairs (Canada)
The Reporter
Review of Politics
Rheinische Merkur
The Russian Review
The Saturday Evening Post
Saturday Review
Shih Pao Tsa Chi (Free China)
Southwest Review
This Week Magazine
Thought (Fordham University)
United Nations World
William and Mary Quarterly
World Liberalism (London)

I am grateful to The Macmillan Company for letting me quote excerpts from their book *The Collected Poems of W. B. Yeats*. George Santayana's "Ode to the Mediterranean," from *Poems* (copyright 1923 by Charles Scribner's Sons), is reprinted by courtesy of the publishers.

The Rediscovery of Values

"A slap in the face against 90 per cent of your kind of readers," comments the first colleague to read this manuscript; "all will agree with some of it; none will stomach much of it." Be that as it may, there is a world problem more urgent than this local American problem of standardized thinking of right and left. What interests the author more urgently is that the "wave of the future," by now a tidal wave blood-red and a mile high, is pounding down in country after country every single value here affirmed.

So be it. "Minute your gesture, but it must be made."

After so total a military victory in 1945, who would have thought that a beleaguered and ever-shrinking world of freedom would soon have to repeat MacNeice's desperate toast of 1936 all over again?

> Our prerogatives as men
> Will be cancelled who knows when;
> Still I drink your health before
> The gun-butt raps upon the door.

But from the 1940 miracle of Britain we have learnt how premature defeatism can be. Defeatism would itself become a cause of defeat. On the other hand: "While three men hold together, the kingdoms are less by three" — the tidal wave is less by three drops.

And bitterness is never motive enough. By itself, the spectacle of intellectual disgrace, rampant and swaggering, provides a motive too negative, inhuman, unsweet. Without the motive of a loftier hour and higher values to turn to, nobody writes gracefully against disgrace, against our devaluation of values. The inspiration throughout this book, the consoling thought that higher values than mammon and expediency can exalt today's struggle for freedom, has been the anti-Nazi resistance movement of 1939-45.

That movement is eternalized by the Battle of Britain and by Winston Churchill. Hence to him the dedication.

The movement is equally eternalized by the continental undergrounds, their sacrifice of life and property to nonmaterial values. We need their ideals and magnanimity more than ever today, if the renewed struggle against brutality is to be fructifying instead of sterile. No book of mere ink can presumptuously hope to be even partly worthy of their blood-sacrifices. But it can at least try to serve their spirit, in a groping and perhaps mistaken fashion. The least unserious of these pages were written with certain war experiences of 1939-45 very concretely in mind. Such pages were goaded into thought by American forgetfulness of the lives sacrificed purposefully and not in vain. Today Americans cannot afford to forget the earlier of our two resistances to totalitarianism.

So may that past ordeal be our future courage. So may a memory become a hope. So may the sunrise of the rediscovery of values dispel that planet-darkening shadow in which Kremlin and Berchtesgaden merge as one.

Then for a second time in one century and by a reversal of astronomy, the sun will rise in the west.

PETER VIERECK

Crass Times Redeemed by Dignity of Souls

(Credo for these pages)

The music of the dignity of souls
Molds every note I hum and hope to write.
I long to tell the Prince of aureoles —
Groper-in-clay and breather-into-dolls,
Kindler of suns, and chord that spans our poles —
What goading reverence His tunes incite.
Then lips whose only sacrament is speech,
Sing Him the way the old unbaptized night
Dreads and
        needs and
                lacks and
                        loves the light.
May yet when sleeked with poise I overreach,
When that high ripening slowness I impeach,
Awe of that music jolt me home contrite:

O harshness of the dignity of souls.

ii

The tenderness of dignity of souls
Sweetens our cheated gusto and consoles.
It shades love's lidless eyes like parasols
And tames the earthquake licking at our soles.
Re-tunes the tensions of the flesh we wear.
Forgives the dissonance our triumphs blare.
And maps the burrows of heart's buried lair
Where furtive furry Wishes hide like moles.
O hear the kind voice, hear it everywhere
(It sings, it sings, it conjures and cajoles)
Prompting us shyly in our half-learnt rôles.
It sprouts the great chromatic vine that lolls
In small black petals on our music scrolls
(It flares, it flowers — it quickens yet controls).
It teaches dance-steps to this uncouth bear
Who hops and stumbles in our skin and howls.

The weight that tortures diamonds out of coals
Is lighter than the skimming hooves of foals

Compared to one old heaviness our souls
Hoist daily, each alone, and cannot share:
To-be-awake, to sense, to-be-aware.
Then even the dusty dreams that clog our skulls,
The rant and thunder of the storm we are,
The sunny silences our prophets hear,
The rainbow of the oil upon the shoals,
The crimes and Christmases of creature-lives,
And all pride's barefoot tarantelle on knives
Are but man's search for dignity of souls.

iii

The searcher for the market price of souls,
Seth the Accuser with the donkey head,[1]
Negation's oldest god, still duns the dead
For these same feathery Egyptian tolls —
But now, bland haggler, deprecates his quest
(The devil proving "devils can't exist").
His boutonnière is a chic asphodel;
He makes Id's whirlpool seem a wishing-well,
Reflecting crowns to outstretched beggar-bowls.
No horns, no claws; that cheap exotic phase
Belonged to his first, gauche, bohemian days.
The nice, the wholesome, and the commonplace
Are Trilbys he manipulates in jest
Till their dear wheedlings subtly swerve our goals: —

MASK ONE: an honest, cleancut, sporting face
Such as will cheer for wrong with righteous grace,
Hiking in shorts through tyranny's Tyrols.
MASK TWO: a round and basking babyface
Distracts our souls, so archly does it beg,
Upblinking like a peevish pink poached-egg.
THIRD MASK: his hide-out is the ageing face
That waits for youth in mirrors like an ambush
And lives our ardent "when"s as yawning "if"s
And, puffing corncobs, drawls between two whiffs,
"Why stick your neck out? Nonsense never pays!"
And rips our aspirations like a thornbush.
Unmasked on tombs by shrieking hieroglyphs,
Seth was his true — his hungry — donkey face,
Nibbling our souls as if their groans were grass,
This grazer on the dignity of souls.

---

[1] The donkey god named Seth or Set on the tombs in Egypt is history's earliest recorded name for evil and negation. Souls were his fodder.

iv

He, the huge bridegroom of all servile souls,
Swaps little jokes with little envious trolls
To snuff the radiance of tragedy
And vend us Pleasure, which turns out to be
An optimistic mechanized despair.
O hear the glib voice, hear it everywhere
(It shouts, it shouts, it cadges and cajoles).
It feeds the earthquake fawning at our soles.
It hands out free omnipotence as doles.
Replaces tall towns with still deeper holes.
To make us God, needs just one hair's-breadth more.

The Agents said, "All ungregarious souls
Are priggish outlaws, stubborn Seminoles."
In Confidential Chats and Friendly Strolls,
They warned us each:
                    "You are alone, you are
The last, you are the lost — O flee — you are
The straggling warrior of the lost last war
To vindicate the dignity of souls."

v

We answered: "Tell the Prince who brays at souls,
Your long-eared Lord with thornless crowns to sell,
That all his halos have a sulphur smell;
And though they flash like flying orioles
Or lure like bonfires on mountain knolls,
These gaudy girandoles are
                           blackness still."

Torn out of blackness, soon to choke on black,
Leaning on nothingness before and back,
Tight-lashed to lies by veins and nerves and Will,
My life is darkness. Yet I live to tell
How shimmering, how gaily freedom prowls
In flesh that guards its consciousness of souls.
Then love that gives and gives and loves the more,
Frees us the way the good and daily light
Heals and
          shreds and
                     liberates the night.

Though blinking — burning — shivering in the white
Blaze that each dust-heap blest with speech extols,
May every dark and kindled "I" revere
In every "you" that selfsame fire-core,
In every soul the soul of all our souls.

From Peter Viereck, *Terror and Decorum* (New York: Charles Scribner's
Sons, 1948).

SHAME AND GLORY
OF THE INTELLECTUALS

Specter and Halos:
The Fundamental Assumptions

"Do not lose heart; we are all here."
HERMANN BROCH

A SPECTER HAUNTS THE COMMUNISTS

The typical book titles of our age are not *The Age of Reason* (typical eighteenth-century title of Paine) but *The Age of Longing, The Age of Anxiety, The Politics of Murder, The Strategy of Terror, The Age of Terror*. Such representative book titles, with their mood of 1983 and eleven months, could only have been written in the century of which Nietzsche had prophesied: "With every growth in man's stature, he grows in depth and terribleness too. Where are the Vandals of the twentieth century?"

Well, here they are. The whole intellectual life of the eighteenth-century "age of reason" was aroused to white-hot indignation over one individual miscarriage of justice: the famous Calas case. Yet in our "age of terror," the mass-murder of millions in Hitler's and Stalin's slave camps was long met with indifference and even appeasement. Why? The communazi "Vandals of the twentieth century" have emerged from both socialist and capitalist economic systems. Therefore, the "why" is found not in economics but in values, in our lack of ethical traffic lights.

Nietzsche had hoped for "a transvaluation of values." This was to lead "beyond good and evil." Instead, our devaluation of values is beneath good and evil.

3

Once man was considered God's image. Today he degenerates into mass-man. Then into ape. Then into a jungle beast of prey. Finally into a mere material object, from whose lard despots make soap and from whose skin the mistresses of despots make lampshades.

The way back to human dignity is for all creeds, right or left, monarchist or republican, capitalist or socialist, to treat man as an end, not a means. Man must be treated as a moral subject to revere individually, not a material object to push around in impersonal blueprints. Conservatives, liberals, parliamentary monarchists, parliamentary republicans, democratic capitalists, democratic socialists: all have in common certain values of humaneness and honest thinking. This is not true of the communazis. They — I refer to the rulers, not to their slaves — are not interested in humaneness and honest thinking to start with. They are howling in the savage outer darkness, beyond the metaphoric Roman *limes* of civilized humanity.

One relativist kind of liberal "knows the price of everything and the *value* of nothing." The function of humanistic conservatism in philosophy and in literature, a function from which political action follows merely as secondary, is the rediscovery of the values of western man. I can imagine a sarcastic liberal replying: "Your kind of conservative knows the value of everything and the realistic market price of nothing."

But have we not made a mess of reality by being too realistic? This is a plea for the material necessity of more idealism, for the economic necessity of more than economics, and for a road back from *Realpolitik* and brutalization.

My mistake in past books and essays: too much fuss about labels. Most labels represent oversimplified half-truths that misunderstand each other. Distinctions between labels and -isms are real enough when properly defined. I continue to stress their importance. But I have now learnt to place greater stress on *what kind of* conservative, liberal, capitalist, or socialist you are. Freedom depends on the means you seek it with. This is never realized by the impatient, monomaniac partisans of any one of the above -isms.

The most effective single piece of revolutionary propaganda is the *Communist Manifesto* of 1848 by Marx and Engels. Its dramatic opening and closing paragraphs (capital letters and all) are today recited religiously by millions in Europe and Asia:

A specter haunts Europe — the specter of communism. All the powers of old Europe have entered into a holy alliance in order to lay this specter: pope and tsar; Metternich and Guizot; French radicals and German police.

. . . . Let the ruling classes tremble at the prospect of a communist revolution. Proletarians have nothing to lose but their chains. They have a world to win.

PROLETARIANS OF ALL LANDS, UNITE!

Several things have happened since 1848. Himmler has happened, and the crematories. Korea has happened, and the misery of the forced-labor camps at Karaganda. As a direct result of these happenings, mankind is beginning to make a rediscovery. The rediscovery involves *three questions:* Do you work for your economic objectives (no matter which ones)

(1)   with ethical self-restraint?
(2)   within a framework of equitable universal values?
(3)   with rigorous intellectual honesty?

A specter — here is freedom's Anti-Communist Manifesto to answer 1848 — a specter haunts the Communists. The specter is mankind's rediscovery that these three questions *matter*. All the powers of left and right totalitarianism have entered into an unholy alliance in order to lay the specter: Commissar and Fuehrer; Mao and Perón; French Communists and German neo-Nazis. . . . Let the ruling secret police tremble at the prospect of an anti-communist revolution. Slave laborers have nothing to lose but their barbed wire. They have their soul to win back, sweeter than conquest of a world. HUMAN BEINGS OF ALL CLASSES, UNITE!

ASSUMPTIONS

This book makes four assumptions. If even one of the four is wrong, then the argument that follows is wrong. If they are acceptable to the reader, then what follows follows. At least it would seem to follow in general logic, even though it may err in particular details. The four assumptions:

(1) The plain duty of every citizen, including the most ivory-tower intellectual, is to fight the totalitarian evil.

(2) The contemporary form taken by the totalitarian evil (now that its Nazi form has at least momentarily had its fangs drawn) is, above all, communism.

(3) The glory of twentieth-century liberal intellectuals is the vigor with which they took the only possible moral position towards the Nazi threat, a position betrayed by the appeasement policies of the wrong kind of anti-communists, conservatives, and capitalists.

(4) The shame of twentieth-century liberal intellectuals is their failure to expose and fight Stalinist totalitarianism with exactly the same vigor they showed against its brown-shirted version.

That American thought is getting too standardized is by now a standard observation. One qualification: often this observation is used indirectly, by men too clever to attack anti-communism directly, in order to discredit — as "standardizing" — anybody who talks back a little too indiscreetly in free debate against fellow-traveler attitudes.

Provided you keep that important qualification in mind, the dangerous increase in standardizing is undeniable. Its cause is not the present lawful prosecution of the lawbreaking members of the conspiratorial CP. The cause in part is the mechanizing trend of a mass society, with mass production of thought capsules. This being so, an independent-minded protest against standardized thinking should start first of all against the one group that ought to know better. Ought to know better because by education they at least — namely the liberal intellectuals — are relatively free from the mass magazines and mass movies and mass kultcher. To re-examine their unconscious standardizing should not be construed as "attacking" liberal intellectuals. On the contrary, to scrape the barnacles off an excellent but aging boat is never considered an attack on it.

Except by the barnacles.

Behind all criticisms of the new liberal standardizers, my first motive is the imperative that once again the intellectual be entitled to say, "I wear no man's livery." These five words were once the glory of the intellectual; they are part of what is meant by "glory" on the title page. Has the slot machine banality of

American and European thought gone too far to let the die-hards of integrity rescue and re-enthrone that exiled glory?

There is a difference between the banality-machine of the old conservatives and that of the new liberals: the latter is more coy and concealed. And therefore more insidious. And therefore more tempting for those intellectual circles that would never be tempted in the first place by the rusty, creaking old conservative slot machine. How many of our headlined Great Liberal Minds are able to say — without an unconscious mendacity so pretentiously fatheaded as to make angels weep — are able to say:

"I wear no man's livery."

TOWARDS A NEW DISSENT

To outlaw the military conspiracy known as communism does not mean to deny the obvious fact that a free society needs dissent. Independent eccentric thinkers and challengers will be needed all the more now that our society is becoming more conscious of being semi-closed rather than wide-open. Without the eccentrics and challengers, our art and thought would grow stale on us. But is the left correct in assuming that all this indispensable dissent comes only or mainly from the left?

On the contrary — in American and European intellectual life today, the most independent and fruitful and challenging dissent comes from conservatives and even from ornery, crotchety reactionaries. The latter provide as stimulating a challenge to blandness and glibness as the ornery, crotchety radicals used to do back in the Coolidge era, before the new orthodoxy of progressivism. Time is a taxidermist — he makes rebels stuffy. Business bossed the Coolidge era — and what were Big Labor bosses but the Wall Street of the New Deal era now ending?

In the coming decades, a new conservative dissent can show our Jeffersonians and Jacksonians, in a spirit of friendly interchange of ideas, what America can learn from neglected independent conservatives like John Adams, Calhoun, Randolph of Roanoke, and that fabulous Burkean Yankee, Rufus Choate (Senator from Massachusetts, 1841-45). Analogously in England, a new conservative dissent can show Laborites and ad-

mirers of Gladstonian liberalism what they can learn from
Coleridge, Burke, Disraeli, Lord Randolph Churchill, and his son.
Above all from Coleridge. His helter-skelter jottings and memos
include the profoundest political and social insights of the last
two centuries, more profound than Rousseau, Voltaire, Karl
Marx, and Adam Smith. And on the European continent, a new
conservative dissent can show worshipers of the liberal rebels
of 1848 what they can learn from Friedrich Gentz, Prince Metternich, de Maistre, de Bonald.

There is no question whatever of losing the liberal heritage of
Jefferson, Jackson, Gladstone, and the best of the revolution-
preventing social reforms — popularly called "liberal" — of the
New Deal. All of this is too deeply rooted in American life as
a whole to let itself be uprooted, no matter which party or
philosophy is in the ascendant. It is a question not of uprooting
the great liberal part of America's complex and pluralist heritage
but of enriching it and deepening its shallow insights — now that
it has grown stereotyped and complacent — with the insights of
the conservative dissent. *There* — if certain liberal educators are
so eager to defend as "dissenters" the conformists of Stalin — is
a dissent really worth their more careful study. For it is a dissent
from their own sort of conformism.

Plenty of hard-hitting radicalism will always be needed in
America, all the more so as soon as you venture out of that
literary-academic world with which this book — being about
"the intellectuals" — is particularly concerned. But let it once
again, as in the good days of Thoreau, be a genuinely radical
radicalism. That is to say, an independent radicalism, not the
present radicalism that never dares dissent too far from its own
frozen gestures of facile dissent. The most boring and most
dangerous of these ritual gestures are a half-baked Marxism, a
full-baked materialism, and a statism which is coercively do-goody
— which assumes it can free the individual by "forcing him" (in
Rousseau's ominous phrase) "to be free."

If there is to be not only a new conservatism but also, and likewise needed, a new radicalism, then let it be the inspiring moral
radicalism of the great utopian socialists and Christian socialists,
the great individualists of philosophical anarchism, the Thoreaus

and Tolstoys, the incorruptible honest Orwells. There or nowhere lies the only creative future for an independent radical dissent.

BASIC DEFINITIONS: LIBERALISM, CONSERVATISM

> "Society cannot exist unless a controlling power upon will and appetite be placed somewhere, and the less of it there is within, the more there must be without."
> —EDMUND BURKE

> "The lesson [about liberalism] to which Wordsworth had been deaf in 1793 had at length been brought home to him by the logic of events such as Burke had foreseen: he had come to perceive that a civil society is not a joint-stock company but a living organism, rooted in the past, and growing not by the application of abstract formulas . . . but by the laws of its own nature, which are embodied in its institutions and discoverable only from its history."
> — J. C. SMITH, *Wordsworth*

"All political systems," observed the poet Paul Valéry, "imply (and are generally not aware that they do imply) a certain conception of man, and even an opinion about the destiny of the species, an entire metaphysic." We should all try to achieve an awareness of what it is we are implying. "Metaphysically" (to use a "conservative" word despised by Enlightened Progressives), the difference between a democratic leftist and a democratic conservative is as follows: The conservative, politically descended from Burke, distrusts human nature and believes (politically speaking) in Original Sin, which must be restrained by the ethical traffic lights of traditionalism. The leftist and the liberal, descended from Rousseau, unconsciously assume the natural goodness of man — the less restrained in power the better.

If human nature were naturally good, then I would join the left-liberals and democratic socialists of the west in trusting a party power-machine to regiment a country's economy without eventually creating a political dictatorship to enforce such vast controls. Both Christianity and Dr. Freud teach a different view of human nature.

Conservatism and *liberalism,* as here used, are not clear or primary criteria for the American electoral scenes of 1952-56 (least of all while both parties are under such similarly middle-of-the-road, anti-extremist amalgams of liberal and conservative motifs as Stevenson and Eisenhower). *Conservative* and *liberal* are long-run "metaphysical" and psychological terms, not short-run practical terms. They cannot suffice to help us choose between electing a Democrat or Republican as village fire chief. In that sense they are "useless" terms to pragmatic activists. In that sense I even *intend* them to be "useless," being interested only in social and psychological speculations, not at all in political propaganda tracts for any particular party or candidate.

But in their "useless," impractical way, the terms *liberal* and *conservative* do enrich our understanding of an important split in human nature, a psychological and literary as well as political split. This is the split between those who trust the "natural goodness" of man and primarily want to release it from *outer* restraints, and those who fear his natural caveman propensities and primarily want to check them with *inner* restraints.

II

A sense of man's limitations — a sense of his precariousness and mystery — is the necessary corrective against megalomaniac efforts to remake the world by force. The brilliant communist atomic spy, Klaus Fuchs, wrote in his court confession that the reading of Karl Marx meant to him, above all, the overcoming of human limitations; this overweening self-assertion of man, ruthlessly remaking society regardless of moral limitations, was (he confessed) the basis of his communist faith: "The idea which gripped me most was . . . that now, for the first time, man understands the historical forces and he is able to control them, and that therefore for the first time he will be really free. I carried this idea over into the personal sphere. . . ."

There are Lenins of religion, as there are Torquemadas of atheism; both equally lack this sense of human limitation. Christianity, rightly understood, teaches it the most wisely and truly. But the formula of "Christianity or communism," high-pressured with the same techniques as a campaign for Ivory Soap instead of God, is much too pat without qualification. What about the Red Dean of Canterbury and communism's Christian "peace" fronts? The formula holds true only if you add "Christianity rightly understood," thereby opening an un-pat debate that would fill volumes. How often is Christianity understood and practiced spiritually rather than as a sociological convention? May not its spiritual ethics sometimes work through decent unbelievers (God "works in mysterious ways") while being betrayed not so much by open godlessness as by drab, leaden-eyed, uninspired lip service?

This Burkean (or today perhaps Niebuhrian) sense of human limitation and frailty, as opposed to the megalomaniac faith in limitless progress through mass-movements and material reforms, is a basic distinction between the conservative temperament and the progressive temperament. I say "temperament," not "political party" or "economic program." This Burkean sense is more basic a test of your outgrowing the illusions of liberalism than your position on the economic laws (introduced by the Republican party) against child labor or the economic laws (introduced by the Democratic party) for minimum wages. If such humane reforms, over the centuries, were a monopoly of liberalism, then who wouldn't be a liberal? What is left to debate if you beg the question by making one -ism synonymous with decency and the other with evil? What decent person today doesn't favor such laws?

No, social reform by itself is no criterion for conservative versus progressive (though the motives behind reform, whether motives of class-war-incitement or class-war-prevention, are obvious criteria). I cannot for a minute take seriously the assertions of America's superficial (merely economic) "conservatives" that they would abolish "all New Deal laws," most of which are the mildest, revolution-preventing reforms, passed by *both* parties. All that is shadow-boxing and campaign oratory. The genuine differences between the conservative and progressive outlooks on life are in the ethical and psychological realm, cutting across the lines of political party, economic class, or nationality.

III

There is no single shiny object to be peddled as *"the* new conservatism." That only raises the question: which kind and conserving what? Let author and reader subordinate labels to contents. I don't care what the views here presented are labeled, in case you prefer to define conservatism differently. One writer suggests, "Instead, call these views the *true* liberalism, which the totalitarian and Popular Front liberals have betrayed." Less dramatic and more pedantic than that, I'd settle for being labeled simply "a value-conserving classical humanist."[1] What difference does it make anyway? Here is the real point: after twenty years of hackneyed liberal conformism in high places and of a cult of revolt-for-its-own-sake among writers and intellectuals, it is time to work out a more human view of humanity. And by "human" I mean a view of society based on ethics and psychology, in contrast with an ethically-relativist and psychologically-superficial view of society based on economics.

Economics, economic determinism, and their nonexistent Economic Man are superannuated Marxist-and-capitalist fads. They reflect the temporarily overwhelming impact — the impact of novelty and of crisis — made upon the nineteenth century by the industrial revolution. In America after the Civil War, this industrial impact corrupted and narrowed the broader and more idealistic conservatism of our founding fathers. Hence, the pejorative misuse of the word today; hence, the need in Section Nine, "Which Kind of Conservatism?" (page 245), to distinguish at considerable length between the true value-conserving kind and the contemporary degenerate kind, which conserves merely economic greed. For the more independent students and younger professors, the new conservatism (in its value-conserving sense) is rapidly becoming the only escape from the stultifying standardization of their cynical, value-denying elders.

---

[1] Except that this sounds more pretentious than intended and would raise the endless, fruitless argument over what "humanism" means. To me it means the human dignity of the traditional classical world, before the Ortegan mass-man; to others it means merely a materialistic and God-baiting deification of man, the opposite of my intention.

THE "LITERARY FALLACY" IS NO FALLACY

> "Ideas may become as valid and distinct, and the feelings accompanying them as vivid, as original impressions. And this may finally make a man independent of his Senses. One use of poetry." — *A jotting in the notebooks of* SAMUEL TAYLOR COLERIDGE

Events have taught the West to appreciate the power of passionate ideas in history and not merely the overrated power of economics (overrated except in so far as faith in economics is itself a passionate idea). In consequence, it has become less easy to minimize the unique importance and social role of what has been sarcastically dismissed as "the literary intellectuals." What Bernard De Voto has called the "literary fallacy" (the tendency of intellectuals to exaggerate their own importance and that of their ideas) is no fallacy. It is correct; it is even an understatement. "Three with a new song's measure" can indeed "trample an empire down." They have done so constantly: in eighteenth-century France, in twentieth-century Germany and Russia. Admittedly, they have done so only in the context of auspicious material and economic conditions. But these material conditions, in turn, were the end result of abstract ideas, in a ceaseless chicken-egg process.

I define intellectuals as all who are full-time servants of the Word or of the word. This means educators in the broadest sense: philosophers, clergymen, artists, professors, poets, and also such undreamy and uncloudy professions as editors and the more serious interpreters of news. When they fulfill their civilizing function, intellectuals are the ethical Geiger counters of their society, the warning-signals of conscience. Their direct influence is almost non-existent. What of it? Indirectly and in the long run, their influence can be decisive, whether today or — for both bad and good — in the French eighteenth century. Even more so today, there being no universal established church as guardian of values.

Americans — all except intellectual Americans — ought to become belligerently pro-intellectual for a change. To be an ethics-dedicated intellectual is subversive, but only of subversion;

of cant, clichés, and armed lies. Such intellectuality is a badge to wear proudly. The nature of those who fear or mock that badge is part of its pride. Not the least part of it. There is a special splendor in being distrusted by the demagogues of cant, clichés, and armed lies.

But what of the intellectual who is not true to his ethical function?

Revolts against reason end up in lynch-law and Dachau. Let us distrust any indiscriminate indictment of intellectuals; that would be a potential American revolt against reason. But to indict discriminately the totalitarian intellectuals, who betray their civilizing function, is no revolt aganst reason. It is the restoration of reason.

THE RESTORATION OF HALOS

"When a sage thinks alone and thinks truthfully,
He can be heard one thousand miles."
— Chinese proverb

"The virtue of this article" (I hear said of an article loosely calling most intellectuals Reds) "is that it strips intellectuals of their halos."

"The virtue of this book" (I hear said of a best-seller calling academic freedom "a myth") "is that it reminds professors they are living on the businessman's wages."

I don't care to see intellectuals stripped of their halos, even those I most disagree with. This is not for the obvious subjective reason. It is, rather, because I don't care for Karl Marx. Therefore, I do not cherish attitudes like the above two quotations on "halos" and "businessman's wages." For they seem to justify one of Marx's unfair allegations: "The bourgeoisie has robbed of their halos various occupations hitherto regarded with awe and veneration. Doctor, lawyer, priest, poet, and scientist have become its wage-laborers."

Academic freedom is not "a myth." Intellectuals are indeed worthy of "awe and veneration." I wish more intellectuals would have the pride to stand up and assert and re-assert, without apology, the glory of their function. They are "wage-laborers" not of bourgeois politicians nor of socialist politicians but of truth and conscience.

Even a totally wrongheaded intellectual still wears a disheveled kind of halo, in the same way that an unfrocked priest still has some kind of link with the apostolic succession. If I did not have so high a view of the intellectual's function, I would not bother being so distressed and angry about the treason of the literary fellow-travelers. Their unforgivable sin: they, at least, should know better. Nobody expects some miserable yellow-press columnist or some idiotic, intellectual-baiting backwoods-reactionary to know any better. Therefore, morally you should feel just a bit less distressed or angry about the latter, "for they know not what they do."

Here is the modern version of "the sin against the Holy Ghost": when an intellectual fails to remain *sérieux;* when he sullies the miracle of human intelligence and the privilege of his educational advantages to become a high-brow demagogue, an intelligent charlatan, like Ilya Ehrenburg, Herr Doktor Goebbels, and the fellow-traveling Dean of Canterbury. The job of intellect is not to serve Big Business or its N.A.M. The job of intellect is not to serve Big Labor or its trade unions. If anything (let's be arrogant about it) the job of business and the job of labor in America is to serve intellect on the condition that intellect serves and ennobles the nation — as a whole. Intellect serves and ennobles whenever it searches for more truth and more beauty, in an unpretentious, impractical, haloed kind of way.

The Table Talk of Gaylord Babbitt

"To purify the diction of our tribe" — MALLARME

"Must we still go on with our affectations and sneaking?
Let faces and theories be turn'd inside out! let meanings be
freely criminal, as well as results!
Let the reformers descend from the stands where they are
forever bawling! let an idiot or insane person appear
on each of the stands!
Let there be no unfashionable wisdom! let such be scorn'd
and derided off from the earth!
Let there be wealthy and immense cities — but still through
any of them, not a single poet, savior, knower, lover!
Let the infidels of These States laugh all faith away!"
— WALT WHITMAN

ABATTOIR AHEAD

Needed, an abattoir for Sacred Cows.

Here are two exasperatingly sacred bovines. Sacred not to the
majority of Americans but to the more indignant readers of these
pages. Sacred to a majority of that strategic small minority, the
respectable (meaning cautiously daring) intellectuals.

1. The stereotyped liberal progressive in politics.
2. The hermetic, avant-garde mandarin in literature.

The stereotyped progressive has made a professional new conformism out of nonconformism: "Why can't you be an independent, convention-defying liberal — just like everybody else?"

The avant-garde mandarin is still revolting against a too crude
clarity, a too insensitive communication in literature. The Pound
and Eliot revolt was needed in 1912. Today, the obscure Bad
Writing is as stereotyped as was the clear Bad Writing of the
lingering Victorians of 1912. Today, the second generation of
Eliotizers and New Critics are the parasitic heirs of paths already
blazed and "battles with Victorianism" won long, long ago.

16

While the trail blazers have become the Sacred Cows of the big magazines, their imitators — the *nouveaux* New Critics — have become the Sacred Calves of the Little Magazines. "Why can't you produce literature that shocks the masses — just like everybody else?"

THE NEW PHILISTINISM

Ever since Matthew Arnold borrowed from Heinrich Heine the word "philistine"[1] to describe an insensitive, cliché-addicted conformism, the word has had certain indefinable but readily recognizable connotations for the English-speaking world. These have been immortalized in their American application by Sinclair Lewis's book, *Babbitt*.

Today philistinism has acquired a new content, a new set of conditioned reflexes. It is still mongering clichés, but the clichés have changed. And the only people still using the old-fashioned epithets "philistine" or "Babbitt" are the Babbitts themselves. The main activity of the new-style philistine has become the facile game of philistine-baiting.

Perhaps every twenty years, the eternal Babbitt dons a new name and a new disguise. Today George Babbitt's imaginary son bears the fancier name I invented for him: Gaylord. George Babbitt boosts and flag-waves; hates slackers and political progressives; and distrusts art. Gaylord Babbitt says: "I go for art and progress in a big way. If there's one thing I can't stand, it's a Babbitt."

The essence of all Babbittry, senior or junior, is stereotypes. The stereotypes of Babbitt Senior are the following words and connotations: solid, reliable, sound, businesslike, wholesome, and knows-how-to-meet-a-payroll. Junior's stereotyped words and connotations are: vital, dynamic, functional, unpuritanical, forward-looking, the masses, and the common man.

The new Babbittry has two different aspects, one literary and one political:

---

[1]Arnold: "Our puritan middle classes present a defective type of religion, a narrow range of intellect and instruction, a stunted sense of beauty, a low standard of manners." Whether or not he read Arnold, Lewis has not essentially added to this definition in his amusing caricatures of 60 years later.

1. *Literary*. A typical book review in a typical Little Magazine unconsciously proclaims Gaylord's would-be-sophisticated line for literature: "We unfortunately miss in this book that rich, surrealistic obscurity which our modern taste has been led to expect." The give-away phrase here is "led to expect." The justification of the modernist revolt against Victorian clichés was to give the public what it did *not* expect; hence, quite properly shocking the public of Babbitt Senior by surrealism, Joycian cross-references, and obscurity in poetry. While Babbitt *père* smugly denounces this obscurity as Long-hair Stuff, Babbitt *fils* with an exactly equal smugness applauds it as à-la-mode. The way to improve a modern art public is by difficult and noble simplicity, not easy obscurity. What shocks, what utterly outrages the Gaylords of modern literary criticism, who dominate the more strategic magazines and English departments, is the movement back to communication in poetry.

2. *Political*. *Père* was a Republican. *Fils* knows it's smart to be left: "As my favorite sophisticated poetess, Dorothy Parker, so aptly put it, 'It's no longer I but We!' " To prove this point, I quote from a recent article by Robert Bendiner, former associate editor of *The Nation* and one of America's ablest liberals:

Out of some 140,000,000 people in the United States, at least 139,500,000 are liberals, to hear them tell it, "liberal" having become a rough synonym for virtuous, decent, humane, and kind to animals. Rare is the citizen who can bring himself to say, "Sure I'm a Conservative. What of it?" And any American would sooner drop dead than proclaim himself a reactionary.

No wonder even Senator Taft makes a big point of calling himself "a liberal." Here is the advertisement put out by a brandnew liberal monthly named *Exposé*: "*Exposé* is independent and liberal, as the great majority of the American people are independent and liberal." . . . To be independent "like the great majority," does that not spoil the original J. S. Millsian ideal of the liberal bravely defying "the great majority" and its mob clichés?

Actually Gaylord, even at his height in the 1940's, never represented the "great majority" of *the* country. What he represented was the great majority of *his* country. I refer to that unmapped

country otherwise known as the intellectual cocktail parties of New York, Boston, and the choicer eastern universities.

Smart to be leftist: not in that big, funny Outside World, of course. But in his own small, cozy world of upper-middlebrow professors and the more presentable and top-drawer journalists, G.B. knows it is smart to have a reputation of "believing in" revolutionary mass-progress. In some vague and safe and supercilious kind of way — oh, out there in the sticks in Asia, say.

Like Shakespeare's hero, G.B. complains, "I lack advancement." And what can help your advancement better in those particular circles than to be regarded with awe as a bold (though never *too* bold) baiter of G.B.'s three Suspected Categories of American life, the three horrendous phalanxes of The Witch Hunt: drunken Legionnaires, sober businessmen, and all Irishmen?

Young Babbitt gets around a lot — what with all those art galleries and *soirées* that are dominated by his flashing repartee — young Babbitt gets around; and if you start thinking, you realize that hardly a day goes by in lower Manhattan and many campuses without your running into him. His name, his face may seem to change. But you can always spot him by the phrases he uses; by his enlightened, emancipated attitude toward everything — in life or art or politics; and even more, by his awareness of how enlightened he is and by the complacency that such awareness gives him. It is the same complacency poor, reactionary old Babbitt Senior used to feel when he strolled through Zenith, Ohio, long ago in that other epoch before 1929 — before the world changed on him and laughed at his ideas.

In contrast, even now almost nobody laughs — dares to laugh — at the ideas of Babbitt Junior. After all, who can dare to laugh at Progress? As his Boswell, I have been recording G.B.'s Table Talk for a long time now. This recording is a time-capsule of the dominant ideas of an epoch, 1929-50. The '29 crash killed off Senior's epoch. Certain world events of the 1950's are at last bringing Junior's epoch to an end. Yet Gaylord himself never ends; always lands on his feet by adjusting his line, even somehow (wait and see) to a post-1952 Republican bandwagon.

But why not let Gaylord speak for himself in the next chapter? (Via a strictly SURREALIST dialogue.)

THE TABLE TALK OF GAYLORD BABBITT: AN EXCLU-
SIVE INTERVIEW IN CAFE CHIC [1]

Only yesterday I had lunch with Gaylord in what he called "one of my little French restaurants." Being in a hurry, I blunderingly suggested having hamburgers at Childs. How quickly he put me in my place, snapping:

"How provincial of you! Speed, speed, what does it get you? Stomach ulcers, that's what being commercial-minded gets you. We second-generation Babbitts always take off two hours for lunch on account of it's more *civilisé*. Oh, poor P.V., will you never learn to be a Man of the World? Why, the way you talk, folks might think you're some Middle Westerner — I mean, some fellow who has never eaten the legs of a single frog!"

"Your wit is in fine fettle today, G.B.," I chortled appreciatively, writing down his epigram in my notebook. As we settled down in Café Chic instead of Childs, I asked him in open-mouthed admiration: "How do you insure so infallibly that your ideas on all subjects are always the most liberal possible, so that you're always protected, never giving anybody an opening to kid you as an old-fogey or an awful, narrow-minded businessman?"

Pouring himself an elegant demitasse of Sparkling Burgundy, his favorite beverage, he answered me frankly:

"That's easy as pie. For example, take politics. Whenever I have to choose between two political ideas, I always choose whatever idea is the more Advanced. If they're equally Advanced so that I can't choose, then I read what my *Nation* and my *New Statesman* say about it. And as for the field of art and sex — you know, art, sex, that kind of thing — why, sometimes my thoughts are so Advanced that I tremble at my own daring. There's nothing more wonderful than being emancipated from medieval superstitions and fearlessly defying conventions. Why, there's no more fearless defier than I; I defy conventions right and left."

"As your Eckermann, I always feel I am boring you, asking

---

[1] Written in 1947 (for a novel about the intellectuals of the 1940's). Revised up-to-date for 1951, as a time capsule to preserve a particular literary and political epoch now slowly drawing to a close.

you for crumbs of your wisdom. It's so difficult sitting here, eating with a genius, instead of reading him at a distance centuries later. Oh, G.B., what must I be like to become worthy of lunching with you? What kind of people do you tolerate? What pet hates have you that I can tactfully avoid?"

"Unfortunately for you, I only tolerate folks who are suave. 'Suave'? — oh, by that I mean anybody who can, on short notice, name an adequate little French restaurant in the East Fifties. And you know what's my latest hate? Not the low-brows: that's all *les neiges de* yesteryear. It's those middle-brows. They're even worse than low-brows. For example, a high-brow like me and a low-brow like you can get along together fine. We can talk for hours enthusing over the comic strips: each from our quite different viewpoints, y'understand; my viewpoint analytical, as befits a social observer of life's *mores,* and your viewpoint toward the comics more spontaneous and naïve. Yes, I can get along with you low-brows, you refreshing primitives, but I'll never get along with those over-avid middle-brows. They're so pretentious; always trying to live beyond their intellectual means."

"A misunderstood dreamer like you," I replied with gentle understanding, "must have trouble finding any merely human company tolerable? Can it be that only Paris is your spiritual home? Is that why you brought me, with your exquisite taste, to this restaurant where they print the menus in the language of Robespierre and Proust?"

At the mention of that sacred city, which he had never visited in person but knew better than any visitor, Gaylord Babbitt clasped his artistic hands and was lost to this sordid American world. In his trance, he keened to himself:

"Gee, it must be glamorous to be out there on the Left Bank and sit there in some café, talking about brand-new Movements like Dada-ism and Folies Bergères and everything. And maybe at the table right smack next to me, nonchalantly sipping absinthe, there'd be Sartre and Mistinguette and Louis Aragon and Alice B. Toklas, all four on a double-date together. Maybe it's the eternal bohemian in me, but I'm an incurable Artist of Life."

"Golly Gaylord, how come you always manage to pick just the Right Names in the world of lit-crit? I'm scared to open my

mouth about criticism or even to mention the name of a single
poet, lest it turn out to be a Wrong Name, so that everybody here
at Café Chic would then laugh behind my back and think I'm
slipping."

"The solution is to pick the right lit-crit culture-hero and ride
his juggernaut like a roller coaster, no matter how sharply it twists
and skids at the curves. I find it indispensable to have the Eliot
literary school telling me when to dislike Milton and when I'm
allowed to like Milton again. In precisely the same way, I found
it indispensable to have a political line telling me in June, 1941,
when it was an imperialist war and when it stopped being one."

This puzzled me, and I objected: "But the literary dictatorship
you follow is by a medieval religious author, while your political
line — slips! I mean *tendance* — is 100 per cent modern and
progressive. Isn't that inconsistent?"

"Yes, there is that admitted inconsistency between my literary
and political *tendances,* but a minor one. The major consistency
between them is: both bait poor old daddy Babbitt; both are
or used to be advance-guard; both get me elected into the intellectual élite. Only instead of daddy's Kiwanis-belongingness, my
literary and political lines make me belong with all those dazzling,
outrageously witty giants of Bloomsbury, Greenwich Village, and
Piazza di Spagna."

"How do you giants recognize each other among all us pygmies
of the intellect?" I asked.

"By the intonation of one single word: by the expression with
which we say 'we.' Best example is to talk like The Master himself. I've spent hours memorizing every sentence in which Eliot
uses the word 'we.' Then I repeat just those sentences every time
I meet a London or New York celebrity who's trying to sniff out if
I belong to the literary ins or the literary outs. It never fails. O the
prestige and banquets of being a lonely *poète maudit!*"

"Tell me a couple of those sentences, pronouncing 'we' in the
right voice," I pleaded. "Then maybe even I can learn how to
talk about poetry."

"Well, I memorized that very short sentence in *The Sacred
Wood* where he says: 'Agreed that we do not greatly enjoy Swinburne.' You gotta say that sentence in such a casual yet authorita-

tive tone that a whole praetorian guard of English departments and Little Magazines will exclaim in chorus: O the bliss of being part of that We, O the leper-agony of being excluded from it!"

"With all your scintillating *explications de texte,*" I marveled, "I guess you Olympians can follow the daily fluctuations of careers in art the same way your dad follows his stock market fluctuations."

"Yup, and with the same rush to sell short a loser and to buy on margin every day's winner."

"Teach me another example of a We-sentence, Gaylord, so I can some day prove worthy of associating with you winners."

"A different kind of We — this time pronounced with a tone of squeamish impatience — comes earlier in *The Sacred Wood,* where Eliot writes: 'We still hear that George Meredith is a master of prose, or even a profound philosopher.' Whenever I repeat that sentence at a Yale or Princeton literary forum, all of us belongers feel like members of Skull and Bones, snubbing some underbred cad. Picture the cad sidling up and sweatingly trying to ingratiate himself by saying too eagerly: 'George Meredith is a master of prose. George Meredith is even a profound philosopher.'"

II

As always, our conversation soon progressed from literature to politics. "Would you like to hear my political credo in a nutshell?" he asked dramatically. "I can boil it down to a sentence."

"I can hardly wait," I gibbered with excitement, while opening my notebook to a fresh page. "This is Dear Diary's lucky day."

"I'm an Independent Fighting Liberal, who thinks for himself. Every morning without fail, I repeat that sentence aloud to myself. There I stand, in front of my mirror, adjusting my lips to a sophisticated sneer, and reciting the same sentence: I'm an Independent Fighting Liberal, who thinks for himself."

Tactfully I inquired: "How do you show your independence from that somewhat overly impetuous brand of liberals known as communists?"

Gaylord Babbitt withered me with his noble eye and explained in a tired, patient voice: "I'm a *non*communist, definitely a *non*-communist — ah. but not an *anti*communist."

"Touché!" I conceded, in panic at having dared to match wits with the great man. "Touché, and I'm sportsman enough to admit it. One *bon mot* from you clears up my political confusion like a flash of lightning at midnight. Alas, since the Big Interests crushed *PM* and *The New York Star* and since the end of cooperation between liberals and our brave Russian allies, you've become so silent about politics. This leaves us, your followers and readers, like ships without rudders. Speak out again, bold and loud, and resolve our doubts. For example, why as a noncommunist do you invariably sign your name to every procommunist petition and 'peace' manifesto that comes your way?"

G.B. glanced daintily into his little pocket periscope to see if the F.B.I. was hiding in the booth behind us. Finding the coast clear, he unveiled the Dostoyevsky-like conflict in his soul. He summed it up in the following heart-rending confession, a true *cri de coeur:*

"What I say now, I've never told before to man or beast, not even my own mother. But as the Boswell of my spiritual Odyssey, you're entitled to the naked truth. I admit that as a noncommunist I shouldn't do it, shouldn't sign my name to all those petitions and manifestoes; and God knows how I've struggled against it — afterwards — in the guilty loneliness of my boudoir. Each time I swear that this is the last time I'll submit to their political advances. But it's no use. The same malign ecstasy overpowers my self-control each time I get in the mail a new communist petition whose wording sounds at all progressive. My hand begins to itch, and the more I reread certain favorite phrases — like Common Man and Exploitation and Dynamic and New and Vital — the more I feel intoxicated and just can't bother reading carefully what it's all about. It's like craving a drug; I just gotta sign."

He paused, trembling and perspiring; took a deep breath; continued more calmly:

"And then later, after I've signed, it's such a marvelous feeling to see my name in print everywhere, until I end up, if I'm lucky, with a Profile of me in the *New Yorker*. Not so easy to get into print nowadays. And people are coming to recognize my name, to know it's a name they can always, as they say, 'count on' for progressive causes. Just think of all the people reading the peti-

tions I sign and saying to themselves — maybe even somebody
Real Big like Rockwell Kent — saying:

" 'This Gaylord Babbitt must be a dashing personality; we
always see his name in the thick of it wherever there's a Good
Cause.' "

Being a noncommunist and therefore against anticommunists,
he totally ignores my questions whenever I ask his superior advice
on things that trouble me in Soviet foreign policy. Instead, he
abruptly changes the subject and asks in that tone of sarcasm he
handles so brilliantly: "Aha, so you've reached the point where
you approve of our State Department playing footsie with Franco
Spain?"

"Footsie" is his favorite political metaphor. Here is an example
of how the great man used it, while pouring his special private
mixture of catsup and Worcestershire sauce over his Strasbourg
snails. I had just asked him how he knew with such absolute
certainty that the Chinese communists were just agrarian reformers
with Titoist tendencies. Totally ignoring my question as usual, he
asked in turn: "While your precious Chiang fascists were raping
prostrate China, what do you think our cookie-pushers in striped
pants were doing? Don't tell me you don't know that our State
Department was playing footsie with the openly conservative
Dalai Lama of Tibet."

I asked why he assumed I was defending fascists when I was
merely asking him to explain communist policy to me. But I
soon repented my naïve bourgeois objectivity when he replied:
"Yes, but the ultimate logic of merely asking such questions about
Russia leads you right up the Franco path. Your questions may
not be open Red-baiting, but they're potential Red-baiting. Subjectively, you're actively participating at this very moment in the
rape of prostrate Spain."

When I asked him to define "potential" Red-baiting, he gave
me his most masterful answer; the more I think of it, the more
I see how true it is:

"Even if a fellow does not so much as mention Russia, the
instant he introduces ethics and that kind of stuff — instead of
economics — as a standard for judging some exciting new Social
Experiment, the instant, I say, that he sneaks in ethics, that instant

he becomes a *potential* Red-baiter and warmonger. Because one thing leads to another — that's logic — and once you begin with a medieval moralizing attitude, you'll end up by asking about Soviet forced-labor camps. Not that I approve of them, not for a single second; anybody who says I approve of them is lying. Those kinds of medieval-minded liars, what they lack is ethics."

The word "medieval-minded" is his favorite epithet. In that painful final break with his family, when Babbitt Senior wanted to cover the torn wallpaper with "Whistler's Mother" while Babbitt Junior insisted on a Picasso, the soul-searing cry of Babbitt Junior as he left Zenith forever was: "Why, you're nothing but a boosting, Rotarian, medieval-minded philistine!"

III

"You asked about my pet hates just now," resumed Gaylord, as the waiter cleared the dishes. "Name-calling is another of my hates. The irresponsibility of it! Whom will they smear next?"

"Before you know it," I shuddered deliciously, "they'll even call a moderate Jeffersonian like Mao a Communist!"

"If that ever happens," panted freedom's sturdy old war horse, "then nobody is safe in America any more. It's all interconnected; you cannot thus slander away the civil liberties of Mao or Stalin without ending by implication the liberties of every American man, woman, and child. Not that I hold the slightest brief for Stalin or Mao; oh, how I hate them! But their freedom from being Red-baited is your freedom and my freedom and the freedom of your poor, innocent grandchildren: you and you and you and you. Can't you picture our unborn grandchildren being dragged by our Gestapo in front of the Inquisition? I mean, the way they dragged Shirley Temple that time — she was still a baby then, why practically an embryo — in front of the Committee on Un-American Activities."

"But even worse than the witch hunts," I shivered, "are the spy hunts. They call Fuchs a spy, Greenglass a spy, Ethel Rosenberg a spy, Judy Coplon a spy, our Canadian neighbor Sam Carr a spy; in short, anybody who opposes war or believes in academic freedom."

"Those narsty name-callers even call an almost-nearly Mayflower

American like Prince Charming Alger Hiss a spy. When they pulled *that* red herring on us, it showed no American is safe from persecution any more. Next thing you know, some ex-Red, turned informer, will even call *me* almost a fellow-traveler or something, doing so for strictly psychopathic reasons, of course. Oh la, those ex-Reds! If there has to be any baiting, then what we liberals love is to bait not Reds but ex-Reds. Anyway, according to the dictionary, witches don't exist. By definition, all witch-hunts hunt the non-existent. That means Fuchs, Coplon, Greenglass, and Hiss never existed. What does not exist, cannot be guilty, so why all the national hysteria?"

"Q.E.D." I intoned piously. "But why stop there? Our kind of civil liberties must assume that no Communists at all exist, no Red Army exists, no Red atom bomb exists. Never deign to mention such mirages in your editorials or conversation. Mention only the real danger: the Pentagon dictatorship right at home."

"You're learning from me fast," beamed my mentor. "Whatever spoils our argument, doesn't exist. That's the beauty of an immortal book, called *Witch Hunt,* by Carey McWilliams of *The Nation*. It proves its case against the witch hunters by *never once even mentioning* the names Hiss, Fuchs, or Stalin. Look up those three names in the index, and you won't even find them there. Being witches, they don't exist, and whoever mentions or even thinks of names like Stalin is 'hysterical.' Books and magazines like that are written on the tacit assumption that Joe McCarthy is President of the U.S.A., without a single voice opposing him except on the far left. We Gaylord Babbitts encourage and need the McCarthys. Their actions prove the correctness of our indictment of anticommunism. Without them we'd be lost. What ammunition would we have left if, God forbid, McCarthy were beaten for re-election? Our only solution is to save him."

"What a dandy solution," I chuckled, "for saving the psychological need of liberals to be forever aghast at some right-wing menace inside America. But since you use the label 'fascist' against practically everybody, I wonder why you protested furiously against applying it to an American poet who during the war preached Nazi pogroms and mutiny to American troops over Mussolini's radio?"

"Two reasons. First: that particular poetry cult in my career as a beauty lover means the same kind of advancement that buttering up the Four Hundred means in my wife's social career. Second: that particular literary genius actually supported the Italian political party that openly called itself fascist. And my policy is never to use that word for actual fascist parties. I use it only for those skulking conservatives who refuse to admit they're fascists; that is, for anybody whose politics I don't like. Take members of the Republican party, for example. Call any ordinary Republican a fascist, and you'll never hear me protest that you're using language loosely. But as soon as you call a fascist a fascist, I get my fighting dander up; that's smearing, that's guilt by association, just like calling a communist a communist."

"Your answer satisfies me completely," I recited reverently. "And since you are supplying me with the right thunderbolts to strike down our detractors, tell me what to answer when friends heckle me about the Soviet peasants or about Hiss and Chambers. How rebut such wild charges?"

"Well, even if poor Alger *is* just a teeny-weeny bit guilty of treason (and how can he be? — somebody so successful, handsome, fashionable), yet our duty is to keep silent as clams about Hiss. Concentrate exclusively on inventing Freudian explanations for Whittaker Chambers. There's no surer way to become a social leper in Respectable Circles than to say a good word for a pariah like Chambers. Self-interest is the first law of modern emancipated man. When a fellow gives up a good magazine job and his good name merely to serve a rotten capitalist fraud like the United States of America and merely because some itsy-bitsy treason is going on, his motive must be pathological. Because obviously there are no motives outside Freud or Marx. Honor? Patriotism? Freedom? It's all a gyp!"

"But what about those peasants? The hecklers and spoil-sports say that ten million were deliberately starved to death."

"According to my own, more objective research, the great Five Year Plan only killed five million. That proves you can only believe one half of what the kept press says against Russia. Seeing it's not ten million but a mere handful of five million, you can ask the hecklers: why should a wilful handful stand in the way of

the blueprints of progress? Anyway, it's chauvinism to worry
about mere physical assassination abroad when something far
worse, namely character assassination, is raging in America.
Starvation is not really so bad, especially for insensitive ox-like
creatures like peasants; after the first three weeks the stomach
shrinks from pain, and then the agony gets gradually less. The real
pain is character assassination. Five million stomach pangs are
nothing compared with the anxiety a sensitive intellectual feels
under an ordeal-by-slander."

"You mean there's two kinds of pain, G.B.?"

"Naturally. Most peasants are reactionaries anyway, believing
in stuff like God and family and individualism. If they cling with
vicious kulak stubbornness to such notions, there's nothing left
but rolling over them with the impersonal steam roller of social
engineering. Those hicks can't feel pain the way a New York
intellectual can, who's been made super-wincing by reading Kahlil
Gibran and visiting 57th Street art galleries, something no peasant
would ever do. Marx conceded that peasants are an inferior kind
of people because they just won't revolt when you tell them to.
Regard those five million not as humans but as plow animals.
Why, gee whiz, a peasant or some thick-skinned, bigoted conservative can no more feel real pain than do the earthworms I
like to squash with my heel at my country club every time I'm
annoyed by losing a point at golf."

At this point an ugly-looking cripple at the next table, some
kind of Russian or Baltic refugee who had long been lowering the
bon ton of our bistro, limped out rapidly with his hand over his
mouth, as if he were throwing up. This taught him a good lesson
against eavesdropping, I'll bet!

IV

For future historians of the 1930's and '40's, I must define
further what Gaylord Babbitt meant during those years by being
"noncommunist." It meant that he boycotted all Party members
personally, but hobnobbed socially as much as possible with rich,
fashionable, fellow-traveler sympathizers, was "thrilled to meet"
the Dean of Canterbury, paid lavishly for tickets to hear and

applaud every visiting Fadeyev. Yet when some poor Alabama Negro is in trouble, being framed up by local police and accused quite erroneously of being a "Red" by Ku Klux demagogues, then G.B. will not contribute a penny of what he gives to banquets for Soviet-American Friendship. In one such case he sternly ordered the Negro not to write him letters appealing for a bail fund "lest it get me into hot water."

"I'm an *Independent* Liberal," G.B. explained to me logically and convincingly about this. "No sir, it's no man's Party Line for Gaylord Babbitt — especially when it might prejudice the FBI against me and prevent me from getting an important job as morale builder in Washington in case of World War III. During World War II, I kept up soldier morale by writing — for their *Know Your Allies* Information Series — my morale building pamphlet, 'I SALUTE YOU, ANA PAUKER!' And listen to my human interest subtitle: 'An Epic of Jeffersonian Agrarian Reform under the Pin-Up Girl of the Carpathians.' Well, why can't I do the same kind of inspiration of the young in the next world war? And the next and the next. I can already recite how I'd begin my inspiration leaflet for Our Boys in Siberia:

"Dear G.I.s. Sitting here in Washington this winter and suffering silently (like a loyal soldier of the pen) from these overheated radiators, I ask myself: of what does the name of this capital city remind me? Washington? Washington? It sounds so familiar.

"Suddenly I know! It reminds me of that great Independent Liberal who was our first president and derived his name from the name of this city. George Washington! Our martyr president! What a privilege to be able to share George Washington's sacred ordeal, by camping out there in Siberia. You, and you alone, can know what the Father of Our Country felt like during that First Hard Winter that tried men's souls in the snows of Valley Forge."

As you can see from this, G.B.'s attitude toward Stalinism is undergoing a rapid and still inconsistent flux. This is in prudent accord with what Hegel calls the Weltgeist, meaning the local Spirit of the Moment. That is why the 1950's and Korea are the *end* of an epoch. Babbitt's sympathies with labor are stronger than ever, so long as it is a question of attending a testimonial dinner in tuxedos for a popular labor leader at $50 a plate. But his sympathy with labor leaders now suddenly ceases when they get into any danger. This had always been true of democratic, anti-Stalinist leaders, whom he accused of "Trotskyite sapping of our unity with the Soviet Union." But in 1950, the turning-point year, he turned for the first time against the eleven Stalinists who had been convicted under Judge Medina in 1949:

"Just because I sign all those petitions for Soviet friendship that I never even read before signing, they ask me to 'stand by' them in their 'hour of trial.' It was different standing by them in the easy pre-Korea 30's, in the days of Loyalist Spain. Why shucks, *all* the smart boys I admire were doing it then. You should've seen all the debutantes who came to my charity ball for sending a platinum corset to La Passionaria.

"But now," he sounded plaintive and hurt and bewildered, "everything's suddenly different. No more liberal solidarity. And boy, am I getting cold feet! Gotta think of my own skin occasionally; can't be crusading for oppressed humanity *all* the time. Don't tell anybody yet, but I can switch from the toiling-humanity bandwagon of the '30's to the McCormick-McCarthy jeep of the '50's just as quickly as I switched from interventionism to isolationism the day of the Hitler-Stalin Pact. Mind you, I'm not saying I'll do that necessarily; we Babbitts first wait and see, to make triply sure which way Progress is really marching in the 1950's. Meanwhile, as my forthcoming liberal novel will show you, I'm marking time: like a dying swan barking up the wrong tree in a final *ave atque vale* to destiny before the changing of the guard."

"Sometimes, Gaylord, you're just too idealistic to live," I marveled, with eyes not utterly untouched by the tell-tale moisture of a strong man in presence of the sublime. "That's what the ancients called 'selfless love': the way you force yourself to change your line in order to serve the Progress of mankind. Every change in your politics is like a new act in some cosmic Greek tragedy."

"Of course," resumed G.B., "I'm always 100 per cent on the side of revolutionists; that's the liberal thing to be; but I draw the line at — well, at subversiveness. No Babbitt — and here for once dad and I agree — no Babbitt ever wastes sympathy on anybody who resists the police. That goes for America if times should change, just as for the good old Gay-Pay-whatcha-call-it in Russia."

"But then what rocklike principle can you give us through the crisis?"

"Liberty!" boomed Babbitt reassuringly. "The main thing is to be always in the front ranks of martyrs of liberty. How you define liberty is of secondary importance; that depends on what part of the country you happen to live in. If I lived down south, I would have signed my name to the Dixiecrat Party petitions and would define liberty as State Rights. Similarly in New York I signed petitions in 1948 to put the Wallace Party on the ballot. My point is: real integrity in politics — (and I'm a glutton for integrity) — depends on having an Open Mind and adjusting it 100 per cent to your neighbors. That's what I call sympathizing with the aspirations of the toiling masses amongst whom you dwell."

"Which mass-aspiration is it best for a live-wire writer to tie up with in this eastern part of the country?" I asked.

"If you've really got your ear to the ground in New York, then you'll agree with me that antibigotry is still the big thing. Moreover, that's the one slogan of our former Popular Front days that is still negotiable currency. This leads up to the subject of my movie scenario — I mean, novel, being published next Monday. Now don't confuse me with the old-fashioned, soft kind of liberal who also fights bigotry. He does it merely for some sissy purpose like compassion and understanding and reform. My novel wastes no time on that old stuff. My aim is not compassion or reform but to turn a quick dollar by *commercializing,* as a hard-headed salesmanship technique, the soft-headed reforming or compassion-ate impulses of the public. I got the idea for cashing in on this when I read the ads of a big commercial publisher playing up, as a book-selling technique, something called 'Brotherhood Week.' Playing skilfully on the liberal conscience of modern readers, the ad told them to celebrate Brotherhood Week not by *acting* for FEPC but by *spending money* for lurid pulp novels on racial minorities, alcoholics, excitingly tortured lunatics, and whatever new kind of misery we creative artists can commercialize next."

"The highest idealism is a practical idealism," I nodded sym-pathetically, "which knows its dollars and cents. The lofty, quixotic head of you is ever soaring to the clouds, hitching its wagon to following the muses, but those big earthy feet of you remain hard-headed on the solid ground. Like all genuises, your *mens sana* remains the *Weltschmerz* in your *sano corpore*."

"My novel will be my way of getting into the antibigotry business on the ground floor and cleaning up in four ways. Yes, four ways; that's because of my original plot. Promise not to give the plot away before the day of publication; it'll make novelists like Charles Jackson burst with envy. Mere one-way tolerance is small-time stuff, like using an electric shaver with only one head. My book has race tolerance, sex tolerance, it's got everything."

"I'm all ears," I wheezed, breathless with sheer suspense. "Tell me the title. Tell me the plot. I won't tell a soul."

"The title of my novel is: *Must Such Things Be?* That's indignation, get it? There's money in any kind of tolerance; but four-way antibigotry protection — like a four-headed Remington dry shaver — will really hit the jackpot. Now, who are the four most important underdogs in current movies and fiction? You know the answer: it's Negroes, homosexuals, alcoholics, and the People of Israel. I hit upon the formula when I heard somebody remark that, since people buy books about Lincoln, doctors, and dogs, a sure best seller must be called *Lincoln's Doctor's Dog*. Let's shift this formula to *Lincoln's Doctor's Underdog*. Give the public a four-way underdog for the price of one, and the book writes itself. The inner voice of my Muse tells me I've produced the Great American Novel that we all dream of in secret.

"My fearlessly frank psychological novel has a hero who suffers from feeling somehow alienated from society because he is a very, very sensitive homosexual Negro of Hebrew religion, afflicted with alcoholism caused by his name not being included in the New York Social Register. His nervous breakdown, caused by the Social Register trauma, will give Metro-Goldwyn-Mayer a chance for a thrilling insane asylum sequence, where the brutal White Protestant heterosexual guards torture my hero by telling him he doesn't 'belong.' "

"Think only what the movie and television rights will be," I panted. "A more stupendous picture than *Pinky, Gentleman's Agreement, Snake Pit,* and *Lost Week End* put together. How proud I am to be allowed to talk with you, almost like an equal."

"Patience, while I get back to the main story. The hero's

lawyer, who is also a psychoanalyst and a crusader against Victorian Puritanism, will be played by Paul Muni. Brandishing aloft the guilty volume of the Social Register, Paul Muni swears to 'fight this thing through every court in the land till the American people undo this wrong.' Meanwhile, his idealistic client becomes a national hero by writing a humanitarian muckraking pamphlet on the U.S. Navy, demanding that the oppressed sailors be allowed more nights of shore leave in New York. In order to reward his achieving this forward-looking reform for the toilers of the sea, the Social Register tycoons repent and put his name at the very head of their book. Like the name Abou ben Adhem heading the list. This happy dénouement at once cures his alcoholism and his sense of not belonging. There's psychology for you!

"The scenario — I mean, the novel — ends with the hero (now appointed Scout Master in the most socially élite section of New York) holding what he calls a 'Tolerance Jamboree.' In *Ballad for Americans* fashion, the hero sings an appeal for religious, racial, and sexual tolerance. His audience consists of cheering Eagle Scouts, who in wholesome young voices chorus, 'Lynch them, string 'em up!' each time he assails 'those sinister groups who look as if they might secretly be harboring intolerant thoughts.' On the boy scout refrain of 'Lynch them,' the curtain falls — I mean, the novel ends."

"Your every word purges me of pity and terror," I sputtered, moved to the quick. "You mince no words in your unmasking of social shams. I reel aghast at your passionate indictment of what man has made of man. Yet you inspire me with your battle cry on behalf of the downtrodden."

"Battle cry — there's the right phrase for Yours Truly," bantered Babbitt in that charming, whimsical way of his. "Not for nothing did they call me 'Battling Babbitt' at college when I founded the Social Conscience Powwow Parlor in an old, abandoned N.A.M. hall after it got foreclosed on in 1929. I'm a strong-chinned crusader for the Welfare State, who believes in pushing around all people who believe in pushing people around."

"What will Babbitt Senior think of your novel, G.B.?"

"It's this kind of urge for higher things that my dad was never able to understand in me. Read this letter that just arrived from the old boy, accompanying the monthly check on which I'm unfortunately still entirely dependent. Nothing confidential; just go ahead and read it. It proves my point that he doesn't see the difference between him and me. Doesn't see that I'm the Creative Type, just an intellectual Don Quixote forever following the Gleam."

While my friend chatted in slow precise French with the headwaiter, saying, "Moi, je suis un gourmet, pas un gourmand; très au courant avec le paté de foie gras," I skimmed the closing lines of the letter from Babbitt Senior:

"Though I stayed behind in Zenith and you left for Manhattan, though I still drink my Bourbon in 'Ye Chummy Steak House' while you sip wine in 'Café Chic,' we're not so different as you like to think. Son, you're just a chip off the ole block."

Vignettes on Thin Ice

"The truth of existence is always classical if we had but
the wit to see it, but immersion in our animal cares prevents
us from raising our eyes."   — GEORGE SANTAYANA

VIGNETTES ABOUT VALUES

Seven Times Around Values

For reasons it would take years to prove and which the reader
will either sense in a second or not at all, the modern intellectual
feels he needs to be able to make value judgments ("This is *better*
than that") in order to sustain his own sanity and the freedom
of his society. He feels he can no longer make value judgments on
the basis of his former liberal dogmas: economic determinism,
Deweyite pragmatism, the cultural relativism of the anthropologists
he used to admire, the ethical relativism of the semanticists he used
to quote.

Such is his dilemma. Solution? — I don't know it. Am not
sure there is any. Need there be?

But I do know this: to think this value dilemma all the way
through, to ponder and assess its rival solutions, religious or
humanistic, is the most challenging and important intellectual activity possible today for all who are revolting against the relativist-
materialist revolt.

Just as communists are less numerous than anti-anticommunists,
so those who believe in God are less numerous than those for
whom I suggest the term anti-anti-God. These anti-agnostics believe they believe because they are afraid of being afraid. What
they are afraid of — and with good reason — are the social consequences of pragmatism and disbelief. Their faithless, naturalistic

reason convinces them that reason is not enough, that faith and supernaturalism are needed to make men obey ethics.

Such considerations help prove my own belief that ultimately the ethics count more — are more innate in man — than the sanction behind the ethics, whether a naturalistic or supernatural sanction. Ethics inhere in man; values *are*.

The phrase "the crisis in values" has become an insufferable banality. Most serious contemporaries are, none the less, concerned with it. Not one of them has stormed his fortress of values, in the opinion of onlookers; not the pragmatists, not the supernaturalists. My handful of vignettes cannot presume even to try to storm it. Instead, like Joshua at Jericho, they merely march seven times around it.

No trumpets.

Bewildered Dignity

Of course, there is no ground for humaneness and for honesty — no ground for resisting the communazi degradation of man — if the dignity of man is merely an idealistic illusion. The credo of these pages, their tacit unprovable assumption, is that man clings — and clings innately — to some shreds of glory. Like a good sport in a bad comic strip, man grins tearfully through the mess of custard pies with which fate bombards and undignifies his forehead. So doing, he yet clings — and clings inherently — to some bewildered and inalienable dignity.

It matters to cling to glory's shreds. The remnant saveth. The shreds of ideality redeem reality. They are tattered. They are pathetic. They are, we learn, "semantically meaningless." But they are not an illusion. And they are not entirely a gyp, a fake, an operational tool, a rationalization of self-interest, an accidental by-product of sex or economics, a glandular reaction. They exist. They matter. Self-transcendence is part of self.

And self, in turn, is part of all self-transcendence. Self is the cruel practical joke, the old tin can, tied to the tail of transcendence by the neighborhood brats and rattling forth a distinctly tinny laugh at the sublimest moments.

When after a few million years our planet dies of cold or fire; when the carbon, hydrogen, oxygen, and proteins, that strutted about as "life," sink back into their primordial slime; then their last flicker of consciousness will sough, as they ooze back soggily into the ocean:

"Anyhow, for a while it was good to have been man."

This "for a while" is the deep sadness of the human condition. The condition of armorless consciousness. But this "anyhow" is the cry of gladness whose prelude is not pleasure but tragedy.

It is the tragedy of being born neither a stone nor a star but a human being. Mortal, aspiring, and earth-bound. A glory. A muddy and vulnerable glory.

We are all, aren't we, locked in the same firetrap together. No fire escape. The earth is not a "good neighborhood" to settle down in. Definitely on the wrong side of the cosmic railroad tracks. In the long run, earth is one of the "uninhabitable" planets.

There may be a less messy, more decently furnished universe around the corner. Unfortunately that is not the doorbell we rang by arriving as humans. Nobody likes "blind dates." Being born is a blind date.

Innateness of Values

Man is the evaluating animal. Only man has value codes.

Though variously interpreted, the need for value codes and the existence of ethics is innate in man, innate only in man, innate in all men without exception. This becomes obvious through experience, but can never be "proved."

According to Freud, even every criminal has a superego censor-mechanism. According to religion, even every criminal has a conscience. Perhaps more so, in the case of criminals, than other people. Perhaps the criminal has so much greater a sense of ethical self-condemnation that he commits crimes in order to be able to condemn himself. And in order to have a pretext for eventually getting caught. But must fight back his self-condemning desire to be caught by putting up the best possible show of re-sistance up to the eventual moment of getting caught. At which time his self-indicting files may be found readily available in significantly good order. Nazi aspects of this at Nuremberg trial. Any Stalinist aspects?

I do not know whether the Christian ethics are so-called natural or so-called divine in their origin (nor even whether everything natural is not divine; or everything divine natural; or what the distinction is). Being lower than the angels, I never expect to know. But I do deeply believe that values and the Christian ethics not only are innate and universal but are the most important and most distinguishing characteristic of man. Man must prevent their being relativized, pragmatized, and semanticized away — by the dogmatic theologians of science and the absolutists of relativism — into "self-deceptions" or mere "operational tools."

Pragmatism Is Unpragmatic

A seeming paradox yet factually correct: society can only achieve the goals of materialism by an idealistic interpretation of life.

Without the idealistic framework of ethical restraints, materialism can never achieve its material goals. It loses them in the scuffle of the war of all against all. It loses them in the mutually destructive scuffle of rival egotisms. Egotisms of the nation, of the class, or of the individual. Only the idealism of Christian love can save these rival egotisms from each other. And from themselves. Therefore: —

Material self-interest is suicide.

Material sacrifice is survival.

In place of the economic capitalist philosophy of Adam Smith and its parallel, the economic philosophy of Marx, the world through trial and error will come to see the material necessity of antimaterialism, the economic necessity of an anti-economic credo. The economic (if incidental) function of spirituality. The physical function of metaphysics.

Pragmatism is unpragmatic. It won't work.

My Quarrel With My Students

Into the campaign against new tyranny, let us throw ourselves with the old ardor and aspiration. The old ardor that preceded the present pose of urbanity and noncommitment. This anti-communist campaign must not be waged in a nationalistic spirit of "America *über alles*" or of cynical financial profiteering. It must recapture the enthusiasm and international idealism of those anti-Fascist campaigns of which most American intellectuals are proud

veterans today. My quarrel with some of today's representative
students: their sluggish lack of passionate commitments. Any kind
of commitments in any field.

America's college generations alternate regularly between commitment and sophistication. Currently, the choice again is for
sophistication. This is shown in their literary tastes and in their
political indifference. I feel an inadequacy in many of our younger
artists, because they wear their heartlessness on their sleeves; I
wish they dared commit themselves "embarrassingly" to the risk
of attempting lyricism and ecstasy. I feel an inadequacy in some
of our college political groups because, though anticommunist, they
dare not commit themselves "embarrassingly" to an unashamed
crusading spirit in regard to the great drama of Korea and the
Mao-Stalin danger. An earlier college generation was not ashamed
to have this crusading spirit against the Hitler danger.

No, this is not an appeal for "war propaganda" nor for "conformism"; such journalese is the business of the professional
patrioteers, not of the gropers for truth in the universities. This is
an appeal not for belligerency but for compassion. Not for hate
of the oppressor but for a lot more spontaneous sympathy and
aid for the oppressed behind the iron curtain and for the refugees
who flee to the West. The civilians on the campuses can do many
times more than at present to mitigate suffering without becoming
recruiting sergeants. In 1937, many a campus raised funds to send
an ambulance to Loyalist Spain for the victims of fascism. Today,
how many send ambulances to West Berlin or South Korea or
Greece to aid the victims of communism? Or is that somehow
a "different" kind of war? If a five-year-old child is half-starved
and is mangled by barbed wire when its parents flee with it across
the iron curtain to liberty, does this make it a "reactionary,"
unworthy of financial relief or of dignity and sympathy, while a
child fortunate enough to have been persecuted by a right-wing
government is a "progressive" child, worthy of relief rallies in
Madison Square Garden?

The atrophy — or else double standard — of the campus conscience is its failure to organize the same amount of public charity
and sympathy and "refugee committees" for anti-Soviet refugees as

they once did — and did rightly — for refugees from the Axis countries. Not that there is a dearth of student or faculty committees; you'll see plenty of them against teachers' oaths, McCarthyism, and thought control; splendid, but where are all the urgently-needed committees for the tortured refugees from Mao's thought control? Here the issue, which cuts across differences of politics and foreign policy, is again compassion and heartfelt human brotherhood.

In the past the great lyricists of liberty joined Byron in singing their detestation of all "despotism" and not of "despotism in every nation except China, Russia, and Planned Economies." Do the young writers on the campuses today react merely with a superior anti-sentimental shrug to Byron's "plain, sworn, downright detestation of every despotism in *every* nation"? If students and teachers are too clever to commit themselves vulnerably, naively, passionately on the side of humanity in their poems, paintings, and philosophizings today, then it is time for the pendulum between commitment and sophistication to swing once again and to give us less cleverists and more lyricists, saints, enthusiasts, and good old-fashioned drunkards: the four categories not afraid of revealing themselves, spilling teacups, "making scenes."

In reply, the modern collegian will point out the dangers, the blunders that resulted in the past from a gullible ardor in politics, in literature. Logically he is right. These dangers, these blunders I would not deny. Indeed I myself inveigh against them elsewhere. But what of the subtler dangers — the debits and gray debilities — resulting from sophisticated noncommitment?

Look at all the ethical, literary, and political problems piling up in America. They are waiting to be faced. They are waiting for the new generation to feel personally mixed up with them, before they can be solved. When will facing-up-to-things replace superciliousness as the first *noblesse oblige?* To be embarrassed in front of your friends, to make a fool of yourself by your own impetuosity or indignation or genuineness, is an even better social lubricant than good manners. Perpetual poise in front of others, when vital matters are discussed, is the worst, the ultimate offensiveness.

Suaveness is the only unforgivable gaucheness.

Seesaw

When the average religious believer argues with the average pragmatist, in the last resort each uses the other's trump. As crowning argument, the pragmatist justifies pragmatism spiritually, the religious believer justifies religion pragmatically. Though antispiritual, the pragmatist argues that only he can save the values of the spirit: by smuggling them in the back door after banning them from the front door. Though anti-pragmatic, the religious believer argues that only religion can save our material bodies: he assures parents that only religion will guarantee that their boy returns from college without Dangerous Thoughts and their girl without quintuplets.

In their desire to score debating points and to steal each other's trumps, each of the two destroys the dignity and partial truth of his own position.

All over America at this very moment, hundreds of Deweyan instrumentalists are arguing heatedly with hundreds of neo-Thomist religious absolutists. Watch them parrying blow for blow, parrying "progress" against "original sin." Rapping the rapier of "self-expression" against the buckler of "soul." And each is shifting to the other's position, like a seesaw that moves and moves and moves and — gets nowhere. Seesaw: the relativist arguing that Dewey really gives a much firmer foundation for faith in God than religion does ("well anyway, a kind of sort of God"), and the absolutist arguing that "in practice" his absolutes are "applied" with whatever necessary and minor, surely minor adjustments are required ("that's understood, isn't it?") *relative* to the particular facts of every particular situation.

Groping and Fumbling for Values

Our much-needed reaction against certain excesses of pragmatism today may become as much of a band wagon as pragmatism was twenty years ago. This leads to qualms and second thoughts: it is always distasteful to join what may become a band wagon — or, more precisely, an intellectual stampede to the womb, in case antipragmatism really comes to mean (as alleged) an unlimited "clericalism." Yet these qualms and second thoughts about antipragmatism leave me again, as secondary to the need for reaffirming universals, when I read such testimony from our educators as the following:

In the spring of 1942, when the armies of Germany and Japan stood at the very gates of victory, a young lady came up to the writer one day after class and said with deepest sincerity: "I can't see that we have any right to condemn Hitler. After all, he has a different standard of morality and has just as much right to his views as we have to ours." This excellent student reflected the kind of cynical detachment and moral relativism to which American students and the American public had been subjected during the twenties and thirties. The citizen (and the writer is a citizen) who stands by neutral in a struggle between cops and robbers is, in reality, favoring the robbers.[1]

How can you read such moral relativism and hear such words from your students without deep concern? Is it not natural to respond with the laudable naïveté of great emotion: "By God, something should be 'done about' those who foster such attitudes in education!"

My motive is not esthetic love of stained-glass windows, or love of a new Torquemada and a theocratic Inquisition, or alienation from America's democratic pluralist tradition, or anything except "deep concern" when I react to such student-attitudes with emotional antipragmatism. For have not the pragmatics, relativists, instrumentalists, and positivists helped bring us to such nihilism?

I lack the training in technical philosophy to follow the arguments, pro and con, on the theoretical level. Nothing I say presumes to encroach on the proper realm of trained and technical philosophers, whether pragmatists or theologians. I realized my own awkwardness in the realm of technical terminology when I found myself unable to "follow" a controversy in a learned journal about how Dewey hoped to preserve ethical restraints even under instrumentalism. I am eager to concede that the above student quotation, which so disturbed me because so typical, is not at all the intention nor the properly deduced consequence of the Deweyites. On the contrary, they do somehow manage to smuggle in decent values — what I call innate universals — despite themselves. Despite their own relativism.

---

[1] John B. Harrison, *This Age of Global Strife* (Chicago: J. B. Lippincott Co., 1952), foreword, p. vii.

Is their smuggling in of values done by legitimate philosophical logic? Or is it a contradiction? Is it done by their living (in practice) on the past capital of those same Christian absolutes which they (in theory) decry? Neither I nor 99 per cent of my readers are trained to answer these questions. Yet our lives, our entire cultural heritage may depend on the answer.

When all is said and done, leaving aside the theories or rationalizations of the more idealistic and more intellectual pragmatists, the following situation seems clear:—

Just as what the Germans call *Vulgarmarxismus* took the field almost completely from theoretical Marxism, despite Marx himself, so *Vulgarpragmatismus* is an active and malignant value-destroyer and uncivilizer today.[1] This is either because of or despite whatever may be the real meaning of the original Deweyite philosophers. Call it despite. In any case, their direct influence on the world is slight. But their indirect influence — *Vulgarpragmatismus,* meaning "anything goes" — is a menacing reality, sapping the West's resistance to totalitarianism. This reality must be recognized for what it is. Once it becomes recognized by most intellectuals, it must be stamped out — like a prairie fire — by two honest intellectual groups:

(1) the religious but non-Inquisitional antipragmatists;

(2) the nonvulgar, high-minded, theoretical philosophers of pragmatism.

No one can fairly blame the latter group for the misuse to which their ideas are put, on condition that they candidly recognize and combat that misuse. We saw how the Nazis misused the ideas of a basically individualistic — hence, anti-Nazi — philosopher like Nietzsche. Philosophers are not going to be confused with their parasites and vulgarizers — provided they themselves repudiate their fleas. The kind of warning I have in mind against the disastrous misuses and excesses of pragmatism and empiricism is illustrated by the wise words of the pragmatist Sidney Hook: "The

---

[1] So is *Vulgar-antipragmatismus,* to coin another verbal monstrosity, and ideological reality. It operates on the more low-brow level of anti-intellectual demagogy: "Fellers, let's wreck the Pasadena schools because them Dewey educators is a bunch of Red bums." But it is not this kind of aberration that my present readers — assuming them to be pro- and not anti-"intellectual" — are in danger of believing.

empiricists must . . . work out a scientific approach to values which will not end in the strange conclusion that value judgments are meaningless, and so drive those for whom ethical values *are* meaningful into the arms of authoritarianism to save their moral sanity." But far too few pragmatists, empiricists, relativists, and positivists share Professor Hook's value-affirming reasonableness.

It would take years to master the technical terminology and definitions needed to speak out professionally in the value controversy and the pragmatism controversy. Those years would be well-spent, no doubt. But meanwhile life goes on; crises confront us; we must *make immediate decisions* in value problems. Therefore most of us speak out amateurishly, rather than professionally, about "values." And so we should. Even at the admitted risk of catch-as-catch-can terminology about the value problem. It is more important that the nonphilosophers, the 99 per cent who *are* the problem, face the problem than that the philosophers talk it away.

They talk it away, instead of helping us face it and live it. They do so with formulations that are perhaps irrefutable but certainly irrelevant. They talk it away on a rarefied level where *our* question of life-or-death survival becomes *their* sophisticated, unfeeling wordplay.

Now listen carefully, you logical positivists, you progressive educators: this is the Katyn-Belsen decade; it matters to us deeper than tears whether our civilization lives or dies; we need help, and it's no-go telling us again and again — waiting in that line at Katyn together, it's no-go your telling us with a superior, bored patience — that concepts like "ethics," "absolutes," "values," "human dignity," "tragedy," and "death" are incorrect, amateurish semantics or have been "replaced" by non-Aristotelian logic.

The "Anti-Semitism" of the Liberals

Depressing thought: every conformist group has its own equivalent of the scourge of anti-Semitism, a scourge inflicted on any minority it dare not understand for fear of having to think things through. Your "Jew" (your "slacker," your spoil-sport, your inconvenient nonbooster) is whoever distracts you from your television set. Or who asks you "why" instead of "how."

Catholic-baiting is the anti-Semitism of the liberals.

No Crusade for Bingocracy

The Western heritage is not diversity alone nor unity alone but diversity within unity. Being a Christian-Hebraic-Roman-Hellenic amalgam, with inner contradictions sometimes reconciled but sometimes not, the Western heritage allows for a generous dose of tolerant pluralism. If you make no allowance for pluralism and aim at *too* much unity, you will get no unity at all; you will only provoke the same internal strife and chaos that you condemn in those who seek too little unity.

There is the army anecdote about the naïve and arrogant soldier who protested, "Everybody is out of step except me." This is the position of our more extreme religious absolutists. To indict 99 per cent of mankind for being out of step with yourself is a merely emotional (arrogant and naïve) reaction to the liberal relativists. The latter proclaim: "There are no steps at all. To be out of step is the *summum bonum*. That's true freedom and true self-expression, and it feels wonderful!" Neither of these two extremes will bring the needed Western unity against Marxist economic materialism. Both extremes will only increase the ethical crisis, of which both are symptoms.

By always remembering the Western formula of unity-through-diversity, we will avoid the mistake of recoiling from the excessive liberal relativists to the excessive religious absolutists. The latter are usually former liberal pragmatists, now disillusioned, attempting by pious intolerance to shout down that nagging inner voice of doubt, which tells them: "Deep down in your uncontrollable heart, you — like every single twentieth-century intellectual — are still a liberal."

When pragmatic liberals are converted not organically and earnestly but mechanically and glibly (how fashions do change since the Marxist 1930's!) to Eliotizing and neo-Thomizing and value-absolutizing, then they are still pragmatic liberals as much as ever. Only now they are standing on their heads. T. S. Eliot's *Idea of a Christian Society* is not the real alternative to John Dewey's idea of a progressive society. Both secular relativism and an artificial clerical unity are symptoms of the Waste Land, *the former being its self-satisfaction, the latter being its self-hate.*

Psychologically, as opposed to ideologically, Mortimer Adler (for example) is a liberal. Typically, modernly, most unmedievally so. Even though a self-disgruntled one and *malgré lui.*

Professor Universalia-post-rem is standing in front of Alice's magic looking glass, behind which — through which — he will find Saint Universalia-ante-rem.

But suppose instead he finds just plain air, that ultimate derisive Boojum? I am enough Platonized to believe in universal values and in ante-rem; but to hunt such a Snark is not *so easy* as that.

In other words, it is not a matter of mechanical conversion from fashion to fashion, from learning-by-doing and forward-looking kindergartens to dreams about falling downstairs and the Empire State building as a Freudian symbol; then to a freewheeling re-interpretation of Myth, gilding the *Golden Bough;* then to economic democracy and songs of social significance; then to anti-usury and dark hints about international bankers; then to formalist contempla-tion of the Art Object as thing-in-itself while you glow with a hard gem-like flame; then to *Angst* and lots of very public "fear and trembling"; then to unoriginal remarks about original sin and untragic remarks about tragedy. After that: the whole glib cycle all over again, with every member of the cycle sneering at that other, more suburban member who is one jump behind or who enrages you by believing what you will believe one jump later. Deity of the endless merry chase is a certain bitch-goddess against whom William James warned his countrymen, only to have them misuse his name and his pragmatism as a still slicker and shinier rationalization of Success.

This is not nasty mockery in Thersites style of religious conver-sion. It is a plea against — well, let's call it "parlor Christians." I use the phrase as analogous with "parlor pinks." In fact, the same Lit'ry Set who parlored Social Significance in the 1930's are parloring God today. In both cases, it is a matter of being know-ing about the exquisitely "right" phrases. It is a matter of being *au courant* with the more arid dogmas of both. But not *au courant* with the one dogma indispensable both for sincere social reform and sincere religion: "thou shalt love thy neighbor as thyself."

For centuries to come, intellectuals will continue to rotate through their cycle of varying conversions, bouncing between the same two poles of social versus spiritual idealism. But whichever their conversion, at either pole, it will be worth its Attic salt only when its prelude is love-in-the-heart, not ear-to-the-ground.

II

"Clericalisme, c'est l'ennemi!" This secularist and Catholic-baiting war cry of the French Republican Gambetta is still the tacit motto of American liberalism. To that extent, American liberalism is still bogged down in the by-passed, nineteenth-century alternatives. Instead, the proper war cry for our own day should be: "Anything goes," *c'est l'ennemi!*

On the other hand, just as Eliot is not the alternative to Dewey, so the alternative to the rootlessness and the value-vacuum of progressive education is not the arbitrary imposition of values by a new Inquisition. "Anything goes" is neither crushed nor cured by saying "Nothing goes."

Matthew Arnold's warning about Hebraism and Hellenism makes hackneyed and dated reading today. None the less, it will need to be revived and undated. Otherwise, Christian moralism, in its justified indignation against economic materialism, may ignore the classical, rational, and esthetic parts of our pluralist heritage and stress only the Christian-Hebraic. In order to give the former their due, it is important to conserve our values humanistically. This can be done via poetry and the other arts and humanities; via the study of history and of the great Greek and Elizabethan tragedies; and via the direct, personal, spontaneous experience of love. Redeeming love: how comic and inexcusable that most current philosophies about values and ethics should omit, with embarrassment, this emotional reality, which finds it easier to "move the sun and stars" than to move the intellectuals. "Love is the master key."[1]

---

[1] "Saint Thomas Aquinas declares that love for God is the end toward which obedience to a religious superior is the means. In this spiritual perspective the Christian controversy over Obedience is swallowed up in the Christian agreement over Love, and this brings within view the possibility of a common spiritual effort to save our Western civilization by replacing it on its Christian foundations.

"Willing God's will is man's only way of overcoming a disharmony in human nature which is at the root of every crisis in human society. But man cannot will God's will without loving God as man is loved by Him. Love is the master key." — ARNOLD TOYNBEE, preface to *Law, Liberty and Love,* by Columbia Cary-Elwes, N.Y., 1952.

While completely excluding the communazis and their anti-ethics from the unifying framework of civilization, we must remember to honor and include the classical-pagan as well as Christian-Hebraic sources of the ethical code which unites us. The ethical code (more than economics or nationalism) is the basic issue separating America from Stalinism-Hitlerism. It is the only issue I would die for without misgivings; as a last resort, the ethical foundation of freedom justifies even war.

The great Catholic intellectuals and scholars of the Middle Ages and the Renaissance were steeped in Greek literature and classical, pre-Christian philosophy. This made them better, not worse Christians. Some of their present residuary legatees have no time to waste on such trifles, being too busy picketing un-Puritan movies. This suggests a question. Is the honorable adjective "Roman Catholic" truly merited by America's middleclass-Jansenist Catholicism, puritanized, Calvinized, and dehydrated (reaching America in the nineteenth century, via indirect stages, from the Jansenist seminaries of seventeenth- and eighteenth-century France)?

Today the Christian-Hebraic-Roman-Hellenic-shaped West is rightly and properly "crusading." The crusade is against Marxist materialism and the communazi anti-ethics. As an eclectic sympathizer with many Catholic teachings (Mr. Blanshard classifies me as a sinister "fellow-traveler of the Vatican"), I venture to hint that the purpose of this great crusade, being spiritual, is not exclusively to enable Cardinal Spellman to march victoriously up the steps of the Kremlin, solemnly rededicating the former meeting-hall of the Politburo to Bingo-Games-Every-Sunday.

VIGNETTES ABOUT MONSTERS

"A child would like to sit in his lap and a dog would sidle up to him." — *Ambassador* JOSEPH E. DAVIES *characterizing Stalin in* Mission to Moscow

"To choose one's victim, to prepare one's plans minutely, to slake an implacable vengeance and then to go to bed . . . there is nothing sweeter in the world." — STALIN (*to his friend and later victim, Chief of Secret Police Dzerzhinsky*)

Portrait of a Monster

Who or what was he?

Riding the nationalist-militarist tide of the history he thought he was making, was the most headlined name and most dreaded radio voice and most familiar front-page face of twentieth-century Europe. Now that World War II has passed, leaving 22 million[1] corpses in a Europe of rubble, what is there to say about the mentality behind the little moustache and forelock, the mentality that unleashed the greatest catastrophe ever recorded? What can the historian say, or the moralist, or the psychologist, or each bereaved mother? Once so big an event, and now so incredibly little left to say about it.

This lower-middle-class Siegfried with the grand-opera rhetoric wanted so hard to be considered respectable.

And tried to achieve respectability by conquering the world.

And in the process passed out of the category of "humanity," as defined before the devaluation of values, and instead became a monster; a respectable, patriotic, petit-bourgeois Corporal of monsterdom; murdering more human beings more inhumanly than any other tyrant in history.

And then pulled down half of Europe to be a quilt for his deathbed, as in the *Twilight of the Gods* of his beloved Richard Wagner.

And in every minute of the dozen years of what he called his "thousand-year Reich," was the most ignorant and surly slave of slaves; the cast-off waste matter of nineteenth-century romanticism, nationalism, and industrialism; the casual blunt weapon snatched up for suicide by that "European History" in which he had received in 1905, in a peaceful, provincial, Austrian schoolhouse, the grade of "C minus."

The Secret of the Other Monster

As Marx rightly remarked: after a certain point quantitative differences become qualitative in effect. When the number of peasants murdered by deliberate starvation exceeds five million in the 1930's, when those thousands of Polish prisoners of war

---

[1] "22 million": according to a Vatican study, released Nov. 21, 1945, including civilians killed in Nazi death-camps as well as military deaths.

are secretly butchered at one swoop in 1940 in Katyn, when official Soviet law imposed death sentences of a bullet through the neck upon deviationists aged twelve (*sic!*), and when ten million slave laborers undergo torture in concentration camps at this very moment, then the ravaging criminal who decrees all this is no longer a human being. He is not even an evil human being, the way ordinary criminals are merely quantitatively evil. Instead, such a creature has passed qualitatively out of the category of humanity. He has joined Hitler in a different and rarer category, that of monster.

What, then, differentiates the monster Hitler from the monster Stalin? The monster Hitler, by openly glorifying war and persecution, said he was a monster. The monster Stalin, by repeating desecratingly the language of democratic idealism, says he is not a monster. By playing the Avuncular Joe of social reform, the monster Stalin can deceive and kill more human beings than if he openly proclaimed, in *Mein Kampf* fashion, his hate of human beings. Who in the West would ever have said "Uncle Adolf"?

In 1939, after their joint aggression against Poland, Stalin himself expressed very prettily this difference between the two monsters. On September 27, German diplomats drafted for Stalin a joint communiqué, boasting of the successful joint aggression. While agreeing with this, Stalin protested that "it presented the facts *all too frankly*" — the most typical words he ever spoke. Instead, he caused the Nazi-Soviet allies to publish a benevolent reworded communiqué of September 28, saying the Nazi-Soviet armies were taking over Poland for its own good in order to "help the Polish people."

The Polish people were not told that Stalin later sent the Nazi foreign minister a confidential telegram exulting that German-Russian "friendship" would be "lasting and firm" because it was "cemented by blood" of the butchered Poles. The Polish people, like the Koreans today, were told that the only Soviet aim was to bring peace and prosperity. You are going to hear ever more of this pseudo peace propaganda. It will be parroted by many duped, peace-loving, noncommunist Americans, including some highly-respected pacifist branches of the Christian church. To them, you must repeat again and again Stalin's private boasts of aggression to Hitler. You must repeat Stalin's confession of un-bourgeois prejudice against ever "presenting the facts all too frankly."

Not one man but the whole international Communist network follows this same skilful propaganda technique. In 1924 the French Communist party received the following official directive from its Politburo: "Those elected must make purely demonstrative proposals, conceived not with a view to their adoption, but for propaganda and agitation."[1] This directive is still considered valid. It, too, is a communist maxim to quote and requote. Every time the government with the largest army in history proposes Stockholm peace pledges and proposes atomic disarmament without proper controls, let us repeat: "Purely demonstrative proposals, conceived not with a view to their adoption, but for propaganda."

Whoever still takes seriously any communist promise of co-operation, disarmament, or peaceful coexistence, ought to ponder the following solemn promise, made in 1947 by Clement Gottwald, today communist dictator of Czechoslovakia:

> Dictatorship is not the only road to socialism. Czechoslovakia alone is in a position to show the world how collective economy and individual liberty can be combined.
> We believe in democracy. We practice democracy. We do not for a moment propose to deviate from such a course. There is *not a word of truth* in the assertion that the Communist Party of Czechoslovakia cannot operate with other parties and that sooner or later it must strive for dictatorship.[2]

Soviet imperialism has a far larger fifth column in the West than did German imperialism. Why? Part of the answer lies in the difference between their propaganda methods. It reflects the secret difference between the monster Hitler and the monster Stalin: Hitler was "all too frankly" the wolf while Stalin tells Little Red Ridinghood he is a grandmother. All who hate war and are struggling to preserve peace, must reply to Soviet "peace" proposals:

"Grandmother, what big teeth you have!"

---

[1] Einaudi, Domenach, and Garosci, *Communism in Western Europe* (Ithaca, N. Y., 1951), p. 120.

[2] Italics mine. *Socialist Commentary,* London, April, 1948. *Politics,* New York, Spring 1948.

Twins but not Identical Twins

Communism and nazism are alike in their main business: total and permanent war upon mankind and the murder of millions of innocents. Compared with this main business, political and economic programs and ideologies may seem secondary. Yet communism and nazism do differ deeply psychologically in how they go about this main business. The Nazis murdered melodramatically and sadistically (see reports of concentration camps). The communists murder in an unlurid, businesslike fashion (see reports on slave camps and Katyn). Such reliable eye-witness accounts as Jerzy Gliksman's *Tell the West* confirm this difference.

In interrogating prisoners, the typical communist tortures to get results, not to get fun, as with the SS-men. For a Nazi or fascist, killing is an art; for a communist, a utilitarian science. The Hell created by the former looks like a grand opera by Wagner. The Hell created by the latter looks like the prosaic imitation of a Ford assemblyline. Nazism was a synthesis of romanticism and Prussianism. Communism is a synthesis of the old Tartar autocracy and modern technocracy; in Lenin's definition, "Soviet government plus electrification;" in Herzen's epigram of a century ago (prematurely applied to Nicholas I), "Genghis Khan plus the telegraph."

Esthetically I prefer the astringent sobriety of a Stalin speech to the cloudy rhetoric of a Hitler speech. Ethically, of course, there is no choice. Both are forced to use force because their programs violate nature: trying to change into herd animals the descendants of individualistic simians. But a very special kind of herd animals: in either of its forms, let us define the totalitarian state as a flock of carnivorous sheep.

Two Sets of Photographs

Communists and Nazis differ also in appearance. Gone are the days of beard and bomb; the modern Soviet leaders, in contrast with Nazis and fascists, look petty, dull, and bureaucratic. Look at any recent photo of the dowdy Politburo! Suppose you did not know ahead the long list of genocidal crimes and even more destructive blunders attached to each one's name, the deportation of whole cities, the starvation of entire provinces. You would innocently imagine some retired hick constable in his anecdotage was boring you with his home-talent Rogues' Gallery: two rows of swaggering, small-town "fixers" (each tensing self-consciously his fake "strong chin"), flanked by prissy apprentice-counterfeiters with mean eyes.

Each looks like a third assistant bookkeeper in the act of rising Napoleonically to second assistant bookkeeper. Not Wagnerian Hitler-types but prosaic Himmler-types. It is always the sober pedants of massacre — was not the incorruptible Robespierre another? — and not the bloodthirsty thugs who make the worst killers. How rightly you would apply to most of them what Lenin himself had said so maliciously of Molotov: "Russia's best filing clerk" — (Molotov, the only member of Lenin's Politburos whom Stalin bothered to let survive the palæobolshevikocide of 1936-39).

Among the rest, only the *petite,* Hitler-forelocked Malenkov gives signs of being a monster on the grand scale of the two Masters. Among all those ungracious scowls and surly stares, only his has a flash of the genuine old paranoia, though obsequiously restrained until Big Brother creates a vacuum for new supermen by passing on to the Marxist dialectical Valhalla.

Photographed at their political celebrations, the Nazis look at first glance more presentable and at second glance less presentable than the Politburo. They can be distinguished from the Politburo in two quite different ways; they look less respectable, yet more "elegant."

Less respectable: only Himmler (Beria's twin) has that reliable filing-clerk face. Most of the rest look more bohemian; shopkeepers, yes, but shopkeepers with a raffish "artistic temperament." And indeed, an amazingly large percentage, including Hitler, were romantic artists *manqués.* Wee Goebbels: looking like an evil-minded Charles Addams infant that had been slightly nibbled by rats and then discarded as poisonous. Ley and Streicher: trying to smile benevolently, that benign smile of cadgers of free drinks and pinchers of very young girls. Hess, Rosenberg, and Schirach: trying to look wholesome and reputable in their neat uniforms but only looking like boy scouts suddenly caught abusing themselves.

And yet more "elegant": like con-men in a British colonial seaport, affecting the dashing air of the black-sheep "remittance man" of the fanciest London families. "Von" Ribbentrop: looking like a traveling-salesman parodying mercilessly a Ruritanian diplomat's attempt to imitate an English gentleman. The strutting, dressy, and winking Goering: obviously a landlady. Of the frowsy, slovenly, bursting-at-the-seams genre. Once (it is hinted) a glamor star of the Ziegfeld Follies of 1913, and now tittering like a pachydermic kitten: "Whoops! you should have seen me the time Diamond Jim Brady drank Ribbentrop's champagne from my slipper."

VIGNETTES ABOUT CREDOS

Unlaughing and Untragic

American letters lack and need some equivalent of the Parisian *feuilletoniste*. The latter expression may denote mere froth and superficiality. But it need not do so. The function of the feuilleton is to be serious unpedantically, to be heavy lightly, to worship what Nietzsche called *la gaia scienza*. Does not all Joyful Wisdom have a Mediterranean — an unfoggy — sky? Today its devotees must reluctantly record the alternation between the halcyon and the horrendous: between the blue of Mozart's sweet eighteenth century (Talleyrand's *la douceur de vivre* before 1789) and the thunder-claps from 1984. Even so, it may be maintained, with Swift, Pope, and Nietzsche, that the brief and light touch, the feuilleton touch, is the least embarrassing approach to a tragic reality.

Reality has become too extreme for even the extremest adjectives of overstatement. Reality can no longer be expressed by an exhausted vocabulary of apocalyptic apoplexies. Consider the fate of the apocalyptic word "colossal," and it is clear why a tragic reality requires the Golden Laughter of *la gaia scienza*. Properly applied, the golden brand of laughter is the highest seriousness. It has nothing in common with the irresponsible pose of capering at the edge of the abyss. For that, there is too much suffering in the contemporary world: uneasy lies the clown that wears a head.

This is not an advocacy of the romanticism and tearfully-smiling sentimentality of a Pagliacci but of the neo-classicism and dry witty bitterness of Swift. His light-heavy eighteenth-century touch is still the most understanding approach — the least embarrassing, the least patronizing or crocodile-tearful approach — to the brotherhood of suffering.

In turn, the ability to rejoice goldenly is achieved only by the insights of tragedy. Every "ode to joy" is a tragic insight. It transfigures the predicament of being human. In "The Gyres," Yeats sang this on his deathbed, as World War II was breaking forth:

> Irrational streams of blood are staining earth;
> Empedocles has thrown all things about;
> Hector is dead and there's a light in Troy;
> We that look on but laugh in tragic joy.

And again in "Lapis Lazuli":

> All perform their tragic play,
> There struts Hamlet, there is Lear,
> That's Ophelia, that Cordelia;
> Yet they, should the last scene be there,
> The great stage curtain about to drop,
> If worthy their prominent part in the play,
> Do not break up their lines to weep.
> They know that Hamlet and Lear are gay;
> Gaiety transfiguring all that dread. . . .
> All things fall and are built again,
> And those that build them again are gay.

Even after reading Swift, Burke, Nietzsche, Dostoyevsky, Freud, and Yeats, many Anglo-American progressives still cling to their Rousseauistic faith in the infinite perfectability of human nature. In their politics and in their literature (their naturalistic novels, from Zola to James Jones), they can see happiness and unhappiness but are color-blind to tragedy.

Or else, they define tragedy superficially: for the rich, "emotional maladjustment"; for the poor, the unavailability of bathtubs. No room for saints, no room for drunkards; both must be "psycho-analyzed" until they "adjust."

What American Live Wires hail as progressivism is what Yeats scorned as Whiggery:

> Whether they knew or not,
> Goldsmith and Burke, Swift and the Bishop of Cloyne
> All hated Whiggery; but what is Whiggery?
> A levelling, rancorous, rational sort of mind
> That never looked out of the eye of a saint
>   Or out of a drunkard's eye.

Whiggery, with its boosting cult of material progress, is found equally among our capitalists and among our radical reformers. It stands for optimism. But a whining optimism. It faces television sets to avoid facing the abyss. Such optimism is more nihilistic than a tragic sense that stares back at the abyss.

A tragic sense faces the reality of the communazi terror-camps instead of the illusions of Hollywood. It faces its corpses as they are, instead of prettied and rouged and *endimanchés* by optimistic morticians who never mention the tragic word "death."

Whining and evasive optimism is afraid to brood "morbidly" — that is to say, honestly — about death. This fear and this optimism have been streamlined into a big business. Examples are all around us. Listen to this promotional book blurb from one of the biggest publishers. The title of the book is *Don't Think About It.* The author is described as "the glamorous star of *Ben Hur* and many other silent movies." Having thus established her qualifications as a philosopher, the blurb confides: "Her philosophy is strongly inspirational." Such use of the word "inspiration," a word once associated with Socrates and Saint Francis, is itself a devaluation of values. Its message is a "realistic," mass-produced evasion of tragedy:

> It offers a proven source of practical help and comfort for all who suffer a personal loss or misfortune. . . . She was enjoying a completely happy existence when suddenly her beloved husband died. In her efforts to regain a worthwhile and healthy life with her children and friends, she discovered the simple philosophy which she explains in this book. "Don't brood," she advises, "but focus your mental and physical energies on other activities."

In a different context, some of this may make therapeutic good sense, just because it is not the route to a Shakespeare or Dostoyevsky. But what makes this blurb my candidate for a time capsule of Americana, to be preserved a thousand years in an atomic-proof pyramid, is its concluding sentence:

> Currently, she has her own television show, and is the active president of the DON'T THINK CLUB.

Spearheaded by a "president" who is no mere figurehead but "active" and even "inspirational," and reaching millions via television, a network of these clubs should encircle the globe in no time at all. Finally the entire human race, after evolving for millions of years from the trees into the nuisance of intellect, will become a single, planetary DON'T THINK CLUB. Or is this perhaps not quite what Victoria's laureate meant by "that one, far-off, divine event towards which the whole creation moves"?

"Nothing So Much Resembles a Bump as a Hollow"

Marxism ("religion is the opiate of the people") is the opiate of the People's Democracies.

Stalinism is the fascism of the Marxists. Anti-Semitism, "agin' the bankers," is the socialism of the fascists. "Cosmopolitan"-baiting is the anti-Semitism of the Stalinists.

The "welfare state" is the religion of the materialists. "Pie in the sky" is the materialism of the religious.

Tariffs are the welfare state of the free-enterprisers.

Lattimore-McCarthy

The most interesting thing about McCarthy and Lattimore is what they have in common. Namely, their aid to communism.

Lattimore aided communism by the way he defended it.

McCarthy is aiding communism by the way he attacks it.

Proportion

Loose accusations result in witch-hunts. Loose exonerations — in this day of Hiss, Fuchs, Remington — result in America's "liberal" version of McCarthyism: the witch-hunt against "witch-hunts."

Both brands of irresponsibles are destroying the American *sense of proportion* on which civil liberties depend, until the bewildered public wonders: Which is witch?

It is a case of the crackpot calling the kettle red.

Rehabilitate "Conspicuous Waste"

If it is to preserve individualism, as befits America's pluralistic pattern, then democracy must not merely tolerate but encourage variety. Only the guillotine (in Robespierre's phrase "the dictatorship of liberty") can prevent variety in cultural styles of living and in economic standards of living. *Liberté,* being more than *égalité,* consists of more than economic or cultural leveling. There is a false note, an exaggerated — because concealed — Puritanism, in the horror of "conspicuous waste" that runs through Thorstein Veblen's *Theory of the Leisure Class.*

Boswell, at his best when observing not Johnson but society, made what today would be a "shockingly reactionary" observation; in other words, an observation of courageous, undemagogic clarity:

> Luxury is the great incitement to everything great and elegant in society, to all our commerce, and to almost all our arts.

Today add "conspicuous waste" to "luxury" in that statement. In their end results, luxury and conspicuous waste are less wasteful than thrift, sobriety, and a drab, standardized leveling.

Instead of condemning all idleness and *joie de vivre* as lacking what the 1930's called "social significance," distinguish between ungracious and gracious idleness. The artistic and social magic of the latter has enough dream-nexus value to atone for the lack of cash-nexus. You may generalize from examples like this: French democracy maintaining the expensive upkeep of the royal Versailles gardens. The tax-paying beholder votes to support this expense for the sake of his society's artistic and magical aspirations — and not only for the sake of the tourist trade.

Today democracy needs to abjure the joyless utilitarianism and Puritanism of Bentham and Veblen and to cherish the few feudal relics it still has left. The modern urban or suburban, poor or rich, is emotionally starved for "the unperturbed and courtly images" of custom, ceremony, and stately calm. Let there be more village fairs, strolling troubadours (Vachel Lindsay tried to be one), and even a few Madame Pompadours and Magda Lupescus thrown in. It would cost surprisingly little to add such touches of colorful frivolity to our gray utility of gray factory soot.

Behind the N.A.M. murmurings against excess-profits taxes, there emerges no more dazzling pageantry than the double-breasted business suit. Would there were more conspicuous waste in those quarters, instead of a tight-fisted secularization of Calvinism. We of the sinful profession of professors, currently unmasked as subverters of Adam Smith, may be more willing to limp along at our less-than-bricklayer's salaries if we know that our uneducated economic superiors are *at least having fun*. But I protest when they don't even spend their dividends on courtesans, horses, and champagne, but merely on Worthwhile Investments, donations to Worthy Causes (tax deductible), and nonalcoholic, ulcer-coddling celery juice.

Restraining Reckless Middle-Age

Can you still remember the plot of the play and movie, *The Male Animal?* It typified the culture-hero of the 1920's and 1930's: the young radical boldly revolting against a smug faculty and reactionary trustees. *God and Man at Yale*[1] is the inverted mirror image of *The Male Animal*. This time we have the young capitalist — future culture-hero of the 1950's? — boldly revolting against a smugly radical faculty and not-reactionary-enough trustees. Both books have the gadfly virtue of anti-smugness. Yet both inaugurated a new smugness of their own. Well, so now America may await the spectacle of a thousand Buckleys as campus soap-boxers of the 1950's (twins of a thousand leftist campus-martyrs of the 1930's). The spectacle is worthy of the satiric quatrain by Yeats, "On Hearing That the Students of Our New University Have Joined the Agitation Against Immoral Literature":

> Where, where but here have Pride and Truth,
> That long to give themselves for wage,
> To shake their wicked sides at youth
> Restraining reckless middle-age?

Nominally his book is about Yale education. Actually it is about American politics. While editor of the Yale undergraduate newspaper, William F. Buckley, Jr., had social acceptance (Skull and Bones and other clubs) but understandably resented exclusion from intellectual acceptance by a dominant liberalism. Culmination of these frictions was the suppression by the Yale administration of a prepared address he had been invited to give to the Yale alumni. I can see no excuse for this suppression, especially by those who today are rightly defending academic freedom against his resultant book. The suppression has given vastly more

---

[1] William F. Buckley, Jr., *God and Man at Yale* (Chicago: Regnery, 1951).

publicity to his charges of Yale socialism and atheism than if he had been allowed to blow off steam through free speech, as every radical of right or left is entitled to do (short of conspiracy).

Whether real or imagined, such persecution gave our young capitalist rebel the same kind of radical underdog reaction as it did the left-wing hero of *The Male Animal*. But this time the underdog reaction is linked incongruously with the topdog reflexes of big business. Such a curious linkage has produced a curious book.

The book is an unrestrained attack on nineteenth-century liberalism in education, politics, and religion (but not in economics). This attack is the best way today of combining underdog and top-dog protests. Via so militant a plutocracy, an intellectual out-group combines with an economic in-group. Both poles of the Nietzsche polarity — slave morality and master morality — apply to this book and this whole nation-wide movement. That makes it psychologically more complex than realized by the outraged liberals. Their natural reflex was to dismiss this neo-plutocrat revolt against their New Deal status quo as merely the yawp of crude and un-complex boors. I fear it will not be so easily dismissed as all that. This movement needs to be not snubbed but faced up to, freely and fully debated, and then thoroughly refuted. The process of refutation will require our smugger liberals and New Dealers to re-examine their own fallacies and platitudes as well as the more obvious fallacies of their opponents, who imagine that a return to full laissez faire is possible.

II

To Buckley's credit: he does correctly insist on a return to certain much-needed principles, even though he then goes on to misapply them. These principles are that man has a moral nature, that statism threatens it, and that unmoral materialism results in a suicidal tolerance debunking all values as equally "relative." Above all, he attacks "statism and atheism" on the Yale campus and alleges they rule the roost.

But what is his alternative to their materialism? Nothing more inspiring than the most sterile tradesman-materialism of the McKinley era. Is it not humorless, or else blasphemous, for this eloquent advocate of Christianity, an unworldly and anti-economic religion, to enshrine jointly as equally sacrosanct: "Adam Smith and Ricardo, Jesus and Saint Paul"?

In this urgent crisis, when our survival against Soviet aggression depends on co-operating *both* with capitalists and with anti-Red heroes like the socialist Reuter in Europe, the author (unbelievably) treats not only mild social democracy but even most social reform as almost cryptocommunism. He damns communism, our main enemy, not half so violently as lesser enemies like the income tax and inheritance tax. Words will really fail you when you reach the book's final "message": trustees and alumni should violate the legally established academic freedom to "banish from the classroom" not merely communists but all professors deviating from Adam Smith! (Such neo-plutocrat threats are discussed later in the section on academic freedom, page 293.)

Has a young Saint Paul emerged from the Yale class of 1950 to bring us the long-awaited Good Tidings of a New Conservatism and Old Morality? The trumpets of national publicity imply it. But this Paul-in-a-hurry skips the prerequisite of first being a rebel Saul. The difference between a shallow and a profound conservatism is the difference between an easy, booster-ish yea-saying to the old order and a hard-won, tragic yea-saying. True, we need, as Buckley argues, to conserve traditional morality. But it must be earned and actually lived by open-eyed and free rediscovery, not by blind and coercive indoctrination of slaves. It must be earned by sacrifice, not by glibly being "his class's Bright Young Man" (to quote the Yale 1950 Class History on Buckley).

Great conservatives — immortals like Burke, Hamilton, Disraeli, Churchill, or the poets Pope and Swift — earned the right to be sunnily conservative by their long dark nights. You can earn it by being a tortured romantic Irishman like Burke, an outcast bastard pauper from the West Indies like Hamilton, or a cruelly-snubbed Jew like Disraeli. You can earn it by Churchill's bitter decade before his great hour in 1940. Or by having Pope's hump on your back or Swift's insanity in your skull.[1] But you do not earn a heartfelt and conviction-carrying traditionalism and conservatism by the shortcuts of a popular campus clubman, without the in-

---

[1] Yeats: "Through Jonathan Swift's dark grove he passed, and there Plucked bitter wisdom that enriched his blood."

spiring agony of lonely, unrespectable soul-searching.

Not for economic privilege but for ethical and antimaterialist reasons, some of us have preached a conservative "revolt against revolt." If the laboring mountain of the new campus conservatism can produce no more imaginative vision than some moth-eaten mouse of petty economic privilege, then we shall soon need a revolt against the revolt against revolt.

This symptomatic, best-selling book is merely the outworn Old Guard antithesis to the outworn Marxist thesis. Here is not the liberty-security synthesis the future cries for. Some day Buckley may give us the hard-won, dark-night wisdom of synthesis. But for that, he will find need to add, to his many splendid existing virtues, three new ones: sensitivity, compassion, and an inkling of the tragic paradoxes of *la condition humaine*.

A Pretentious-Sounding Reply, but That's How I Feel About It[1]

Dear —————,

Thanks for your kind and flattering proposal (which I must decline). It recalls the days when you and I felt it a privilege to be allowed to join the "Committee to Defend America by Aiding the Allies." That was a time when Hitler seemed almost certain of defeating the Allies; the situation then was one of real and not artificial necessity, so much so that every single citizen ought to have contributed by joining the committee. But joining an emergency committee is a long step from joining nonemergency committees, even for so worthy a cause as yours. Among so many worthy committees and causes, must we not, as primarily nonpolitical artists, develop in America a more rigorous criterion than worthiness before joining things?

Like Hitler in 1940, today Russia and communism are the winning side. (This is not a prediction — sufficient sacrifice for freedom can still rescue the future — but a statistical statement of fact.) When communism is winning at the rate of conquering

---

[1] This letter — pompous, humorless, but making points that have got to be made — was written to decline political contacts. It was in reply to a kind invitation to be listed in "national publicity" with writers and artists "actively supporting" an excellent presidential candidate in 1952.

one hundred million men a year since 1945, it is not ungallant nor opportunistic to defend the proto-underground of the globe's remaining embattled anticommunists. When I decline your offer of being publicly listed as "active" for the candidate for whom I may (as it happens) vote, it is partly because his looks like the winning side. Bandwagon-joining, even in a good cause, can become a *trahison des clercs* for anybody whose main concern is nonpolitical and literary. It hampers the *clerc*'s function of independent, nonpartisan criticism of all sides, especially of all winners.

Whatever value a poet's or historian's comments on politics may have depends on his independence. He must keep strictly free from party labels and their party lines. Temperamentally an anti-"joiner," I belong to neither American party and never shall. Both are untotalitarian. Politically I am very partisan indeed, but only against actual totalitarianism and its fellow-travelers.

It is a matter of principle that writers, though passionate partisans for liberty in any extraordinary crisis, shall never forsake their workshops for any ordinary party campaign. They shall forsake them only to support a great losing cause or a truly endangered liberty; this emergency support neither party nor candidate can claim exclusively today. Naturally I'll freely write about my preferences between rival parties or candidates when I feel like it, but without ever joining any formal political group. Really, the point is: thumbs down on all professors who'll have you know they are "needed in Washington":

> "They liked their dictaphones a lot;
> They met some big-wheels, and do not
> Let you forget it."

But What About the Fourth Stage?

Three stages:

Having begun by being annoyed with the hysteria of the McCarthyites (who are blind to the thought control danger) and then having followed that up by being annoyed with the hysteria-about-hysteria of the liberals (who are blind to the fellow-traveler danger), I'm now becoming disgusted with the hysteria about the hysteria-about-hysteria of the more paranoid anticommunists (who are blind to the distinction between mistakes and conspiracies).

1929: Trauma of the Over-Forty

In no discussion of ideas must the material context be forgotten. Without the two material infernos of the 1930's — namely, nazism plus the depression — the ideas of Marxism and revolt would have remained ideas and not actions. But conversely, nazism and the depression, these two material "actions," were partly the result of "mere ideas" — bad ideas because grounded in bad ethics.

The overemphasis on economics among American liberal intellectuals over forty is understandable in view of the cataclysmic effect of 1929. But this cataclysm is no norm, need not recur. I don't predict there will be no more vast capitalist depressions in America; I only say there need not be. Not if subsequent governments retain what has been learnt since 1929 about credit control, etc. It is an exciting psychological fact as well as an economic fact that American capitalism, prematurely buried by the novelists and social thinkers of the 1930's, has become viable.

It sounds ominously like the *hybris* of Ajax inviting the lightning; nevertheless, there seems to be substantial truth in the conclusion reached by J. K. Galbraith's book, *American Capitalism,* 1952: "There are no problems on the side of depression with which the American economy and polity cannot, if it must, contend." Intellectuals over forty often still tend to be obsessed with what they call "the unsolvable contradictions of capitalism, the doom of the American way of life." Therefore, they are living in an old, dead world and give wrong answers for the present world. Because their trauma was 1929, they lack faith in the entirely different America of the 1950's.

VIGNETTES ABOUT GAYLORD

The Greater Peril

Old George Babbitt merely hates art.
Gaylord Babbitt hugs it to death.

Twilight of the Godless

The autumn of any sophisticated civilization, the twilight of the godless, begins on that hour when the suburb becomes sophisticated. And reads (in Nero's day) Petronius, "arbiter of elegance." Or (in the eighteenth century) the *Spectator Papers*. Or (today) the *New Yorker*.

Definition of a suburb: any congregation of would-be city slickers who are deadly afraid of seeming suburban.

The New Yorker-*ization of Main Street*

When in 1925 he founded the *New Yorker,* editor Harold Ross best defined its style by announcing, "It will *not* be for the old lady in Dubuque." Best evidence of the intervening changes is that in 1951 the *New Yorker* had a batch of loyal subscribers in — Dubuque.

Years of Helen Hokinson cartoons have shamed the "old lady in Dubuque" into being Babbitt Junior's streamlined mother before she is Babbitt Senior's sentimental pioneer mother. In the 1950's the "old lady" reads the svelte perfume and cuisine ads in the *New Yorker* with the same romantic *Bovarysme* with which she read Sears Roebuck ads in 1925. It is Gaylord's favorite magazine, just as much as the Chamber of Commerce bulletin was George Babbitt's favorite. Mrs. Gaylord Babbitt will now tell you, "I met the quaintest taxicab driver the other day; he was priceless; he said the most whimsical things." In other words, the *New Yorker* line has been taken over by the very people the magazine was originally created to satirize. Its humor and its literary standards (both of the highest) have not changed. But society has changed; the philistine has changed his party line.

The changed role of this magazine is a clue to the intervening changes in the American cultural situation. The *New Yorker* no longer provides élite titillations for a small circle of smoothies. It now means big business, big advertising, big circulation. Or to put the same thing differently, its fun has now become — predictable. This parallels the deadliest change in American and European culture as a whole: the substitution of technique for art; the substitution of the just-as-good for the real thing. What once resulted from the painful and inspired craftsmanship of an experimental and audacious individual is now mass-produced in painless, safe, and uninspired capsules. Is this not true today of every field of intellectual and artistic endeavor?

The sensitive perceptions over which a Katherine Mansfield bled her heart out, the new stream of consciousness for which James Joyce wrestled with his angels, are today imitated by a dozen nimble mass-producers of the *"New-Yorker-*type short story." And imitated with considerable technical skill: no pain, no risk, no inspiration. But most modern readers are not even bothered by the difference between such a good machine job and the individual product of heart's anguish. Nescafé is replacing coffee.

The phenomenon of the New Hick: Our country cousin has replaced the haywisp in his hair with the *New Yorker* under his arm. He arrives at the station with a well-worn copy of it, with checkmarks next to its lists of the choicer exhibits at the Museum of Modern Art and the subtler revivals of French and German movies of the 1920's. He makes knowing inquiries, with just the right note of playful nostalgia, about the fate of the double-decker Fifth Avenue buses. Or of Tryon Park, way up there. Or of "that little — you know — that little Breton bistro near the El."

As a New Yorker by birth, who lived most of his life right here in the Dubuquization of Manhattan, I am interested neither in whimsy, nor charm, nor art of living, nor the onion soup served in the East Fifties but am obsessively interested in the price of hogs in Iowa. I intend to talk of nothing else except hogs to the next Iowan who arrives at Grand Central reading the *New Yorker* and who tells me in a voice of urbane banter, "I am a bittersweet observer of life's little ironies. Why have you no feeling for nuance?"

Feast of Reason on Eighth Street

Let us apply this analysis of highbrow philistinism very concretely. Apply it to a very specific ad in *Partisan Review.* The advertiser (his name doesn't matter) is one of those book "shoppes" that dump all kinds of leftover pseudo-avant-garde junk on Babbitt Junior by appealing to his snobbism. Address: West Eighth Street, of course. Sufficient to characterize it is the diction of its ad:

"Avant-garde fiction in French or English; poetry; literary criticism; psychiatry — YOU know."

The capitalization of "YOU know" is entirely theirs, with its tone of cosy in-group mateyness. If I had to write my Ph.D. thesis all over again, I should like to write it entirely on the *juxtaposition* of the three words "avant-garde," "criticism," and "psychiatry." Still another Ph.D. thesis would trace the long, complex process of history and psychology making it inevitable that a Greenwich Village ad, in any Little Magazine in the America of 1952, must put the adjective "French" in front of the adjective "English."

In this advanced salon of Eighth Street — let us not sordidly call it a "store" — I have never dared set foot. I dassn't. Like the country bumpkin afraid of making a *faux pas* in the boudoir of a Parisian glamor queen, I tremble at my inability to "keep up with" the sophisticated repartee — O the mad, gay wit of it all! — that undoubtedly flashes between the clerks and salesmen at its book counters. But at least I can dream, can't I? — I can admire their ceaseless Feast of Reason from afar. Why, within that last refuge from "commercialized America," life must be just like one of Mallarmé's more sensitive gatherings. Just like one of Mallarmé's Tuesdays, only — YOU know — without Mallarmé.

Modern Versus Modernist

The old Babbitt derides good poetry, good music, good painting for being modern and difficult. The new Babbitt praises bad poetry, bad music, bad painting for being modernist and obscure. Thereby both are sacrificing imagination and originality to new or old stereotypes.

Respect what is modern and what is traditional; reject what is modernist and what is moribund.

Sheer accident! T. S. Eliot, being asked by his publisher to lengthen his manuscript, thereupon happened to insert those famous notes at the end of his *Waste Land*. Disastrous consequence of this accident: his "knowing" tone of literary references has been imitated by a generation of modernists, whose model was not the great art of the *Waste Land* but its footnotes.

Modernist poetry is a snore and an allusion.

Are Your Hands "Wrong"?

What about the "danger of playing into The Wrong Hands"? You are constantly hearing that this results from venturing "even justified criticisms" of any brand of intellectual or of self-styled liberal. This objection is a tactic of diversionary heckling. It pursues any intellectual (writer, artist, professor) who allegedly "betrays his fellow-intellectuals."

By "betrayal," the hecklers mean: giving away the show. By "selling out to the philistines" or to "the big interests," the hecklers mean: publicly unfrocking those pseudo-intellectual devaluators of values who apply double standards in judging Russia and the rest of the world.

Unfortunately for his bank account, no professor who discusses abstract ideas will be popularly read, no matter how good he is at writing badly. This is true by definition; by the very fact of being an idea-monger, no matter what kind of ideas. The lucrative joys of "prostituting your art" are easier said than done.

So let my lachrymose Friendly Warners, with their over-solicitous qualms about misuse, rest assured. Nobody who would persecute their Advanced Intellectuality, nobody who would vote for their ear-splitting demon symbol from Wisconsin, nobody who moves his lips while reading his tabloids in the subway, will ever immortalize the white page now before you with the thumbprint of his Wrong Hands.

Chic Revisited

> "Earth gape. O, no, it will not harbor me."
> — MARLOWE, *Doctor Faustus*

A year later, after the interview solemnly recorded on pages 20-35, I again had the privilege of a personal luncheon engagement with the great man. We again went to Café Chic at 56th Street. We sat at the same table as last time. We drank the same fizzing Burgundy. Everything was the same, exactly the same.

And not the same; not at all the same at the very end, which I wish I could forget.

"How happy and proud and successful you must be," I began merrily, "now that the movie they made from your novel has broken all box-office records. It's comforting, Gaylord, to think that minds like yours have at least partly dictated American intellectual life for two jolly decades. Outlooks like yours have molded our education, our paintings, our liberal weeklies, and to some extent even —until a few years ago — our foreign policy. And look with what glorious results!"

Purring at my heartfelt tribute and drawing himself up like an Elder Statesman, G.B. commented:

"Though 'modesty' is my middle name, I cannot help feeling — ahem — legitimate satisfaction at all we Babbitt Juniors have accomplished in twenty years. In both literature and politics. With both pen and sword. Think of China. Just one instance among many. What we helped accomplish there for the common man, by preventing Wall Street interference, is enough to stamp our mark on history for centuries to come. I feel like God resting on the seventh day; looking around at the world I built, I, too, 'find it good'."

"That apt remark deserves another bottle to celebrate it," I suggested. Later I wished I had not suggested that. For soon we were finishing the second large bottle, with Gaylord, who seemed less relaxed than last year, drinking almost all of it — and showing it.

"But about China," I resumed. "Just between us, don't all the new books give you Gaylord Babbitts more credit than you deserve for that thrilling mass-ferment against feudalism there? There is a weird rumor — neither McCarthy nor you progressives will like this kind of rumor — saying that Mao drafted most of his millions of fighting soldiers right inside China and Russia and not in the offices of the New York book review sections."

"Unofficially that's true," replied G.B. "But neither my team nor McCarthy's team can afford to let so dangerous a rumor leak out. Just between us, we G.B.'s gave only a helpful push and not a causation to China. Even so, what we did do was plenty: we coached American intellectual opinion to swallow it all uncomplainingly — China, Poland, and all that — for two whole postwar years, by which time saving the old order was probably — wait and see — *too late*."

"What I still don't see is: how did you G.B.'s manage to accomplish so much with so little opposition from the very society you were burying? How did you work it so beautifully?"

"Shucks, it was nothing," drawled G.B., spreading out his hands disarmingly in mock awkwardness, like a boyish athletic hero.

"Even more amazing is that we accomplished so much without having a bit more literary ability or political education than the next fellow. Confidentially, few of us literary and political Authorities — with all our honorary degrees and solemn commencement addresses to the young — ever read a serious book in our lives. Not since the day the tutoring-bureau crammed us through college. Then how did we triumph? We did it all with mirrors. I mean, our publicity techniques and mutual admiration societies got our political and literary tastes accepted as *dernier cri*. It's a matter of intellectual climbing, the equivalent of Long Island social climbing. As a result, no independent intellectual in the Western world could criticize our political and artistic Sacred Dogmas and Sacred Cows without being at once howled down, or else ignored as old-hat. Resting here successfully on my seventh day, I can only despise all liberals of the past; they never accomplished anything like this, those old dodos of liberalism like Mill and Zola and Lincoln. At heart they were really as stupidly *conservative* as those five million individualist peasants who refused to be collectivized."

"Yes," I said, "you are right about the difference between New Liberals and Old Liberals. The stick-in-the-mud Old Liberals — Mill, Zola, Lincoln — were warped by unscientific prejudices against the infliction of suffering, no matter who or where. New Liberals are too busy serving mankind in general to waste their emotions on the suffering of mere individuals (except the mental suffering of slandered fellow-liberals). Today the Old Liberals would waste time worrying about the mass-executions of millions in Democratic China. You never hear a word about that from the New Liberal. He is too busy denouncing that sinister fascist China Lobby."

"And rightly so," interjected G.B. "Because here's how the New Liberal differs from the Old: he replaces warm human sympathies (mere sentimental nonsense) with a wonderfully cool and dry concern about what really matters, the legalistic technicalities of civil liberties. Especially the civil liberties of American and French communists. That shows how splendidly liberalism has matured and ripened into tough-minded realism. 'Ripeness,' sang our silver-throated swan of Avon, 'is all.' "

"But why," I wondered, "does it give you such happiness to see the old order dynamited in Europe and China? Mightn't you accidentally stub your toe, too, when you rightly punish this stubbornly conservative old planet by blowing it sky-high? Just what's your motive anyway?"

"No real happiness and no real motive. (Yoo-hoo, *garçon,* pour me a third bottle with that Old World bouquet.) My detractors get me all wrong when they think my motive is a plot, a well-thought-out plan of any kind at all, or even a sympathy with communism. Even my leftist sympathies are only a surface affectation; I wouldn't tell you this sober, but even my radicalism has never been serious; my only deep and serious motive is dilettantism. I like to monkey around with big ideas and feel important, without even thinking of plans and plots beyond that. All I ask is to satisfy my two sincerest emotions: resentment and snobbism."

"You can't mean that, Gaylord! Not even after two bottles. You're only impishly joking, of course, when you speak of resentment and snobbism as if they were — well, legitimate emotions."

"Both are legitimate. Both are justified in the context of *America being what it is.* My fine American regular-fellows humiliated me; they made me feel permanently 'alienated' — that's a word I picked up from *Partisan Review* — when I was a kid. Here I was, a small-town kid, vainly begging their sympathy for my artistic yonely learnings — hic, lonely yearnings. And by God and H. L. Mencken, I'll make every small town in America pay for this in counterhumiliation. They'll pay and pay and pay because their own mediocrity crippled too many like me, a million resentful mental cripples. I'll be remembered as a type, just as people remember the courtiers of the declining Byzantine empire. My type is the supreme anticlimax of American history *after* Horatio Alger; I am in person the liquidation of all the American Buddenbrooks."

"Oh, the evils of alcohol!" I ululated fecklessly, like a Lapland shepherd helplessly watching his thatched cottage of a lifetime burn down.

"Yes, resentment and snobbism, snobbism and resentment. Resentment against middleclass-middlewest mediocrity. I hate it so because I belong to it so. I'll back anything anywhere that baits it, regardless of terrible consequences; I just plain don't give a damn — I'm not really serious enough — to think things through and worry about consequences. Snobbism is merely the reverse side of my resentment. To my business world relatives, who won't appreciate my intellect, who think I'm a joke instead of a sensitive — gulp, fagic trigure; to all those Kiwanis relatives, my snobbism says, 'Fellers, I'm not fired; I quit! You'll hear from me again when I'm gloriously part of the Chosen We of every progressive movement in art and intellect. Every movement that's modernist. And therefore obscure to you. And therefore counterhumiliates you.' "

Trying not to listen, I was speechless with embarrassment at such unexpected self-pity — never hinted before — in my happy and proud and successful idol. He spoke one sentence more, the following sentence, and then fell asleep in his chair:

"All over the world now, a million G.B.'s on the march and wide awake at last — hm, this stuff makes me so drowsy — will drown America in an ocean of blood — first China, Korea, then France — blood, blood, blood for what the red-blooded American Coca-Cola drinker and the patriotic *Reader's Digest* reader did to all our wistful childhoods — did to all our shweet — no, shweet — no, sweet yonely learnings."

"Oh, how your disciples would pull their hair out by the roots if they heard you now," I quavered vainly to his deaf ears. "You of all people. You who used to recite so elevatingly *America Was Promises* at the 'Let's Tolerate Culture' Sub-Committee of the P.A.C. But noble you remain even now, in your brand-new role of Prometheus falling. And, of course, you cannot at heart — why, you simply cannot, Gaylord — mean a single word of all you're saying now."

VIGNETTES ON BEHALF OF CLASSICAL HUMANISM

> "O gentle critic! be advised. Do not trust too much to your professional dexterity in the use of the scalping knife and tomahawk. Weapons of diviner mold are wielded by your adversary; and you are meeting him here on his own peculiar ground, the ground of Idea, of Thought, and of inspiration."
>
> — COLERIDGE (*on behalf of humanist idealism*)

Manifesto Growled by the Two Stone Lions

(*Note de l'éditeur: Regard, my old, these two animals formidable, with their sad eyes of philosopher, guarding actually — I ignore since how many years — the "New York Public Library" at the 42nd street.*)

There is no civilization but the Middle Sea, and Romanized Gaul is its prophet. Necessary to coin at once the verb "to mediterraneanize": lucidity, serenity, proportion, grace. I mediterraneanize, thou mediterraneanizest, he she or it mediterraneanizes. Why all American writers go to Italy:

> Of these the Northman by his beachèd galley
> Dreamt . . . O sacred Mediterranean.
> Unseen he loved thee; for the heart within him
> Knew earth had gardens where he might be blessed,
> Putting away long dreams and aimless barbarous
>   Hunger for battle.
> Thy langours thawed his bosom. . . . His racked spirit,
> By thy breath tempered and the light that clothes thee,
>   Forgot the monstrous gods.[1]

Clarity and reasonableness more exciting than visceral enthusiasm or sublime vagueness. Consequently, special homage to Samuel Johnson (memo to Modern Language Association: revise textbooks accordingly). No more southern Californias.

No Untergang, no Decline and Fall; the regeneration of the West through the dignity and purity of Form; man as personality instead of man as insect.

The esthetic sense once more in control of the utilitarian sense, today inhibiting it, tomorrow fulfilling it; not only cloudward to ivory towers but earthward to ivory factories. Except for the lowest indispensable minimum, no more cowering and groveling

---

[1] George Santayana, "Odes," V.

before the muscular adjective "Practical"; ringside tipsters whisper he is a mere debating-point champion and shows poor footwork in wrestling with angels; through jiujitsu, he can be forced to concede that only death is "Practical" in the "long run" and that nothing else "really works" because only death is "here to stay."

Announcement of integrity test:

Attention all honorable men. Candidates wanted for integrity test. "Many are the thyrsus-bearers, but few are the true Bacchantes." Volunteers will assemble secretly at dawn in Axel's castle, after burning all dependents and private papers. Integrity prize for the highest combined score under the following three categories (Erasmus, De Tocqueville, and Spinoza as final judges of integrity in case of tie):

1. any intellectual who refrains from anti-intellectualism; (inevitable progression from romantic *Bovarysme* to *trahison des clercs*).

2. any upper-middlebrow who refrains from easy satirizing of lower-middlebrows; (instead, browbeat the middlebrow-beaters).

3. any twentieth-century American who agrees with Alfred North Whitehead that "almost all we have of any real and lasting value has come to us from Greece. We should be better had we kept a bit more." (Confidential aside to electrician: set up lie-detector chair to determine sincerity of those who agree with Whitehead statement; "accidental" electrocution of any who agree out of mere *snobbisme*).

Back to pure reason (in place of unreasonable rationalism): to be arranged, a lecture series by Thomas Aquinas to make clear to Citizen Tom Paine the genuine urgency of debating how many angels can stand on the point of a pin. Memo for the world bulletin board: wasteful drains on civilization to be stopped at their source; necessary to conserve our Graeco-Roman-Christian-Hebrew value-supply: PLEASE POST.

Four, all four; caution against dropping Graeco from Roman-Christian-Hebrew; lopsided heritage worse than none; as alternative to practicality-cant, not incense-cant but values and taste. Précieux and sinister at same time: idolized, idyllized, and idealized scenario of medieval serfs folk-dancing in folk costumes around Gothic cathedral and strewing anti-trade-union tracts printed on hand-illuminated parchments. For all is lacking if civilian courage is lacking and the moisture of the rights of man is lacking. Though I speak with the tongues of men and angels, and have not Clarity, I am become a sounding brassiness or a tinkling Symbol.

No freedom but through rigor, reverence, tradition, decorum, and high conservatism, which has more in common with the penetrating acuteness of good Marxmanship than with muddle-class-fascist pseudoconservatism but will supersede both tomorrow morning.

When the right virtuous Sir Philip Sidney and I were at the Emperor's court together: Roncevaux, Roncevaux, Roncevaux, morne plaine. Or in clear twelfth-century Norman, the obvious question: Plus valt Mahum que Seint Perre de Rume?[1] And certainly (as in "here I stand, I can do no other") the Sidney-worthy answer: en Rencevals jo irai juindre Rollant!

And always and again (Franceis sunt mult gentilz) the Mediterranean. Graeco-Roman-Christian-Hebrew. The return of every northern — yes and eastern, yes and trans-Atlantic — Völkerwanderung to this fold (this fourfold) of the universal civitas. Let Western man, sun itself, face west again: "returnent Franc en France dulce terre."

— Thus growl the two LAST HUMANISTS; but the wind of autumn is louder

for a little while.

Lasting Issue: Classicism Versus Romanticism

A "party line" for the conservative conservation corps: — not expansive lushness but norm; not expensive plushness but form; bounds and boundaries again; oceans as lakes, cut down to proportion and no nonsense. To the rescue of King Canute.

No freedom in formlessness and free verse and anti-reason and impulse-from-the-vernal-wood. Byron: "Thou shalt believe in Milton, Dryden, Pope. Thou shalt not set up Wordsworth,

---

[1] Medieval French from *Song of Roland.* The opening phrase from Sidney's essay ("at the Emperor's court together") has its sentence logically ended (that era having ended) by Victor Hugo's corny "Waterloo" lament about the Roncevaux (Rencevals) of that other Emperor.

Coleridge, Southey. Because the first is crazed beyond all hope."
And because in 9 A.D. his vernal wood was named Teutoburg.[1]
And eighteen centuries later it was still a Teuton-burg in that
second revolt against that same empire. The second barbarian
revolt against classical and Roman form: when the whole century,
the nineteenth, revolted for German romanticism against Mediterranean classicism; against pattern and balance; against limit and
limes. A barbaric yawp across the rooftops of the Roman *limes.*

Rousseau, Rousseau, give me back my legions.

Two Definitions of the Romantic School

The blood they said they wrote in, was red ink.

Art is an infinite capacity for faking pains.

From Rive Gauche *Back to Pattern*

If the Hudson River at Greenwich Village was what Shakespeare
meant by "the seacoast of Bohemia," sculptured out of plastered-in-
Paris, then how forgive, by what discipline of taste atone for the
rive-gaucheries of our 1920's?

Look shining at — strict styles of architecture, a chain of heart.
For to Hart Crane the Doctor (Zinnser) had said — who was
American also — "You cannot heed the negative, so might go on to
undeserved doom . . . must therefore loose yourself within a
pattern's mastery that you can conceive, that you can yield to —
by which also you win and gain mastery and happiness which is
your own from birth."

Don't Think We Don't Know

Sergeant Economics (says Corporal Ancient Classics), you think
you're pretty smart, but we're watching you. Don't think we don't
know you were only a bootblack in civilian life, back in the Middle
Ages. And now, just because you've been the new Colonel's orderly
since 1789, you — but come, let's make up and be friends; let's
all meet in that nice dark little alley next to the precipice, and
we'll give you a real surprise present to celebrate that fine promotion you won for building such a cheery fire with our books.

---

[1] The defeat of the Roman general Varus by Herman the German at
Teutoburg Forest ("Varus, Varus," wept the Emperor, "give me back my
legions!"), prevented the Romanization of German culture beyond the
barrier of classicism: the *limes.*

The Nature of the Crisis

"Revolution in the USSR is only part of the world revolution, its beginning, and the base for its successful advance."
—STALIN, 1927

THE EUROPEAN CATASTROPHE:
ROOTS OF TOTALITARIANISM[1]

1. Three Nonpolitical Revolutions

The political revolutions of modern times are more famous and familiar than the nonpolitical ones. Yet the latter are just as important. It is precisely the nonpolitical background that explains the political revolutions of communism, fascism, and nazism. Here, then, are the three most influential nonpolitical upheavals of the later nineteenth century in Europe:

1. First, to coin a phrase, the ethical revolution. This will also be referred to as: the revolution in values.

2. The territorial revolution.

3. The second industrial revolution, also called the neo-industrial revolution.

Brief characterization of each:

1. The revolution in values liquidated the ethical restraints

---

[1] The author's main project for the next two years is a detailed history of modern Europe for the Harcourt Brace Company. This brief essay is a series of very sweeping generalizations about the causes of the European catastrophe. They were written in a preliminary, tentative effort to "think through" the general problem of Europe *as a whole,* in preparation for writing the more concrete, more specific project of the two years ahead. As such, these generalizations are likewise directly relevant to the present topic — "The Nature of the Crisis" — and hence included here. Reprinted from *Political Science Quarterly* (September 1952), periodical of the Academy of Political Science.

governing the means society used to reach their ends. Thereby it eventually transformed liberal nationalism into fascist nationalism, and democratic or utopian socialism into bolshevik socialism.

2. The territorial revolution changed the territorial structure of Germany and Italy from the traditional decentralization into a centralized unity.

3. The new industrial revolution extended to these new areas, in an expanded form, the original industrial revolution of England and France.

For all three of these nonpolitical revolutions the key date, the symbolic date, is 1871, and the key place is Paris and its nearby palace of Versailles. This date and this place are the most convenient starting-point for re-examining the roots of the twentieth-century European catastrophe.

On January 18, 1871, in Versailles, under the Prussian chancellor Bismarck, the German princes were proclaiming the foundation of the German Empire. Having invaded and defeated France, the King of Prussia was proclaimed Emperor of a newly-united Germany.

On January 18, 1871, the great Hall of Mirrors in the palace of Versailles reflected and counterreflected, in an endless glittering and counterglittering, the swords which all the princes of Germany flashed from their scabbards, shouting "Hail the Emperor!" ("Hoch der Kaiser!"). This fiery scene of swords in mirrors is the very quintessence of the spirit of war. This shout of triumphant militarist nationalism—"Hoch der Kaiser!"—mingled in a single martial roar with the Prussian cannons bombarding Paris. Both noises seemed to echo all Prussia's and Bismarck's aggressive wars of the past and then reverberate future-ward into the two world wars of 1914 and 1939. By April 3, 1871, the noise of class war was already drowning out the noise of national war, as a radical Paris Commune fought bloodily with a conservative French National Assembly.

Hoisting a red flag as symbol of socialism, the Paris Commune, later glorified in a book by Karl Marx, created a heroic legend for the Russian Bolsheviks of 1917. "Do you want to know what a dictatorship of the proletariat looks like?" asked Engels. "Then look at the Paris Commune" — which Marx said "will be forever

celebrated as the glorious harbinger of a new society." The so-
called "proletarian" dictatorship of this Commune revolution was
in reality a coalition of all brands of socialists and republican radicals, but for the European revolutionary movement the real facts
have been replaced by the Marxist legend about it. It joined with
German nationalism to make the Paris of 1871 a doubly prophetic
place and time, the Year One of contemporary Europe. Symboli-
cally the glass Hall of Mirrors was reflecting the approach of the
two greatest history-making forces of modernity: forces that
changed the map and changed society and trampled upon what
Mussolini was to call "the rotting body of the Goddess of Liberty."
These two forces are militaristic nationalism and militant socialism.

The ethics of this transition, when the European Christian
heritage of "humanity" was exchanged for the pagan war cult of
"nationality," was summed up by Franz Grillparzer (1791-1872),
the great Austrian dramatist. Observing the nationalistic revolutions of 1848, which were wrecking the mellow, international-
minded Hapsburg empire, Grillparzer commented: "The path of
modern culture leads from humanity, through nationality, to
bestiality."

2. Changes in Socialism and Nationalism

Both socialism and nationalism had long been present in Europe.
A bit of socialism and a lot of nationalism had modified — to left
or right — the liberalism of the various uprisings of 1848. But
to a great extent the original pre-Marx socialism and the original
pre-Bismarck nationalism had been peaceful, conciliatory, tolerant,
evolutionary, in the great liberal tradition. The pre-Marxist socialists — Robert Owen (1771-1858), Saint-Simon (1760-1825),
Fourier (1772-1837), Proudhon (1809-65), and the rest — have
been dismissed by Marxist and Soviet writers as mere "utopians."
The label "utopian socialist" continues to cling mockingly to non-
Marxist socialists, who hope to bring about socialism peacefully
without class war. The label is not one to be ashamed of. Its
advocates claim that only through peaceful evolution — as currently in Scandinavia — can their social reforms be achieved without sacrifice of civil liberties. In contrast, Marxist socialism and
Bismarckian nationalism have in common a resort to force, a

contempt for tolerant parliamentary solutions. After the 1870's, these are the strongest kinds of socialism and nationalism.

The pre-Bismarck nationalists — like Herder (1744-1803) in Germany and Mazzini (1805-72) in Italy — are known as "liberal" nationalists. Like their historical brethren, the utopian socialists, they had tried and failed in the revolutions of 1848. Their nationalism was not one of hate for other races but of tolerant cooperation of all nationalities in a peaceful nondespotic Europe.

In deriding the attempt to achieve socialism through parliamentary means, Marx (1818-83) and Soviet writers are exactly as scathing as Bismarck was in deriding his "liberal nationalist" predecessors. Marx and Lenin might have said on behalf of class war and of the proletariat what Bismarck said on behalf of national war and of Prussia in his often-quoted speech of 1862, attacking peaceful parliamentary methods:

The eyes of Germany are fixed not upon Prussia's liberalism, but upon her armed might. . . . The great questions of the day will not be decided by speeches or by majority decisions — that was the mistake of 1848 and 1849 — but by blood and iron!

The "blood and iron" nationalism that followed 1870 culminated eventually in Nazi Germany and fascist Italy. The "blood and iron" Marxist socialism of the 1870's culminated eventually in Soviet Russia and in an Iron Curtain advancing over Europe and Asia. Preferring state omnipotence to individualism and preferring quick violent change to gradual parliamentary change, these are the two new value-systems that arose from the ethical revolution. They arose to challenge the traditional ethics and values.

In contrast with the ethical revolution, man's traditional ethics are either individual or universal or both, being a very individual responsibility to a universally valid code of morality. This is true of Plato, of the Stoics, and of Christian thought. This combination of the *individual* responsibility and the *universal* validity continued through the eighteenth century. It inspired the rationalism of the Enlightenment as well as the "categorical imperative" of Kant's version of the Golden Rule.

The ethical revolution replaced both individual and universal ethics with national ethics. Thereby the national interest, its military power, its economic power, its expansion, became the final criterion of right and wrong. This criterion was openly and gloatingly proclaimed by such political writers as Friedrich A. J. von Bernhardi (1849-1930), German general and nationalist: "Political morality differs from individual morality, because there is *no power above* the state." (The "patriot" who wrote these words claimed to believe in God!) Or in the words of Cavour (1810-61), who achieved the Italian territorial revolution: "If we did for ourselves what we do for our country, what rascals we would be!" That sentence might be taken as the motto for the whole ethical revolution and for the two world wars that followed.

Contrast the above Bernhardi credo about "no power above the state" with its direct opposite: Thomas More's dying words on the scaffold, "I die the king's good servant, but God's first." Substitute "the nation-state" for "king" and substitute "universal ethics" for "God," and you have the perfect contrast between our value-heritage and the revolt against values.

Nationalized ethics has crushed internationalism on the one hand and individualism on the other. This made it the appropriate creed of the new middle-class nationalists born from the industrial and territorial revolutions. So-called Machiavellianism — ruthlessness in world affairs — is, of course, nothing new; has always been with us. But not until after 1870 was it systematized so thoroughly, or thought out so deliberately. Never before the age of Hitler and Stalin was it practiced with such efficient total co-ordination. Never before was it accepted so popularly and widely as replacing Christianity as a religion and system of ethics.

At the same time, a scientific revolution — the "New Science" associated with Darwinism — changed not merely the science of Europe but had important indirect repercussions on its political and social ethics. Political and social misuses of Darwin's theory of "evolution through natural selection" gave a seemingly scientific justification to the ruthlessness accompanying the ethical revolution. National war and class war, the political militarism that followed Bismarck and the social militarism that followed Marx, could now claim to serve man's evolution by weeding out the allegedly "unfit" nations, races, or classes.

3. The Assault on the Heritage

The revolution in values has almost annihiliated the European heritage. Nourished over the centuries by the teachings of Christ and Saint Paul, by Socrates and Pericles, by Aristotle and Erasmus, the European heritage is built on reverence for the precious uniqueness of the individual soul. This heritage, which has absorbed so many social and political changes, is compatible with democratic capitalism or with democratic socialism [1] or with democratic nationalism. It is incompatible with the new totalitarian blood-and-iron nationalism and socialism, whose extremes are fascism and bolshevism. Both are necessarily against the Christian ethic and the democratic polity. Both liquidate the concept of "Europe" and "the West."

The European heritage, expressed in some of the most free and creative cultures of mankind, is an amalgam of the four traditional ancestries of Western man: the stern moral commandments and social justice of Judaism; the love of the free Hellenic mind for beauty and for untrammeled intellectual speculation; the Roman Empire's universalism and its exaltation of objective impersonal rule of law; and the Golden Rule and international, interracial brotherhood of Christianity.

These four ancestries were often mutually conflicting and, still more often, hypocritically evaded. Nevertheless, their ever-shifting amalgam has for some two thousand years given Europeanism its society-building spark, its creative imagination, its urge to discover new continents — new Americas — of the earth and of the mind. Never attained, often betrayed, less often practised than preached, yet never wholly extinguished, these traditional values are what goaded Western man to greatness.

The history of Europe after 1870 relates the decline — not necessarily fall — of Europe. It is the history of how a heritage of two thousand years was smashed in three generations of state worship, power worship, world depressions, and world wars. As a result, the historian of Nazi Europe and communist Europe observes that the typical institution is no longer the parliament,

---

[1] Compatible with democratic socialism: provided it is democratic first and socialist second if forced to choose. For this dilemma see the chapter "The Peculiar Feebleness of Social Democrats" (page 264).

the university, and the cathedral, but the secret police, the gas chamber, and the forced-labor camp.

At first the value-system known as "Europe" did seem to tame the two revolutionary forces of nationalism and socialism, extracting from them what was valuable, changing national frontiers and social frontiers wtihout sacrificing personal liberties. It was a good example of "challenge and response." A seemingly successful absorption of the challenge, a case of practical evolutionary conservatism, marked the history of Europe from 1870 up to World War I. Reactionary tsars and Kaisers and revolutionary socialists and nationalists were all making ever handsomer concessions (no matter how grudgingly) to reasonableness and to parliamentary processes.

By 1914, socialism and nationalism seemed "housebroken." Marxist socialist parties had relaxed into "Social Democrats"; most nationalistic hotheads were calming down into national democrats; for a while there was more talk of the Hague Peace Conferences than of the approaching war. To a great extent, the leading parties of socialism and likewise of nationalism had been assimilated into the European parliamentary system, working in lawful, gradual, parliamentary fashion for the changes they demanded.

That is why World War I was a tragedy so irrevocable. It cut suddenly short the slow, patient taming-process. World War I is the worst single catastrophe in human history. Even worse than World War II, though it killed less millions: for by the time of World War II there was much less freedom and decency left to destroy than in 1914; by 1939 Europe's decline into totalitarianism was already far advanced.

World War I smashed both the moral and economic fabric of European civilization. This is why its advent at the time was hailed so ecstatically by its two chief beneficiaries, Hitler (1889-1945) and Lenin (1870-1924). These two men between them, and what they stood for, brought about the terrible European crisis threatening America's very existence' today. Hitler reduced blood-and-iron nationalism and racism to its ultimate, logical absurdity, just as Lenin was the ultimate extreme of the blood-and-iron socialism of the 1870's.

The foregoing analysis of the pre-1914 European heritage is substantiated by the fact that both men explicitly saw World War I as the salvation of their respective doctrines and as the smashing of the non-blood-and-iron world they despised. In his auto-biographical *Mein Kampf,* Hitler described how he fell on his knees to thank Heaven for this bloodthirsty war:

> The fight of the year 1914 was certainly not forced upon the masses, good God!, but desired by the entire people. . . . To me personally those hours appeared like redemption. . . . Overwhelmed by impassionate enthusiasm, I had fallen on my knees and thanked Heaven out of my overflowing heart that it had granted me the good fortune of being allowed to live in these times.

For Lenin, likewise, "these times" were his "good fortune"; without the moral and economic crash of Europe, he, too, would never have had the chance to remold half a continent nearer to his heart's desire. Lenin, too, was an accurate prophet when he foresaw before 1914 that the sole hope for bolshevism was a big war, adding wistfully (in a letter to Gorki in 1912), "I am afraid that Francis Joseph and Nicholas will not give us this pleasure." When two years later the two rulers did manage to please, they destroyed not only their own dynasties but the hitherto very promising effort of a resilient Europe to absorb nationalism and socialism peacefully and gradually into the traditional value-structure. The conservative, evolutionary solution to Europe became the first casualty of a nihilistic world war.

And the Pan-German nationalists and Pan-Slav nationalists, who between them incited the Austro-Serb and German-Russian clash of 1914 — they, too, were accurate prophets when they proclaimed that only through war could they achieve their dreams. Only through war could they smash the old, law-abiding, parliamentary society of Europe, in which the new nationalism was tempered by a sense of international unity and the new socialism (as "Social Democracy") was tempered by a sense of common liberties and a common noneconomic culture. These common liberties and cultural values transcended all classes and nations and contained a great European spiritual treasure.

Here is a typical example of how by 1914, in the eyes of one of the clearest minds of the time, this great European heritage had seemingly absorbed its opposition. The English historian J. B. Bury wrote in 1913:

> The struggle of reason against authority has ended in what appears now to be decisive and permanent victory for liberty. In the most civilized and progressive countries, freedom of discussion is recognized as a fundamental principle. . . .

That there should ever be a swing back to tyranny and against this "permanent victory for liberty," he deemed in 1913 "improbable."

However, almost as an afterthought, Bury did see one threat to this triumphant European liberty and tolerance. Coercion might return if, in some supposedly remote future,

> a revolutionary social movement prevail, led by men inspired by faith and formulas (like the men of the French revolution) and resolved to impose their creed. . . .

As an historic tragedy, World War I is unequalled, even by World War II, because World War I in a few years of chaos replaced Bury's "permanent victory for liberty" by the fascist and bolshevik revolutions of men "resolved to impose their creed."

In the light of the later Nazi and communist consequences of that war, it is today interesting to recall what Sigmund Freud said of World War I in 1922: "No event ever destroyed so much of the precious heritage of mankind . . . or so thoroughly debased what is highest." This analysis of World War I by the greatest of psychoanalysts was also noted at the time by the intuition of the century's greatest poet. Both are evidence for my view of that war as the worst thing that ever happened to mankind. In the year 1919, contemplating prewar hopes like Bury's, William Butler Yeats observed:

> We too had many pretty toys when young:
> A law indifferent to blame or praise,
> To bribe or threat; habits that made old wrong
> Melt down, as it were wax in the sun's rays;
> Public opinion ripening for so long
> We thought it would outlive all future days.
> O what fine thought we had because we thought
> That the worst rogues and rascals had died out.

All teeth were drawn, all ancient tricks unlearned,
And a great army but a showy thing;
What matter that no cannon had been turned
Into a ploughshare? Parliament and king
Thought that unless a little powder burned
The trumpeters might burst with trumpeting
And yet it lack all glory; and perchance
The guardsmen's drowsy chargers would not prance.

Now days are dragon-ridden, the nightmare
Rides upon sleep: a drunken soldiery
Can leave the mother, murdered at her door,
To crawl in her own blood, and go scot-free;
The night can sweat with terror as before
We pieced our thoughts into philosophy,
And planned to bring the world under a rule,
Who are but weasels fighting in a hole.

Recorded by the historian and confirmed by the psychologist and the poet, this shift in values from peaceful parliamentary gradualism to blood and iron, from stress on good means to exclusive stress on ends, is what I mean by "the ethical revolution" of modern Europe. "Man does not live by bread alone." Therefore, in the long run, the anti-Western and anti-Christian revolution in ethics is an historical earthquake as important as the far more famous industrial and political revolutions of Europe.

4. The Three Industrial Revolutions

Nineteenth-century Europe has witnessed at least two distinct industrial revolutions. Today we are witnessing a third. The three may be conveniently summarized as follows:

1. In the late eighteenth and early nineteenth century, the *first* industrial revolution, beginning in England, swept over Europe:

(a) It replaced hand power and horse power by steam power;

(b) It urbanized a hitherto rural Europe;

(c) It gave impetus to materialism and a worship of science in what had been the domain of religious philosophy;

(d) Needing a broader market than old provincial tariff lines permitted, it gave impetus to nationalism and the formation of the large, capitalist, nationalist state.

2. In the 1870's, centering in Germany, the *second* industrial revolution swept over Europe:

(a) It replaced steam power with electric power;

(b) It replaced small laissez-faire capitalism with large mass-production monopoly capitalism;

(c) It gave impetus to power politics and statism;

(d) It helped transform nationalism into imperialism by directing national aspirations outward to foreign colonial markets and raw materials.

3. The first industrial revolution is symbolized by the railroad, which in turn became the unifying sinew of nationalism, making local provincial markets outdated. The second industrial revolution is symbolized by the transoceanic freighter, speeding to Asia and Africa: the unifying sinew of worldwide imperialism. Similarly, the *third* industrial revolution, centering in America and Soviet Russia and now dawning upon us, may replace electricity by atomic power, just as the second replaced steam power and the first replaced hand power.

As the symbol of the first was the railroad, unifying the nation, and as the symbol of the second was the ocean liner, uniting the globe, so the symbol of the third may some day come to be (incredibly Buck Rogerish as it sounds) the interplanetary rocket ship, uniting all space and time and conquering everything in the material universe except that tiny catalyst, the heart of man. The ethical rightness or wrongness inside the human heart will still determine whether any given physical or economic advance is a blessing or a curse, just as it did when the first caveman invented the first ax in some prehistoric "industrial revolution."

5. The Territorial Revolution

The third great nineteenth-century convulsion, accompanying the ethical and industrial changes, was the territorial revolution of 1859-71. It created two new centralized states: Germany and Italy. It was far more than ideological in scope. But it was set in motion by an ideology: nationalism.

In turn, the territorial revolution altered nationalism. It militarized nationalism. It gave a bigger springboard for expanding a landlocked nationalism into transoceanic imperialism. And it made the new German and Italian nationalism synonymous with the cult of the existing state. The earlier German and Italian nationalism had been a cultural feeling that became political only in order to protest *against* the existing state. After 1871, nationalism and statism at last became reconciled, uniting into a single, overwhelming force.

The territorial revolution occupied the dozen rapid years of aggressive war by which Cavour unified Italy and Bismarck unified Germany. To see how truly revolutionary were these dozen years of unification, it is necessary first to recall the preceding thousand years of a disunited center.

For the thousand years following the breakup of Charlemagne's united Central Europe, the constant factor in the shifting kaleidoscope was the weakness of the European center, the strength of the periphery. The German-French-Italian-Christian empire of the Frankish King, who became Roman Caesar in the year 800, was turned by feudal centrifugality into a jigsaw puzzle, whose fragments never held together. Intermittent successes of a Pope or a Holy Roman Emperor, a Leo or a Hohenstaufen, were the exceptions. The rule was that Germany and Italy were, to use Prince Metternich's phrase for the latter, mere "geographical expressions." These two central areas consisted of many tiny, feeble, divided states while their neighbors to west and north and east — France, England, Sweden, the Grand Duchy and later Tsardom of Moscow, the Ottoman Sublime Porte — were powerful, large, united monarchies.

Nature abhors a vacuum. Into the power vacuum of the German-speaking center, gravitated heathen Viking and Latinized West Frank; Tartar and Turk; Magyar and Pole; Pope and Bourbon and Romanov. The crescendo of this process was the Thirty Years' War (1618-48) when the Hapsburg armies were fighting the armies of Denmark's King Christian, Sweden's Gustav Adolph, and France's Cardinal Richelieu on the two-thirds-devastated soil of the many little "Germanies."

Meanwhile in the south, in the power vacuum of the Italian-speaking center, Scandinavia's Christian pirates beat their swords in Sicily against the scimitars of Africa's Arab-speaking Mussulmans. On the Italian soil they both claimed, the heirs of Constantine debated the heirs of Peter over the endless question of what to render unto God and what to render unto Caesar. In the swamps

of the Neapolitan boot, Spanish Aragon fought French Anjou with
the Italian mercenaries both sides hired and could not pay, until
both crumbled into luxury, corruption, and malaria and were
replaced by the cannily-marrying Hapsburgs. Above all, it was
Austrian and Frenchman who battled in Naples and in Milan;
first with crossbow and then with musket; from the days of a
divinely-anointed Charles and Francis through a brace of plebiscite-
anointed Napoleons.

For ten trampling centuries, up to Cavour (1810-61) and
Bismarck (1815-98), the boot tread and hoof beat of invasion
passed always from east and west and north into the feeble Ger-
man-Italian center. Then suddenly, amazingly, as a result of the
twelve-year territorial revolution of Cavour and Bismarck, the
tide of invasion reversed itself. It now hurtled outward for seventy
years from a strong aggressive center into weak peripheries. Of
this second tide, the crescendo was the Hitler-Mussolini empire,
in which the two former "geographical expressions" mastered their
geography and conquered a continent.

6. Russia Over Europe: The Third Tide

During 1940-43, Nazi Germany and its fascist Italian satellite
ruled all Europe from Norway's Arctic Circle to the Sahara side
of the Mediterranean, from England's French "sleeve" up to the
Volga River's little-known outpost of Stalingrad.

Up to Stalingrad! But Stalingrad is a time as well as place.
In 1943-44 at Stalingrad, the Russian periphery replaced the
German center as the first power in Europe. Like the nationalist
Versailles and socialist Paris of 1871, so Stalingrad in 1944 is
both a time and a tide. It is the opening wave of a third surge over
Europe. The first was from periphery to center and lasted a
thousand years; the second was from center outwards and lasted
some seventy years; the third — "how long, O Lord"?

Hitler's "National Socialism" had no popular appeal outside
Germany. Its "socialist" half was never taken seriously among
the masses abroad. Yet in 1951 the equally bogus "socialism" of
Stalin's equally "fascist" police oligarchy was still being taken very
seriously indeed by the voters of Western Europe. It won almost
37 per cent of the Italian vote in the May elections of 1951. It

won 26.5 per cent of the French vote in the June elections of the same year: the largest percentage of any single French party. Janus-faced, the Soviet woos millions of Asiatics and West Europeans today by promising socialism, while wooing Russians by a more-than-tsarist imperial expansion. Ideologically the strength of the third tide is its synthesis of the two most appealing secular religions of the post-1870 epoch: blood-and-iron nationalism; blood-and-iron socialism.

Such double psychological seductiveness, plus atomic and industrial power, plus three hundred potential infantry divisions, make National Bolshevik Russia the most dangerous aggressor in all history. Today the so-called "Union of Socialist Soviet Republics" is the final fulfilment of the European catastrophes of 1871 and 1914: the revolution in values.

AMERICA'S SECRET THIRTY-YEAR WAR

"The victorious proletariat of that country [where the socialist revolution first takes place], having expropriated the capitalists and organized socialist production at home, will rise against the rest of the capitalist world, attracting the oppressed classes of other countries, raising among them revolts against the capitalists, launching, in case of necessity, *armed forces* against the exploiting classes *and their states.*"

— LENIN, 1915

"We know or believe that Russia's interests, so far as we can anticipate them, do not afford an opportunity for a major difference with us in foreign affairs. . . . They want to maintain friendly relations with us. . . . They are going to see to it that their borders are protected from unfriendly states; and I, for one, do not blame them for it."

— HARRY HOPKINS, *six months after Yalta* (*quoted in* Roosevelt and Hopkins, *edited by Robert Sherwood*)

There is a heaviness dangerous to shoulder, still more dangerous to let go of. Let us call it the American chore. "Manifest destiny" sounds too corny. "Historic mission" sounds too arrogant, dictatorial, and self-appointed for a task requiring humility and service to others. The American chore is to save the free world — and thereby ourselves also — from the communazi aggressors. Acting not as "patriots" in any narrow sense of the word. Not primarily as nationalists nor as capitalists. Acting as servants of the old, true, basic ethics of the free world, as analyzed in the preceding chapter.

The alternative to the rootlessness of revolutionary intellectuals is not the narrow provincial roots of Know-Nothing Americanism but the broadly-anchored older roots of a generous and humane brotherhood of the free world. The essence of Americanism is not the bigoted xenophobia of the patrioteers. It is that spirit of magnanimity and understanding of other viewpoints which made our winning general tell our losing general, after fiercest civil war, that his soldiers need not surrender their battle horses but should use them for next spring's plowing. Such incidents are the essence of our real and not fake Americanism.

The American chore does not mean forcing our values down the throats of the rest of the world. Nor does it mean giving up our own values for the sake of new ones. It means stressing deliberately those values that we and the rest of the West have in common and minimizing those on which we differ.

A patriotic over-stress on the westward movement in American history may make us forget that our basic values, every single one of them, came from before 1776. This includes our religions and our parliamentary institutions, our trial by jury and habeas corpus, our Milton and Shakespeare and King James Bible. Even such typically American material matters as our industrial revolution have their models in the old world prior to our separation from it. The real American traditionalism, as opposed to a star-spangled isolationism, sees us within a broader community, transcending our national boundaries.

The Atlantic community, which must unite to survive the Soviet challenge, must draw closer not only in economic and military agreements but by stressing its joint decencies. In our justified, though romanticized, praise of our frontier traditions, let us never forget the older and still deeper heritage of individual freedom that England gave us. Our own idiosyncratic institutions, our frontier and our jauntier democratic intermingling, are but a widening of this English heritage, not a break with it.

America's greatness has been to diffuse among all its diverse nationalities — and therefore on a less insular, more universal basis — a heritage that previously had belonged only to one particular nationality, the British. Namely, the heritage of the free two-party system and of self-restrained political "fair play." America is the Saint Paul of politics. Paul took the ethical ideas of Judaism and diffused them through all mankind via Christianity. The genius of the American melting pot is also one of successful diffusion. Among all its ethnic groups, it has diffused the Bill of Rights way of life of England. To this it has added the valuable and unique ingredients provided by each of the older, often profounder, non-Anglo-Saxon cultures.

Against this Bill of Rights way, whose championing is the American chore, a deadly counterchampion arose some three decades ago from the European catastrophe that followed 1871 and 1914. Prior to the twentieth century, the most destructive war in history was the Thirty Years' War, 1618-48. It, too, was an intermittent war, in which the line-up of nations fluctuated. From this we can borrow a unifying name for the post-1917 communazi war against the American way. Let us call it the Second Thirty Years' War. But it is a war whose victims did not know it was being fought against them. For its first two decades, it was a secret war.

II

New history books, retracing more rigorously the sources of twentieth-century history, will rewrite it with far less emphasis than in the past upon the occasional rivalry between communists and Nazis and with far greater emphasis on how closely they cooperated against the parliamentary center. Only cooperation between both outlaws was capable of overcoming the free liberalism and conservatism of Europe. Fascism has never triumphed without intentional or unintentional communist aid, and the reverse is equally true. As Max Salvadori points out:

In 1928 Stalin and the Comintern decided that the shortest cut to the triumph of communism in Europe was to *help the authoritarian Right* to destroy the main enemy — Liberalism. The *result* was the sudden appearance of nazism, which proved to be stronger than either liberalism or communism, and which would have destroyed the Soviet

Union if the latter had not been helped by what remained of the liberal states.[1]

By the Trotskyite "trials" of the 1930's, Stalin among other things was eliminating in advance any Marxist opposition at home to his persistent wooing of Nazi militarism. As scapegoats he was accusing his Old Bolshevik victims — again, among other things — of his own unsuccessful pro-German orientation, which at that date was being rebuffed by Hitler.

Stalin's anti-Nazi "Popular Front" policy in the West during the '30's was not only reinsurance against Hitler's appetite for the Ukraine. It also was a shrewd way of increasing Soviet bargaining power with Hitler by publicly blackmailing him into considering Stalin's private alliance offers during those same '30's. The greater Stalin's nuisance potential — for example, in slowing up Axis aggressions against Loyalist Spain — the greater the price (half of Poland and the Balkans) he could demand from Hitler when in 1939 their alliance was finally consummated.

In 1941 Russia's ruler fought Hitler not as an anti-fascist but because he had no choice, being attacked. This cost millions of innocent Russian lives that might have been saved if both Chamberlain and Stalin had stopped the unappeasable Nazi earlier when Churchill warned them to. Stalin's 1939 alliance with Hitler was not an angry short-term reaction to the Western crime of Munich but a calculated long-term culmination of the secret Reichswehr-Soviet military co-operation begun by their Rapallo pact of 1922 and the Berlin treaty of 1926. The almost incredible extent of this co-operation is confirmed from such *entirely separate and independent sources* as the posthumous papers of General von Seeckt, the 1948 memoirs of Ruth Fischer, and many others. "The Rapallo pact started not only the political but the moral rot. It infected the left with parlor-bolshevism, and the right with dreams of a military alliance with Russia and a war of revenge against the West, thereby making things a good deal easier for Hitler and for his present [communist] imitators in East Germany."[2]

In some ways a precursor of Nazi militarism, Seeckt in the 1920's organized the Reichswehr rearmament on Soviet soil, which en-

---

[1] *The Rise of Modern Communism* (New York, 1952), p. 103.
[2] G. L. Arnold in *The Twentieth Century,* issue of August 1952, London.

abled Germany to violate the disarmament provisions of Versailles behind the Iron Curtain. Already then, Seeckt planned a joint Soviet-German attack on Poland, such as eventually started off World War II. His confidential papers were captured with the German Army archives by American troops after the war and are now stored in Washington in the National Archives Building, accessible to scholars.

Here is Ruth Fischer's summary:

In 1928, there were at least 800 men assigned by the Reichswehr Ministry to work with the Red Army. . . . In Leningrad, Perm, Sverdlovsk, and the Ukraine, munition plants were set up and run with expert German assistance. . . . The *continued collaboration* between the two armies has remained one of the *best-kept secrets* of contemporary history. In this relationship, we must seek the basic explanation of many factors of both Stalinism and Nazism. . . . After Hitler came to power, Stalin tried incessantly via army channels to get an alliance with Nazi Germany, a policy that reached its fruition finally in August, 1939. . . . Manipulated from Moscow, [the German Communist Party under the Weimar Republic] was directed into a policy of silent agreement, not disturbed by name-calling, with the Nazis, and virulent opposition to the Democrats and Social Democrats. . . . The anti-Nazis camp was split down the middle, split by an ax wielded by Stalin.[1]

The climax of this long Nazi-Soviet co-operation was reached in their conquest of Poland in 1939 and in Molotov's speech to the Supreme Soviet (on which I should like anti-fascist fellow-traveler liberals to comment):

"One swift blow to Poland, first by the German Army and then by the Red Army, and nothing was left of this ugly offspring of the Versailles Treaty. . . . Germany is . . . for peace, while Great Britain and France, which but yesterday were declaiming against aggression, are . . . opposed to the conclusion of peace. . . . There is absolutely no justification for a war . . . under an ideological flag. . . . One may *accept or reject the ideology of Hitlerism* as well as any other ideological system; that is a matter of political views. . . .

[1] Ruth Fischer, *Stalin and German Communism* (Cambridge, Harvard Univ. Press, 1948); for this quotation and similar material, see pp. 524-36, 655-57, 662-63. Ruth Fischer was General Secretary of the German Communist Party and a member of the Comintern presidium and knew personally the Soviet leaders, including Stalin. In his preface to her memoirs, Harvard's historian of Germany, Sidney B. Fay, vouches for the general historical validity of her assertions about Soviet-German co-operation, which are confirmed by independent sources.

It is, therefore, not only senseless but *criminal to wage such a war as the war for 'the destruction of Hitlerism,'* camouflaged as a fight for 'democracy'. . . . It is the fear of losing world supremacy that dictates to the ruling circles of Great Britain and France the policy of fomenting war against Germany. . . . Today our relations with the German State are based on our friendly relations, on our readiness to support Germany's efforts for peace. . . . We have always held that a strong Germany is an indispensable condition for a durable peace in Europe."[1]

After Hitler defied Reichswehr advice by breaking this Soviet alliance in 1941, it was revived without Hitler by the captured Reichswehr officers of Stalin's "Free Germany Committee" of 1943. Today the same alliance lives on in Germany's Russian-directed "Socialist Unity Party," openly recruited from both Communists and Nazi S.S. men. Vincent Mueller, officer of the communist East German Government, boasted on March 26, 1952, in the Berlin *Taegliche Rundschau,* official organ of the Soviet Control Commission:

Today former members of the Nazi party occupy responsible positions in all [East German] branches of economic, political and cultural life. They are now men of good will fighting for a democratic united Germany.

The evil minority of German industrialists who financed Hitler did this only after Hitlerism was already Germany's most powerful bandwagon; they tried to jump on that wagon but they did not create it. The two forces actually creating Hitlerism were German nationalism (romanticism plus Prussianism plus anti-Versailles) and German communism. Communism was the final decisive factor bringing Hitler into power. Hitler and World War II could have been prevented, had Stalin not ordered his German communist vassals to center their main attack not on nazism but on the Weimar Republic and on the Social Democrats (then called "social fascists").

Once you realize that Hitler's power was created by Stalin — first, by communist undermining of Weimar; second, by secretly

---

[1] Quoted from the full text of Vyacheslav Molotov's report delivered on October 31 in Moscow to the Fifth Extraordinary Session of the Supreme Soviet of the USSR. "Molotov's Report to Supreme Soviet," *Soviet Russia Today,* communist monthly, New York, November, 1939, pp. 5-8, 47-50.

rearming the German army on Soviet soil — you will not be surprised by those new revelations showing that Stalin's preference remained more pro-Hitler than pro-West throughout World War II. Even after Stalingrad, Soviet agents offered the Nazis a separate peace against the Western democracies they both hated. The terms of this peace feeler included restoration of the 1914 boundary between Germany and Russia and a Russian free hand in Asia.[1] Fortunately for the West, the maddened Hitler resisted his importunate Soviet wooers.

The danger of a separate peace by Stalin entirely justifies the wisdom of Roosevelt's lend-lease to Russia during the height of the war. It justifies even many of the most painful Anglo-American concessions to Stalin up to the end of 1944. A separate Soviet peace might have saved Hitler and destroyed the free West. This fact is overlooked by a certain unbalanced, slanderous kind of critic of the Roosevelt foreign policy.

However, by February, 1945 (the surrender of Manchuria at Yalta without consulting the Manchurians), the danger of a German victory was over; and so was the justification for any further concessions to Stalin. Our policy of unnecessary softness and concessions (financial, political, and the cruel repatriation of Russian escapees) continued even after the end of the Pacific war for two more years. In turn, the Pacific war may or may not have seemed to justify at the time — according to rival military experts between whom nobody today is competent to judge in retrospect — our buying from Stalin what turned out to be a worthless Soviet aid against a tottering, surrender-ripe Japan.

III

To fulfill the American chore, Americans must become far better acquainted with the unity behind the secret thirty-year-war of totalitarianism against us. The public must not be confused any longer by the fact that at times the two totalitarians — no honor among thieves — fought each other and found it expedient to ally, in Popular Fronts or Munich Pacts, with the duped West. What of it? Two facts remain basic:

---

[1] Soviet feelers for a separate peace are described in Peter Kleist, *Zwischen Hitler und Stalin,* Bad Godesberg (Athenaeum Verlag, 1950).

1. The democratic parliamentary Russian regime of March-November 1917 was overthrown not by Lenin alone. It fell only because of the *simultaneous* assault against it by the right-wing tsarist militarists of Kornilov and the left-wing Bolsheviks of Lenin.

2. The Weimar Republic was overthrown not by Hitler alone. It fell only because of the *simultaneous* assault against it by Nazis and Communists.

Their basic identity was stressed by no less an authority than Hitler himself. After marching into Vienna in 1938, he gave his famous order that communists but not liberals or conservatives be welcomed into the Nazi party. Goering, Ribbentrop, and other Nazis testified unanimously at Nuremberg that Hitler looked up to no foreign statesman except Stalin. Stalin he admired as a fellow fascist nationalist, who had purged communism in the Trotskyite trials of what Hitler considered "cosmopolitan Jewish internationalists." According to Ribbentrop, Hitler had "great admiration for Stalin" and "was only afraid some radical might come in his place."[1]

The sentiments of Hitler for Stalin were handsomely reciprocated in Stalin's famous champagne toast of 1939 ("I know how much the German people loves its Fuehrer; I should like, therefore, to drink to his health")[2] and by Stalin's telegram to Ribbentrop hailing the cementing of their alliance by Polish blood ("The friendship of the peoples of Germany and of the Soviet Union, cemented by *blood,* has all grounds to be prolonged and stable").[3] Stalin "personally always advocated a friendly relationship between Germany and the Soviet Union" and "was a *convinced adherent of the Axis* and an opponent of England and America."[4]

Unlike the more primitive Hitler, the Stalinists are too sophisticated to believe racial prejudices privately (even though Stalin, in

---

[1] Goering, Ley, Ribbentrop, etc., are quoted about Hitler-Stalin in G. M. Gilbert, *Nuremberg Diary* (New York, 1947), pp. 85, 228, and Douglas Kelley, *22 Cells in Nuremberg* (New York, 1947), p. 163.

[2] *Nazi-Soviet Relations, 1939-1941* ("documents from the archives of the German Foreign Office as released by the Department of State"), ed. by R. J. Sontag and J. S. Beddie (New York, Didier, 1948), p. 75.

[3] Published in New York *Daily Worker,* communist newspaper, Dec. 26, 1939.

[4] *Nazi-Soviet Relations,* p. 324. For Stalin's pro-German leanings, see also pp. 335-6.

an article in *Bakinskii Proletarii* after a tsarist pogrom, was highly amused by a fellow-Bolshevik's jest that "the Mensheviks are a Jewish faction, the Bolsheviks a Russian faction, whence it wouldn't be a bad idea for us Bolsheviks to arrange a pogrom in the party.")[1] But even though privately no racists, they are increasingly turning to public incitement of anti-Semitism and public lynch trials of Jewish "cosmopolitans" in order to distract the masses from the poverty innate in the Soviet system. A characteristic example of communism as communazism was the anti-Semitic pogrom of 1951, unleashed by the communist government in Budapest.

The deportation of Jews into the deadly slave-labor camps was superintended by Hungarian Nazi collaborators, the very same individuals (like General Laszlo Piros) who had done the same function during Hitler's occupation of Hungary and who now are high communist officials. For example, see Dr. Bela Fabian's articles about this in *Commentary* magazine, entitled "Hungary's and Rumania's Nazis-in-Red" (May 1951) and "Hungary's Jewry Faces Liquidation: Again the Concentration Camps" (November 1951). These articles are being distributed by the American Jewish Committee as valid evidence of the extermination of East European Jews as "cosmopolitans," etc. Dr. Fabian describes how arrested Jewish leaders were coerced into signing false statements to the outside world that "no Jews were being deported *as Jews*," and how some committed suicide as protest against this untruth. The Fabian article supplies names and specific evidence about these butcheries. It concludes:

The parallel to the policy of Nazi extermination is almost complete: the only difference is the denial that "Jews as Jews" are being mistreated, and the fact that, at the end of the line, instead of the extermination camps of Auschwitz and Treblinka, there are the slave labor camps of Karaganda and Kolyma and the cotton fields of Tashkent and Alma-Ata. Indeed, the parallel may well be even closer. Minister Istvan Kossa, charged with the handling of ecclesiastical matters since the beginning of May 1951, is a convinced anti-Semite. Lieutenant General Laszlo Piros, charged with the supervision of deportation and of frontier control, was one of the infamous participants in the Miskolc pogrom, in 1946. Many Jews walked silently into the streets with the

---

[1] Stalin, *Collected Works* (Russian edition, Moscow, 1946), II, 50-1.

yellow stars of the Nazi occupation sewed on their clothes, in protest — the wearers were immediately seized and deported.

Almost all the Czech Communists purged by the Kremlin in 1951-52 were Jews. That is to say, "cosmopolitans" — the standard Soviet double-talk for Jews. The Czech press issued the following justification for the communist incitement of a pogrom mood against "the behavior of the Jews":

The common people had not dared to express their *indignation at the behavior of the Jews,* for fear that they might be charged with anti-Semitism or Fascism. It is a pity that we did not know how to distinguish between the sound instinct of the people and anti-Semitism, and it is even more regrettable that it [the sound instinct] was suppressed by the "cosmopolitans" [Jews] who had *infiltrated into the leadership of the party.* By now, these enemies of our country have been unmasked, and the sound voice of the working people will no longer be stifled.[1]

However, it is absurdly oversimple to single out the anti-Semitic aspect of communazism, important though it is. Or to single out the anticapitalist aspect or anti-trade-union aspect. What counts is that *human beings* are being bestially massacred, no matter of what "race" or religion or economic "class." By definition, the very essence of communazism is a pogrom against the human race as a whole. A communazi globe — and at crucial moments during the Battle of Britain and today again in Europe and Korea, one random Anglo-American loss of nerve could bring it about — means the whole globe as a single huge gas chamber or slave-labor camp, into which (as Mussolini's American apologists once boasted) "the trains will run on time."

It is oversimple to make too much of listing all the practical instances of fascist-communist co-operation (for example, most recently their joint backing of Perón against America). It is equally oversimple for the other side to list the undoubted instances when, for tactical reasons, communists and fascists fight each other. What counts is not practical-tactical shifts in either direction, motivated by Realpolitik. What counts is their basic long-run identity of attitude toward the ethics of ends and means, and

[1] Published in the communist newspaper *Lud,* Bratislava, January 26, 1952.

toward the parliamentary system of peaceful change, and toward the relationship of state and individual.

Churchill was one of the only statesmen with vision enough to comprehend the new thirty-years-war at its birth. Hence, his much-slandered intervention policy in 1918. Churchill intervened not against the Russian people but for them. He intervened on behalf of England's ally of World War I, the Russian people, against the small bolshevik minority, who had been voted down by an over-whelming majority of the Russian people in the free elections of late 1917. At that time Churchill publicly prophesied that all mankind would pay a terrible price in the future unless Russia's allies helped Russia's struggle for liberation from the bolshevist police state. Unfortunately the Western intervention was too tiny and halfhearted to help war-weary Russians resist with bullets the bolshevik minority they had just defeated with ballots.

A second time Churchill's imagination grasped the communazi danger: when he dramatically warned an appeasing England against Hitler's rise and against Hitler's intentions. A third time: when, during World War II, he kept warning of the postwar political dangers while most American leaders thought only of immediate military victory. A fourth time: when his Fulton speech of 1946, in the nick of time, woke up the West to the Soviet postwar expansion policies. Truly Winston Churchill, more than any other man alive, merits the title of the Cassandra of freedom.

America may not have realized war was being waged against its very existence from November 1917 through today. Many Americans combined the greed of the hog with the isolationism of the ostrich. They combined the spirit of Déat's "why die for Danzig?" with Cain's "am I my brother's keeper?" They never realized their own complacently-slouched shoulders were the target, every time a communazi whip hissed through the air in the murder camps of Europe. But the communazis did realize it; they knew it every moment and said so openly: in *Mein Kampf,* in the homilies of Lenin and Stalin. They wrote it down, but we did not have eyes to see; and so we let them grab half the globe while we dawdled and disarmed, Muniched and Yalta'd, and used our vast steel production for TV sets while the long fuse was sputtering from Moscow toward Korea.

IV

The pages that follow concentrate more on communist psychology than on fascist psychology. This is not because either is inherently viler than the other. Nor is it merely because communism, in the constant protean shift between these twins, happens to be so much more dangerous than fascism at this particular brief moment of history. The purpose, rather, is to avoid repeating here the material about fascism appearing in a separate book, *Never Forget This: The Nazi Mind,*[1] a companion-volume to the present one.

Though the contrary was true of other circles, there was never any danger that the circle of liberal literary intellectuals in America and England would be neutralist toward the crude and obvious danger of fascism. Their peculiarly characteristic temptation was and is a neutral or unmilitant attitude toward communist fellow-traveling. Partly a "lost generation" of moral saboteurs: in the whole thirty years of the secret Soviet war against American ideals, it was the Gaylord kind of intellectuals, not workers or businessmen, who sabotaged the American anticommunist fervor (not "hysteria" but sane and necessary fervor). By thus failing to keep their own house clean, it is they who are partly guilty of causing that vicious McCarthyite anti-intellectualism which they wrongly blame on anticommunist fervor. To cut the ground from under McCarthyism, let American intellectuals today sabotage their own sabotaging by taking the lead in uniting the West behind an anti-communism more fervent than before, yet more fairminded. This can still become their glory, as once it was when intellectuals were the spearhead of anti-Nazi militancy.

Once America realizes a war to destroy it has gone on for thirty years, the next task is to see that America serves its chore constructively and never with hate. No good can ever come from hate, even if it is hate for as good a cause as liberty. No matter how mellifluous his tune, toads instead of words leap out of the hater's mouth (as in the old fairy tale about the witch).

When *The New Statesman* implies something called Wall Street is to blame for Soviet aggressions, when Del Vayo in *The Nation*

---

[1] To be published by the Beacon Press (title tentative).

gloatingly blames American foreign policy instead of communism for Jan Masaryk's death, or when a die-hard America-First isolationist blames Roosevelt and Marshall for Hitler's war, you can visualize an ugly toad leaping from their mouths at every word, so hot is the wave of hate, hate, hate emanating from their pages. Yet these same able and courageous critics of our foreign policy, if minus the hate, would be indispensable to our national welfare. Democracy cannot function without such severe criticism of its rulers and policies as a perpetual corrective, and without presentation of all independent, uncontrolled viewpoints, including wrong ones. The lesson is not that we should prevent free criticism of our foreign policy but that political criticisms, like private ones, go sour unless they proceed out of love.

We must resist the Politburo's thirty-year-war against the West not out of hate for it but out of compassion for its Russian and foreign victims and out of a fiery love for our value-heritage. It is simply not true that hate must be drummed up as a motive for resistance in a just war. A love for humanity was an even more compelling motive in inspiring the millions who died resisting Hitler and Stalin. What finally makes the governments of Mao, Hitler, and Stalin identical is that the verb "hate" is the most prominent in the vocabulary of all three. They and their satellite countries taught and teach hate to innocent young schoolchildren as the chief item in their curriculum.

For example, the Chinese Reds organize what they candidly call "hate sessions" to inflame their people to "hate Uncle Sam" and to pretend that the imperialist invader of China is American democracy and not Soviet fascism. In November, 1950, an article called "How to Understand the United States" was published in Peking in *Shih-shih Shou-ts'e* (*Current Affairs Journal*). This key article has become the basis for the "three views movement" officially sponsored by Red China as necessary for a "dialectically correct understanding of America." Here is the translation of the "three views" being instilled into millions of Chinese children:

1. "Hate the United States, for she is the deadly enemy of the Chinese people;"
2. "Despise the United States, for she is a rotten imperialist nation, the headquarters of reactionary degeneracy in the whole world;"

3. "Look with contempt upon the United States, for she is a paper tiger and can fully be defeated."

After being converted to liberty, one of Germany's top communist intellectuals (who must still remain anonymous) addressed these memorable words to the West:

The Soviet power itself can only be conquered by might. Communism as theory, *Weltanschauung,* and religion, however, which rationalizes every absurdity of practice, can only be conquered through the one thing for which there is no place in the system: liberty of the personality, the freedom of the spirit. And through that other power, which together with liberty first confers humanity upon man, which ensures the freedom of the other, because it respects him and recognizes itself in him: love and compassion.

The best way to fight Communism is to let those who are suffering under it, and those fallen intellectuals whose soul is still alive, experience understanding and sympathy, love and help, from the free world — those qualities, in short, that are foreign to the system. If I think back to the Moscow prison cell, I find that neither there nor at the Academy, neither from Soviet officers in the camps nor in the East Berlin Central Committee, nor anywhere in the Party did I ever hear the words "love" or "compassion." They are missing in the vocabulary of Communism just as they are missing in the *History of the CPSU (B).* They don't even exist as concepts. Stalin knows why.

When you hear eye-witness accounts of North Korean Reds throwing the American defenders of collective security into bonfires and burning them alive, when communist leaders in Berlin smash the helpless body of the crippled democratic deputy Jeanette Wolff (crippled in a Nazi concentration camp) while shouting anti-Semitic slogans at her because she favors civil liberties, and when you hear not one faint, subsonic peep of indignation against this from many who in America, England, and France pose as champions of civil liberties, then to avoid emotions of counterhate does become difficult for *our* side of the barricades. Difficult yet indispensable. He who looks too deep into the abyss, said Nietzsche, should beware lest the abyss look into him. He who confronts monsters should beware lest he himself become monstrous. Atrocities tend to beget atrocities. Hate on our part would hurt us more than our enemies. Hate would trick our anticommunist struggle into hysterical errors of judgment, from which only communism would gain.

Not hate is called for on our part but sympathy for the tortured Chinese and Russian peoples, pity and sternness toward their miserably sick and unhappy oppressors, and a granite determination that this time the globe is too small to be left merely half-liberated from the communazi thirty-years-war.

IGNORANCE IS BI-PARTISAN

"Beaverbrook noted of Stalin, 'We had got to like him; a *kindly* man.' . . . In his records of this conference [in the Kremlin], Beaverbrook has given an interesting glimpse of Stalin's doodling habits: while Litvinov was translating the Russian words into English, 'Stalin occupied himself by drawing numberless pictures of wolves on paper and filling in the background with *red* pencil.' "

— *from* SHERWOOD, *Roosevelt and Hopkins*

"The wolves are playing in the courtyard, but the hare will not escape them."   — *from a fantasy by* KAFKA

In 1948, when Taft and Wallace were the top mentors of the far right and the far left in America, both reacted the same way to the Czech disaster by saying it did not greatly concern America. No wonder one of them voted against the Atlantic Pact when it first passed the Senate and the other denounced it as aggressive, although both belatedly accept it today. Even moderate Democrats (who in 1945, including the President, sometimes distrusted British imperialism more than communism) and even moderate Republicans (who in 1945 joined the self-destructive cry to "bring the boys back home") were not always much better than such extremists as Taft and Wallace.

Not only foreign policy but foreign folly is usually bi-partisan. Since at least 1944, there has been ignorance in high places of the nature-of-the-crisis. This ignorance has been so evenly distributed that it should not be made a narrow political issue to indict either Republicans or Democrats alone. It indicts both or none.

It is not irreverence and impertinence toward high dignitaries but reverence for pertinent facts that necessitates the adjective "ignorant" for the following two quotations. One is from a not uninfluential New Dealer. The other is from the largest circulating Republican newspaper. The New Dealer in question counted on his charm to tame the nature-of-the-crisis, as the isolationist Republican counted on his selfish cynicism.

Editorial of March 12, 1952, in the Republican isolationist *Daily News*:

> So long as Batista keeps the Communists under screws in his country [Cuba], and doesn't let sugar or rum shipments to the U.S.A. be seriously interrupted, we should think Americans could afford to remain calm about this revolution. Apparently the Cubans can be happy, anyway, only if they have such a show at regular intervals.

Of course, Americans cannot "afford to remain calm" about any tyranny, right or left. The whole present crisis comes from too much initial calm about Lenin and Hitler. What is dangerous is not some ephemeral Batista or any other banana-republic dictator, whom nobody but a fellow-traveler or anti-anticommunist would equate with Stalin as a menace. What is indeed dangerous is not the Batistas abroad but these shortsighted American cynics right at home, who imagine they can stop communism by buying foreign dictators instead of arming foreign freemen.

Roosevelt (in reply to a warning that Stalin sought world conquest):

> "I just have a hunch that Stalin isn't that kind of man. Harry [Hopkins] tells me he's not, and that he doesn't want anything but security for his country." [Hopkins, of course, could not really know.] "I think that if I give him everything I possibly can" [at someone else's expense] "and ask for nothing in return" [not even effective safeguards for the victims] "he won't try to annex anything" [beyond twelve countries], "and will work with me for a world of peace and democracy" [People's Democracy]. "It is my responsibility, not yours" [it is indeed], "and I'm going to play my hunch." [It was played.][1]

When the head of the American government was taking this view of the nature-of-the-crisis at the time of Yalta, may he be pardoned as merely reflecting the universal advice of democratic, anti-fascist authorities? It does not seem so. The correct analysis of the crisis was made, not through hindsight but at the very moment of Yalta, by a leading democratic hero of the coalition war against Hitler. He and others had the irrefutable information about

---

[1] Analyzed by Lord Vansittart, *Even Now* (London, [1949?]), pp. 115-116. This book is one of the most interesting British indictments of communazism.

Soviet intentions. But they were not listened to in 1945. The man I refer to is Tomasz Arciszewski, the last legitimate prime minister of Poland. Let us close with his prediction, after having heard both Republican ignorance and New Deal ignorance about the nature-of-the-crisis. Arciszewski in 1945:

Remember, so long as one free country is left, the men in the Kremlin will never feel safe. No matter how peaceful its desires and its policy may be, they will never be satisfied until they bring it down, by intrigue or force, or a combination of both.

Far from being a tool of American right-wing reactionaries, serious anticommunism cuts equally across the lines of both our parties. Fellow-travelers had infiltrated the Republican Mac-Arthur's SCAP organization in Tokyo and not only the Democratic State Department. When a high State Department official remonstrated with MacArthur about this danger, he replied:

Of course, we have Communists in SCAP. They have them in the Defense Department. You have them in the State Department. But they don't matter. We can take care of them.[1]

Such a statement was never made by Acheson but by MacArthur; it was made in 1948; it is food for thought during the mudslinging of the 1950's.

Partisan anticommunism, directed exclusively at either one of our two parties, is discounted by independent voters as petty politics. As a result, it fails to be taken seriously, even when it deserves to be, and fails to injure our communist foes. What we need is a justice-dedicated, bi-partisan anticommunism. This will hammer away relentlessly at the evasive Democratic State Department to get the full story of its hushed-up *Amerasia* case. Equally it will hammer away for the full story behind the following serious allegation by Richard Deverall, MacArthur's Chief of Labor Education and now A.F. of L. representative in India:

A group of Communists and pro-Communists in MacArthur's headquarters played a dramatic part during the early days of the Occupation in turning over press, radio, and movie facilities in Japan to native

---

[1] This unrepudiated quotation is cited in Rovere and Schlesinger, *The General and the President* (New York, 1951), p. 202, note.

Communist elements. . . . Those of us who combated this plot against America inside MacArthur's own headquarters were forced to resign "because you are too anti-Communist."

Not in the slightest do such reflections cancel out or condone the hair-raising initial complacency of the Truman-Acheson Administration toward the rise of Chinese communism. But most of the mistakes about China and communism were diffused nationwide — neither party wanted to vote the money and troops they ought to have voted to stop the Chinese Reds while there was still time — and cannot be pinned on any one scapegoat. On the other hand, the influence of the semi-infiltrated [1] Institute of Pacific Relations is definitely a score against the Democrats and not the Republicans. For the net effect of that osmosing influence — with its ubiquitous book reviewers and professors in the cultural world and with its experts and consultants in the political world — was obviously favorable to Mao's aggressive ambitions; this holds true regardless of whether you evasively try to deny the existence of that influence, as do the Democratic State Department apologists, or whether you wildly exaggerate the effect of that limited influence upon the more important local causes in Asia of Chiang's defeat, as does the McCarthy chorus of Furies.

When the scene shifts from Democratic mistakes in China to foresight in Europe, the score tends to favor the Democrats instead and not the semi-isolationist and China-oriented Republicans. This holds true only after 1947, when the statesmanlike Truman Doctrine of anticommunist intervention in Greece replaced the costly earlier illusions of "post-war co-operation." The joint support of the wise and indispensable Marshall Plan and Atlantic Pact by the Democrats Acheson and Truman and the Republicans Eisenhower and Vandenberg did rather more to stop communism than

---

[1] Semi-infiltrated: the communist Frederick Vanderbilt Field was executive secretary for many years of IPR's American Council; the then fellow-traveling (but not communist) Owen Lattimore was a key policy-maker; and a number of IPR figures under oath refused to answer questions about communist-party membership on grounds of self-incrimination. But alongside them, significantly in less strategic posts than the Fields, was a far larger number of honest university scholars, valuable researchers, and staunch anti-communists, whose undoubted integrity is being shockingly smeared by any unqualified blanket indictment of IPR. To untangle that complex web would take a book by itself.

did McCarthy's vote against the Marshall Plan ("operation rat-hole") and the rightist-leftist Taft-Wallace campaign against the Atlantic Pact. Such foresight and such ignorance both cut completely across party lines. Neither party has a monopoly on patriotism.

"BLOODY-MINDED PROFESSORS": SHAME OF THE INTELLECTUALS

"The power of vested interests is usually exaggerated when compared with the gradual *encroachment of ideas*. . . . Indeed the world is ruled by little else. . . . Madmen in authority, who hear voices in the air, are distilling their frenzy from some *academic* scribbler of a few years back."
— JOHN MAYNARD KEYNES

"If we liberals were right on certain single aspects of the Russian Revolution, we were wrong, disgracefully wrong, on the question as a whole. We were wrong because, in our . . . vision of a new world springing from the womb of this Russian experiment, we permitted ourselves to condone wrongs that we knew must be wrongs." — JOHN HAYNES HOLMES, *America's leading liberal clergyman, 1939 (after the Hitler-Stalin pact)*

In one of his breathtakingly apt phrases, Winston Churchill called our communists and their sympathizers *not* a gang of ruthless and bloody-minded gangsters but "a gang of ruthless and bloody-minded professors." The phrase is apt because Churchill, by implication, has spotted a central problem of our century: the strike of the middle-class intellectuals, their reluctance to conserve the very heritage that protects from Russia their freedom and their security.

Just as American workingmen have an innate impulse toward Red-baiting and toward capitalist democracy, so many bourgeois intellectuals, artists, and writers (what Churchill means by "professors") still have an innate soft spot for some kind of almost unconscious fellow-traveling with communism. I wish more of my fellow "professors," to use Churchill's phrase a third time, would analyze the reasons for their (our) soft spot — in addition to spending so much of their leisure deploring loyalty oaths for professors. We will fight these potentially dangerous oaths more effectively, and protect more effectively our indispensable academic freedom, by analyzing objectively our own soft spot. To replace our alienation from our own society with greater mutual trust, we must improve — rather than servilely accept — our imperfect society. But equally we must improve — rather than self-pity — our own imperfect selves.

Conversely, on the opposite side of this social split, I wish more business tycoons would spend more of their leisure analyzing the following question. Since America is not merely prosperous but a relatively free and decent place to live in, why are its patriotic and capitalist slogans so unattractive, psychologically and esthetically, that they repel educated Americans and attract only the uneducated?

Totalitarianism has had an innate attraction for an able minority of literary intellectuals as far back as Plato. He in turn expelled his fellow poets from his totalitarian republic, thus anticipating the modern popular impulse to send "all long-hair radicals back where they came from." Bad tempers on all sides may abate if all sides remember that it is nothing new — has been true for centuries — that *some* intellectuals have an inherent soft spot for totalitarian revolution and that, therefore, *all* intellectuals are distrusted by their nonintellectual fellows. We have seen it all before: the sensitive artists saying (with Wordsworth) of a brutal, insensitive revolution, "Bliss was it in that dawn to be alive," and the victims of that revolution chanting:

> Je suis tombé à terre,
> Le nez dans le ruisseau;
> C'est la faute à Voltaire,
> C'est la faute à Rousseau![1]

Today American victims of a later world revolution, paying a price in Korea for the illusion that you can appease the Soviet terror, are chanting prose versions of this old anti-Jacobin ditty: "C'est la faute à. . . ." For Voltaire, they are substituting any number of more recent and less distinguished intellectuals and ideologues, including all the professors who reassured America that communists are not communists but agrarians, Chinese Jeffersons, fellow-pro-

---

[1] "I crashed to the ground, my nose in the gutter;
It's the fault of Voltaire, it's the fault of Rousseau!"

gressives in a Popular Front, or (to quote one book title) "people on our side."

Then as now, the guilt of intellectuals and educators gets wildly exaggerated. Then as now, there has been some truth — amid the obvious exaggerations — in some of the accusations. Intellectuals are more susceptible to the leftist totalitarian lure than any other group in America: only a small minority of them, of course, but proportionately a higher minority than of such other groups as farmers, businessmen, and manual workers. Why? The question cannot be fully answered here, but let us now rethink some neglected aspects of it.

II

"Utopias" are constantly being written — or thought silently — by intellectual idealists. As Thomas More and Samuel Butler knew, every Erewhon is Nowhere. The seeking of an impossible heaven-on-earth leads to more hell-on-earth than the seeking of a possible second best; the unattainability of the best invites ever more violent and coercive measures from the midwives of an un-co-operative Clio. In his heart every revolutionary Caesar, from the first one through Napoleon and Stalin, prefers Clio to Cleo. He prefers the muse of history to the cherchez-la-femme of history. The revolutionary-totalitarian mind is always in a hurry to get perfection aborning right here and now, so that totalitarian Caesarism is necessarily violent: a Caesarian operation on history. (See the compulsive recurrence of the midwife metaphor in the writings of the Old Bolsheviks.)

The impossibility of any very rapid social improvement leads to an ever more ruthless attempt to force it on human nature by terrorism. In consequence, the abstract theorists of the most perfect democracy again and again end up as the concrete apologists for the most imperfect dictatorship. So ended even such appealing figures as Lincoln Steffens, John Reed, and the Webbs. Note that Tom Paine, once the champion of a liberal perfectionism in England, ended up in France as the "fifth column" intellectual of his day. This treasonable Englishman was so shameless in his treason that he even offered to guide the unliberal dictator Napoleon in an invasion of parliamentary England.

Among those intellectuals who continue to fellow-travel, after the true nature of "the God that failed" is no longer a secret, a lust for power replaces impatient idealism as the motive. This power lust is consistent with the paranoiac trends found more frequently in that social group, the intellectuals, which is the most rootless, isolated, and abstract. Like spiders embracing the universe in their webs of *systematized* delusions, they spin their beautiful and insubstantial outer worlds from their own insides.

The intellectual's neutral aloofness from his society can change imperceptibly into unconscious hostility. This happens almost automatically in a society that does not appreciate his ideas as much as its electric dishwashers. The alienation of the introvert is nothing new either; the symbolism of Socrates, executed by his own unappreciative society, has always had a suspicious fascination for intellectuals in all ages. Their instinctive self-identification with Socrates may suggest a self-destructive masochism or may suggest its apparent opposite, an aggressive resentment against the square-shouldered, rosy-cheeked extroverts. Or perhaps, instead of either of these alternatives, it merely suggests an all-too-correct sense of realistic prophecy.

If you rationalize the lack of esthetic appreciation you receive from the Babbitt warrens, you may end up by fighting them also in politics and in economics; thereby you can save your offended pride secretly and your pocketbook openly. Hell hath no fury like an intellectual scorned; the semi-Stalinist fellow-traveling sometimes found in America's largest circulating liberal weekly, and also in England's, is one way of saying: "I'm not fired, I quit."

Ancestor of this attitude was the nineteenth-century distrust between Paris and *la province,* that duel between the farm and the café or between the countinghouse and the salon; this theme runs through the most influential nineteenth-century French novels (Balzac, Flaubert, Stendhal). American artistic circles know amazingly little of their own co-operative, compromise-minded, and relatively-classless society. They naturally know best the society they have studied best: the society portrayed in the French and other novels that composed their own youthful *éducation sentimentale.* This is a society seen through the colored glasses of a literary (at first nonpolitical) anti-bourgeois crusade. In the Roman holiday of the bourgeois arena, the intellectual is alternately the martyr and the lion. And there is more than one kind of lion. Among literary intellectuals, the lion of the barricades (reread Wagner's and Baudelaire's fascinating and parallel accounts of their revolutionary role in 1848) may be the salon-lion *manqué* or not yet arrived. The baitee becomes the baiter; the sissies of the Right Bank become *les fauves* ("the wild beasts") on the Left Bank.

How many American intellectuals, knowing little of their own country, still identify themselves with the victims of bourgeois misunderstanding in Joyce's *Portrait of the Artist as a Young Man* and Flaubert's *Madame Bovary!* Sinclair Lewis's *Main Street* is merely the twentieth-century American version of this nineteenth-century European duel. The Young Werther of our time is the self-pitying intellectual "crucified" upon some bourgeois philistine's "cross of gold." Through political and economic radicalism the crucified esthete, "L'Albatros" of Baudelaire, can get revenge against the cross of gold. The romantic-esthetic pose of the introverted stare ("yond Cassius has a lean and hungry look") can make heads roll in the sand of bloodthirsty politics. "Such men are dangerous," as Caesar knew.

So far as this is a human duel, a psychological and noneconomic one, it has an esthetic root. But an economic root is added readily by the insecurities of the business cycle, with the underpaid professors and un-unionized white-collar workers crushed between the millstones of both kinds of bigness: big business and big trade-unions. In the impersonal hustle and bustle of modern industrialism, the intellectual gets rudely pushed about as a barely-tolerated court jester. Without being allowed even the court privileges and indulgently-applauded impertinences of the medieval jester. Then, one day, in his humiliation, he discovers Marxism. Purely by accident and yet somehow inevitably. Suddenly everything makes sense again, or seems to; in a jungle of blind commercialism, he again finds a purpose for society; for himself, he finds at last a more dignified role than court jester or court prostitute. Precisely because he understands not one word of Marx's materialistic economic jargon, this nonspiritual church comes to him as a spiritual salvation, a Damascus vision, a reason for going on living. Marxism provides a vast political "system" to canalize and seemingly "explain scientifically" the nonpolitical, psychological resentments of Werther, Emma Bovary, the Artist as a Young Man, and our own poor Carol Kennicott of *Main Street,* America's homespun version of the "sensitive" hero.

How well these resentments are expressed in the song of Jenny, in Bertholt Brecht's *Dreigroschenoper,* dreaming of a sudden murderous pirate fleet to queen her and to unking bourgeois society! Is the psychology of Jenny's bloodthirsty song unconnected with the recent decision of the gifted Brecht to leave the free world and cross the Iron Curtain to his beloved pirates?

Or turn to a noncommunist poet like Vachel Lindsay. Few writers have traveled so widely and observantly in America as this Dante of Fundamentalism whose Rome was Springfield, Illinois; whose medieval crusade against the Saracens was the Anti-Saloon League; whose Virgil through his Inferno was Johnny Appleseed. In the early 1920's Lindsay wrote: "I went through the usual Middle West crucifixion of the artist." The revealing word is "usual," even more than "Middle West" or "crucifixion" ("crucifixion" is merely the "usual" self-sentimentalizing of paranoiac artists, a silly habit no doubt but productive often of magnificent diction). The intentions of Lindsay's above statement were esthetic, unpolitical. That only made it all the more a portent of future political dynamite in the trek of artists from ivory tower to politics after 1929.

Political Marxism; plus the bourgeois-baiting, nonpolitical novel; plus the self-pitying Socrates-hemlock identification; plus genuine social wrongs (and not even the best society attainable by mortals will eliminate all occasions for Tennyson's "Cursèd be the social wants") — this quadruple combination still won't turn the Western intellectual into a communist; party membership requires too Calvinistic, almost too bourgeois a discipline; but it does turn him into the familiar blend of an "aristocratic" snob in art and a fellow-traveling "progressive" in politics. If you are not lucky enough to be endowed with Baudelaire's bitter eyes and resentful chin, then as second best this familiar blend will enable you to strike the twin poses of dandy and stormy petrel at your publisher's cocktail party for buttered-up book reviewers.

Every artist steeped in the magnificent French literature of the last century — that is to say, every typical American literary-intellectual — will see that this snob-plus-progressive pose is neither new nor indigenous. Open at random Stendhal, for example, and you find in his autobiographical *Vie de Henri Brulard:*

I had, and still have, the most aristocratic of tastes. I would do everything in my power to ensure the happiness of the masses. But I think I'd rather spend a fortnight of every month in prison than have to live with shopkeepers. . . . My family were the most aristocratic people in the town. This meant I became a fanatic republican on the spot.

The American Middle West was the scene of the most influential Lewis novels. This has made it today — in part unfairly, merely as a literary convenience — the accepted international symbol of the babbittry once represented by the French *provinces* of Flaubert and Balzac. The love-hate relationship between our Middle West and its tormented rebel artists is worth a separate book in itself: Hart Crane ("I could not pull the arrows from my side"), Pound (finding civilization "a bitch gone in the teeth"), Henry Miller, and the others.

Sulking in a Paris café, writing the following lines, there sits typically not a Parisian city slicker but the thoroughly Midwestern — practically corn-fed — Henry Miller: "All my life I felt a great kinship with the madman and the criminal . . . Civilization is rotten . . . Release the instinctive vitality of the primitive." This stale romantic pose, which equips every Sauk Center and Kalamazoo with its drugstore Lucifer and its cracker-box Prometheus Unbound as innately as with its "Y" and its Chamber of Commerce, was harmless enough for years. Then, suddenly, it got catapulted by October 1929 into politics, where the old *New Masses* became its lucky heir. (At first the legacy amusingly embarrassed the heir, for The Party takes a dim view of bohemianism.)

At heart nonpolitical (except in the unusual context of that terrible economic depression), this pose was struck so much better — that is, with profounder insight — by Charles Baudelaire when it was not yet stale. In the revolution of 1848, gun in hand, he leapt joyously onto the anti-bourgeois side of the barricades, later explaining:

What was the nature of my intoxication in 1848? Thirst for revenge. Natural delight in destruction. A literary intoxication, the memories of books I had read. . . . The dandy's . . . opposition and revolt.

This great poet was temporarily drawn to the barricades not by political theory nor economic suffering but by esthetic "thirst for revenge" against France's proto-Middle West and its hucksters-in-embryo.

On the surface, America's literary defenders of Hiss, Coplon, Fuchs, and the eleven convicted communist leaders have motives more plausible, less romantic. On the surface, the motives are all pure reason and civil liberties, not Miller's "kinship with the madman and the criminal" nor Baudelaire's "natural delight in destruction." But this libertarian surface plausibility evaporates in many (not all) cases when you consider two ignored facts: 1. communist civil liberties are less impaired in America today than ever in our history; contrast the lawless Palmer raids of the 1920's with the long, fair, painstakingly lawful trials of Hiss, Coplon, and the eleven. Even though communism is murdering Americans in Korea and jailing them illegally in Europe, not one communist inside America — not one — has been deprived of habeas corpus, due process of law, his own legal aid, and unlimited free speech in his *Daily Worker*. 2. Most of these same intellectuals did not protest when many thousands of innocent Japanese-Americans during the war had their civil liberties impaired incomparably more than any communist today.

These two facts justify the following speculation: to what extent, within the infinite complexity of human motives, are the intellectual defenders of the "persecuted communists" excited not by their civil-liberties rationalization but by a sneaking sympathy with any kind of conspiracy against their hated "booboisie"? Beneath the seemingly detached defense of "communist rights," or of the analogous fascist "martyr" Pound, there often lurks a savage joy at the thought that a conspiracy against "rotten civilization" — against the bourgeois "bitch gone in the teeth" — will release Miller's "vitality of the primitive" and Baudelaire's "revenge and revolt." These speculations concern only a minority; they do not concern the genuine civil-libertarian defender of communist civic rights, a defense perfectly tenable so long as it defends only communist civil liberties and not communist conspiracies. But the minority motivated by the above savage joy happens to include many leading figures in the intellectual and artistic world; this fact offers priceless psychological clues to the otherwise inexplicable communism of such world-famous scientists as Pontecorvo, Fuchs, Allan Nunn May, and Joliot-Curie or such artists as Picasso.

The proper rebuttal to this savage joy is not to defend an indefensible burgher stodginess or huckster crassness. Unnecessary! Nor are pompous orations on "God Bless America" needed; that would only startle your quarry. All you need point out is this: the mean and prosaic qualities which are *rightly* resented in burghers by the literary intellectuals are found ten thousand times more in the mean and prosaic bureaucracy of the slummy U.S.S.R.

Fortunately newer and younger writers are starting to see American capitalism as it really is — a relatively democratized mixed economy — and not according to catchy false analogies with the 1789 tradition of class struggle in France or with the predatory, class-line capitalism which socialists *rightly* denounced in America and Europe in the early nineteenth century. No poltroonish conformism! I am not saying: stop attacking America's many faults. They are in many ways greater than Europe's. But they are a different kind of faults. They need to be attacked — and studied — in their own context, not that of either French cafés or Russian samovars.

By his French or Russian analogies, the American intellectual has added an artificial and unjustified alienation to that natural and justified alienation which native commercialism has already created. The American context lacks any class-conscious proletarians. It cannot be subjected, without violence to truth, to the "radical" (actually highly conventional) analysis of Marxist clichés. Not "boosting" of America nor a censorship of dissent but more self-knowledge and more knowledge of America are the cure for what ails our literary world.

III

The cultural inroads of pro-communism are many, many times more influential than their often-exaggerated political inroads or the feeble electoral campaigns of the tiny Party itself. Merely one example among many: consider the cultural damage — I am thinking of good books rejected as well as bad books published — that could be done by the presence of Angus Cameron until 1951 in one of our finest publishing firms. He put the priceless imprimatur of *respectability* on the pro-communist books published under him by communist propagandists like Howard Fast, Albert Kahn, and others.

With the characteristic hatred of literary Stalinoids for democratic socialists (a hatred more frenzied and frothing than any they expend on fascists), Cameron also was among those who after the war prevented Little Brown from publishing George Orwell's anticommunist satire, *Animal Farm*. Some eighteen to twenty publishers, almost all the leading ones, turned down the best anti-Soviet satire of our time. In view of its wit, its readability, its salability, and its democratic outlook, the most likely motive for these rejections can be the brilliantly successful infiltration (then, not now) of Stalinoid sympathizers in the book world: the world that does more than Congress to mold the attitude of literary Americans toward Russia and foreign policy. "Witch-hunt"? "McCarthyism"? Yes — but from the left and against the free speech of *anti*communists. The fact that the book finally did get published and with triumphant éclat — in the end serious literature does triumph — cautions us not to exaggerate Stalinoid infiltrations paranoiacally. But not to overlook them schizophrenically either. The mentality revealed by this attempt to prevent American readers from freely hearing Orwell's free speech about despotism made Arthur Schlesinger, Jr., cancel his contract with Little Brown,[1] writing them (in days when that still took real courage):

Each day increases my sense of shame at ever having been associated with your house. I would never have signed up in 1939 if one of your leading members had been an active pro-Nazi, and I have no intention of being published by Little, Brown today when one of your leading members [Angus Cameron] is taking an active part in opposing the democratic effort to check the spread of Soviet totalitarianism.

During those same incredible years when Cameron was pub-

---

[1] Be it stressed that today Little Brown is a wholly admirable firm, publishing admirable books without any more Angus Camerons to purge it of the freedom-loving Orwells, the genuine liberals and democratic socialists.

lishing the communist propaganda of Albert Kahn in an excellent old firm and was organizing his branch of the communist-controlled Progressive party, Alger Hiss was helping Stettinius draw up the agenda for Yalta, superintending the San Francisco Conference, directing the Carnegie Peace Foundation, and serving as special assistant to the Director of the Office of Far Eastern Affairs in the State Department. Until recently, even to notice such facts was considered hysterical. That this should have been so considered, is the same disgrace as the earlier indifference of Americans to the Nazi danger.

Allegedly, anticommunists are exaggerating — out of malice or persecution complex — the powerful, camouflaged role of fellow-travelers in the intellectual world. Allegedly, we exaggerate the damaging influence of those noble-sounding front organizations of the 1930's, all those American Writer Congresses, those Leagues Against War and Fascism and (*after* the Pact) Leagues for Peace and Democracy. It is up to allegers to prove their allegations. This charge of exaggeration can be checked on. Enough American and English writers are alive in the 1950's to testify as to the very real power of the fellow-traveler intellectual during 1930-47. Ask any writer who tried to tell the truth about Russia or about those Chinese "agrarian reformers" during those years. Ask him to tell you what reactions he got in the literary and academic world. For example, ask him what happened to even his literary, nonpolitical books.

There are literary wrongs that still need to be righted, assassinations of character and of literary reputation. Tactful forgetfulness today may be convenient to the assassins but will not serve the duty that wrongs must be righted. How many present readers still remember the suddenness with which progressive critics discovered, before the war, that the novels of Dos Passos and James T. Farrell had no literary merit after all? This "discovery" took place the instant these two writers happened to break with communism. These are merely two random examples — Eastman and Lyons are others — to whom a belated atonement for injustice is overdue.

Unless there really was a Pink Terror of social pressure in favor of fellow-traveler conformism, Bertrand Russell would not have confirmed that

he lost more friends by his criticism of Soviet terror than by his absolute pacifism during a war in which his country was locked in a battle
of life and death with Germany.[1]

In other words, in intellectual circles (in contrast with the nonintellectual "outer world") it was safer to attack your own free
country in wartime than to criticize a certain sacred foreign country
for its despotism.

At the same time, remember that in the 1930's many anti-
fascist idealists seemed fellow-travelers merely because they felt
(mistakenly but honestly) that only communism opposed a Munich
appeasement policy and because they were justifiably disgusted
with that kind of capitalist who used to say, "Better Hitler than
Léon Blum." Such anti-fascist idealists should not be retroactively
slandered as "Reds" today, provided they passed the key test of
left-wing decency by ceasing to fellow-travel when the 1939 pact
revealed Stalin as merely a Soviet version of Hitler. Of course,
this is what communism was all along from 1917 on; clearer heads
knew this long before the pact, having studied the Moscow trials,
the slave labor, and the deliberate starving of peasants in the 1930's.
But this does not allow us indiscriminately to impugn the high
motive of those who, though less informed about Russia than some
of us before 1939, rendered priceless aid and self-sacrifice to the
anti-Nazi cause. Today, needless to say, there is no such extenuat-
ing circumstance for "softness" toward the Soviet as there was in
the shameful Munich year of 1938. Today the Soviet is not the
seeming alternative to fascism but *is* fascism incarnate.

In America, fellow-traveling has never been a working-class
movement or a spontaneous people's movement. American pro-
communism, and even much of European communism, is a spontaneous movement only among the educated intellectuals of the
upper middle class. It arises among that section of them which is
psychologically — *not* economically — discontented and self-out-
lawed. (That these, in turn, with their educational leadership, may
set a mass movement in motion under certain unusual economic
conditions, is another and *later* matter.)

Marx, Engels, Lenin, Trotsky, Bukharin — most of the original

---

[1]Julien Steinberg (ed.), *Verdict of Three Decades* (New York, 1950),
quoted by Sidney Hook, p. 612.

communist leaders — were intellectuals of the upper middle class, not suffering economically but suffering intensely psychologically. This must be qualified by adding that Lenin's family belonged to the petty nobility (the Tsar's professional service-aristocracy) as well as to the rich upper middle class. Among top communists, Stalin was one of the few to spring (like Hitler and Mussolini) from humble — so-called democratic — origins. But this fact had far less to do in shaping Stalin than his being picked by the Greek Orthodox church as one of the favored semi-intellectuals trained for the priesthood. Thereby he, too, was able to find his way indirectly to the alienated upper classes, the first prerequisite to communism.

Evidence is available about the composition and origins of the small Bolshevik party that seized power in November, 1917. The overwhelming majority of its members were definitely not workers, but middle-class intellectuals. Is this fact sufficiently known and sufficiently analyzed in America? As late as 1921-22, even after the triumph of the revolution and the adherence of some of the propagandized masses to the Bolshevik party, a *majority* of its members were still not workers but intellectuals.[1]

Even more, far more is this true of America. The American worker is the most anticommunist bulwark of freedom in the world today. He believes in democratic trade unionism, working *within* the capitalist system for increased living standards and increased civil liberties. Though intended as slander, there is reassuring truth in the definition of "Trade unions" in the 1951 edition of the *Soviet Dictionary of Foreign Words:* "primarily opportunists and adherents of class collaboration with the bourgeoisie."

It is only half the story to explain the anticommunism of American workers by their having the highest living standards of any workers in the world. Just as the pro-communism of rich middle-class intellectuals defies economic determinism, so does the anti-communism of American workers; it, too, is partly motivated also by noneconomic factors. For trade unionism has a rarely-discussed psychological appeal in addition to its much-discussed and obvious economic appeal. Communism appeals to those suffering from the frustration and loneliness of an impersonal, cash-nexus rela-

---

[1] E. H. Carr, *The Bolshevik Revolution* (New York, 1951), p. 207.

tionship with their neighbors. The middle class suffers most from
that; in consequence, its intellectuals become the leaders of communism in all countries. Trade unions not only bring obvious
economic gains to the Anglo-American worker. They also replace
for him the cash-nexus with a sense of belonging. They give him
a human, cultural, social, and recreational unity with his neighbors,
not merely an economic one. They give him an organic sense of
community, more medieval (guild-style) than modern — if modern
means a separatist, atomistic liberalism.

Therefore, America's anticommunist trade-unions (in contrast
with the reckless, revolution-provoking anarchism of the Republican Old Guard) are our most conservative, revolution-preventing
force. Their *voluntary* sense of community is the best guaranty
against communist or fascist collectivism, which appeals — with its
coercive sense of community — to all who are starved for an
organic human nexus. Part of the same pattern is the much-mocked
bar (pub in England); it, too, gives the worker but never the
middle-class clerk a belonging-ness that undercuts the psychological
appeal of communism-fascism. Despite "Seven Nights on the
Barroom Floor" and "The Drunkard's Progress," I would even put
in a good word for the saloon, the old-fashioned pre-Prohibition
saloon, which so horrified the "properly" educated (that is, half-
educated) middle class, whose lace-curtain psychology barred them
from participating in this great American folklore. In that same
unifying folklore, the unmentionable burlesque show also occupies
an honorable place, as the only spontaneous, non-fancied-up folk
art of our day.

Since the problem is global, let the camera flash back for an
instant to a very different continent:

> The significant thing about all these [pro-communist] leaders . . .
> is that they almost without exception are middle-class, and most of
> them from the fairly well-to-do middle class with a tendency toward
> the intellectual side. Many of them are somewhat bookish men. . . .
> They feel that their talents are not appreciated, a common disease of
> the intellectual, particularly in the Orient.

These words by a reliable American foreign correspondent[1] were

[1] Albion Ross, "Iran's 'Secret' Tudeh Party," despatch of August 16 from
Teheran in New York *Times,* August 17, 1952, Sunday editorial section.

not written of the Russian Bolsheviks of 1917 nor of American fellow-travelers — though they might just as well have been — but of communist sympathizers in the Iran of 1952. Over three different continents, a single world-wide pattern of the pro-communist personality emerges.

In 1945, Elmo Roper took a poll on whether America should offer still greater concessions to communist Russia. Roper classified the responses according to the education and income of those who replied. A sharp split in American opinion was revealed. Workers and low-income groups distrusted Russia and opposed concessions. Rich Americans, what Marx would call the bourgeoisie, trusted Russia and wanted still further American concessions to Russia. Roper classified these answers not only by wealth but by intellectuality and by knowledge of Russian and world affairs. The uneducated and the nonintellectual, in Roper's words of 1945,

were much less aware of the necessity of co-operation with Russia and much more inclined to charge Russia with dark and sinister intentions. . . . Those who knew something about Russia gave broad, balanced, opinions — critical on some scores and laudatory on others, but with the balance leaning strongly toward friendly understanding.

In 1946, a Gallup poll asked: "Do you believe Russia is trying to build herself up to a ruling power, or is Russia just building up protection against being attacked in another war?" Again answers were classified by education and income. The most optimistic replies came from "the professional and business group." They split almost 50-50 on this question. The most pessimistic replies came from what Gallup called the uneducated "manual workers." Sixty per cent of these "oppressed proletarians" predicted — in contrast with experts and professors — that Russia aimed for world power and expansion.

In other words, the main obstacle to understanding that communists are communists (not good neighbors, not agrarian reformers) was the possession of education, intellect, or great wealth. No wonder one editor made the following comment on all this in 1952: "to predict accurately in 1945 that Russia would act as Russia has acted, you had to be as dumb and poorly informed as an ox."

IV

The misinterpretation of Soviet world conquest by the best-educated non-oxen of the West did not merely affect the realm of abstract theory. It affected the course of actual history. To what extent it did so, cannot be accurately assessed. Here we enter the imponderable realm of the indirect influence exerted by "intellectual atmosphere" — in this case, a trust-Russia atmosphere. One assessment of the historical results of this atmosphere has been formulated by Norman Angell, the winner of the Nobel peace prize. He can hardly be called an imperialist warmonger, or unliberal, or anti-intellectual. His assessment of the trust-Russia atmosphere, among our unproletarian, upper-middle-class liberals, probably exaggerates its concrete territorial or military influences and consequences. But he does offer a real insight into at least the spirit of what was happening:

We defeated Hitler in a second war for democracy and then (against all the counsels of the "imperialist" Churchill) insisted upon a strategy which left the military domination of those states to Stalin, largely *because liberals and leftists* in both Britain and the United States believed Stalin and what he stood for to be so much more democratic than Churchill and what that "Tory imperialist" stood for.[1]

To Angell's insufficiently-qualified comment, you must add: Stalin could have and probably would have taken Eastern Europe militarily (though hardly Manchuria) even without Yalta. For this was a time when armed resistance to Soviet expansion would have been politically impossible in terms of the still deceived, still Popular Fronting public opinion of western Europe.

But the issue is not: what would he have taken anyway? The issue is: why did we give the seal of Western moral approval upon what would otherwise have been an open act of highway robbery? Confronted by such an open act, without the Yalta moral sugar-coating, our public opinion — which hampered resistance to Russian aggression till 1947 — would at least have hardened earlier. This would have permitted rearmament and a Truman doctrine and an Atlantic pact many months earlier, instead of having to undergo that fatal delay of unilateral disarmament — until Churchill's noble

---

[1] Norman Angell, *The New Leader*, May 26, 1952, p. 11. Italics mine.

Fulton speech and Stalin's own actions brought Stalin's Western dupes back to their senses. Back from the Popular Front illusion.

That illusion may be defined as the view that communists are merely misguided, overhasty liberals, moving in the same general "forward-looking" and "anti-fascist" direction as the rest of us. This illusion views communists as a problem of "civil liberties for nonconformists," instead of as a murderous Red army of invasion on behalf of a Russian fascist ruling class. This illusion made well-groomed and plausible-sounding maniacs of precisely the highest intellectual liberal circles, as shown not only by their above Roper-poll reactions but by their books, lecture courses, and liberal weeklies.

If you have forgotten the prevalence of this illusion — so I wrote in an *Atlantic Monthly* article of April 1940, and so I repeat again today — then simply read the list of 165 (allegedly 400) supposedly liberal intellectuals, not the worst nor the best elements of our culture, who in August 1939 signed a disgraceful pro-communist manifesto. This denounced "the fantastic falsehood that the fascist states and Soviet Russia equally menace the democratic way"; it called "Soviet and fascist policies diametrically opposed," and called Russia the great "bulwark" of peace. To repeat the list of signers now, in part the élite of the world of liberal weeklies, would embarrass some honest men who subsequently changed their minds for the better. Suffice it to recall again in 1952, as my article originally did in 1940, one tragi-comic coincidence: this manifesto was featured in *The Nation* the very week of the Hitler-Stalin pact!

Originating in the '30's, the Popular Front illusion provided during 1944-47 the moral sugar-coating to Russia's aggressions. It did so by blending into what might be called the optimistic "Yalta spirit," namely the spirit of thinking that Stalin would behave more peacefully and democratically than Hitler. Thereby the Popular Front illusion has dealt a blow to peace and liberty, and likewise to lucid reasoning, of still unassessed proportions. Just possibly it will turn out to be (if Russia annihilates the West) the most antisocial act ever committed in the history of mankind by any comparably decent and well-intentioned intelligentsia.

Today American intellectuals are rejecting these misconceptions, so far as foreign policy toward aggression in Korea goes. But they have still not rejected sufficiently the most successful communist hoax ever perpetrated: the confusion of criminal deeds with free thought, the confusion of communist military conspiracy with the sacred cause of civil liberties. One can only echo and underline the phrase, "so grave and urgent that a man breaks out in a cold sweat," in the following comment on this whole problem by John Dos Passos:

A living organism that fails to react to danger is sick or dying. The questions raised in the mind by the moral lynching of Whittaker Chambers by the right-thinking people of this country are so grave and urgent that a man breaks out in a cold sweat to think of them. Can it be that the "liberals" who control communications in the press and the radio and the schools and the colleges . . . refuse, in the light of all the evidence, to recognize the existence of a conspiracy of assassins bent on the destruction of the right-thinking liberals, as much as on the destruction of the rest of us? The day that this mystery becomes clear, the day when this strange delusion is swept out of the public mind, that day we will be able to go to bed secure in the thought that, if the United States is doomed by forces of history too great for us to overcome, at least we will go down fighting.[1]

EVIL

> "See, how on the unsubstantial air
> I kick, bleating my private woe
> As upside down my rolling sight
> Somersaults, and frantically I try to set my world upright;
> Too late learning why I'm hung here. . . .
> I, too, misjudged the real
> Purpose of this huge shed I'm herded in: not for my love
> Or lovely wool am I here,
> But to make some world a meal."
>
> — ALFRED HAYES, *The Slaughter-House*

Robert Gorham Davis is the author of a noble essay called "America's Intellectuals and the Idea of Love."[2] For those who have not read it, its two main points may be summarized something like this: The answer to despotism is not counterdespotism but

---

[1] *Saturday Review*, May 24, 1952; p. 11.
[2] *The New Leader*, March 10, 1952.

joyous, spontaneous individualism. Defying embarrassment, we must restore love to its rightful priority as catalyst of a free culture. Not only do I agree; I think it egregiously incumbent upon "us" Red-baiters to search our own conscience: to insure that our motive is not hate of Russia but love of human beings.

Alas, certain internal psychological dangers and external military dangers threaten Davis's two points of love and individualism. American liberalism, with its dogma of Original Sinlessness, is congenitally susceptible to these dangers. To build up resistance against them, let us evoke that surrealist sadistic nightmare which has already become realist for one-third of mankind. If that inspires an empathy into these dangers and makes their obscenity feelable and convincing, it may persuade vacillating liberal readers to add to Davis's love-plus-freedom some ethical and physical disciplines. These are needed to shield his love-plus-freedom psychologically and militarily — that is, within and without the heart — from the infernal darkness of hate-plus-slavery. Is not the darkness masked (Baudelaire's devil proving scientifically that devils don't exist) as progress, "peace" drives, and a materialistic welfare state? Owing to America's origin in the eighteenth century, the century of a top-of-the-brain rationalist optimism, our country must still learn to face the existence of evil. The realness of evil.

Suppose, by ignoring that evil is as instinctive as love, Americans interpret love merely as instinct and as maudlin self-indulgence. Suppose we discard, as allegedly "unjoyous," love's shell of ethical and physical disciplines. In that case, we would oversimplify "love" (against Davis's intentions) into romanticism. We would sentimentalize love's message into merely another pseudo-poetic exhortation to go dance pantheistically on the greensward of Arcadia or pan-Bacchically *sur les toits de Paris*. About to do so, we are sobered by one unanswered question: does not this stress on sweet "spontaneity" (like other messages of optimistic liberalism) open a Pandora-box: the all-too-spontaneous evil in the twofold, bittersweet heart of man?

Suppose such a beguiling Hymn to Life sends us all caroling into the streets with vine leaves in our hair? What exactly — let's examine closely — will we find in the streets? Will it be serene-eyed, high-foreheaded swains and maidens from a Grecian urn? —

hugging each other in unneurotic, pre-Christian innocence, between bouts of seeing life steadily and seeing it whole. Or will we, instead, find a surprise party waiting for us? Will we find — *Them,* impatiently consulting their 1945-bartered Mickey Mouse watches? Those familiar faces! — who of us will be the first to recognize and identify them, name by name, the dumpy little mediocrities from the Politburo photo? There they wait, the mean-eyed mousy supermen, the filing-clerk Prometheans of world arson, prissily instructing us to dig our own graves, stuff a handful of sawdust in our mouths, and pile in like sardines. (That Katyn burial drill.)

Each of the 15,000 sardines — or will it be 150 million[1] fresh and plump ones across the Atlantic? — will be neatly packaged by the "Katyn Russian Caviar Company" (trademark), individually wrapped in a very open-minded, very understanding editorial of the future by Gaylord Babbitt. Caption of his editorial: "No Progress-Omelette Without Breaking Eggs."

Look up wistfully, Chloris and Daphnis; it again is springtime in your pastoral; your delicately-awakening valleys are just as green as they always were, before Hitler-Stalin-Mao. And everywhere, from Prague to Peiping, *something* is popping up just like your crocuses. Dear playmates, what can it be?

That jolly, springtime pop is the budding sound of dragon's teeth. They are sown by the immoral optimism of decent dupes, who tried twice — 1938, 1945 — to evade a tragic but necessary moral decision. They tried to be isolated "from." They tried to coexist "with." Chummily "with" Hitler-Stalin satanism.

II

Unless the West devises (it is not too late) greater material sacrifices, greater unity, and more imaginative counterrevolutionary appeals against those who love war and hate peace, we must ahead

---

[1] The basic "ideology" or "five-year plan" of all monsters, even before the present monster, was formulated by Caligula: *"Utinam populus Romanus unam cervicem haberet."* Tacit motto of Stalin-Hitler nihilism: would that all kulaks, Jews, cosmopolitans, capitalists, social democrats, the 150 million Americans — ultimately the two billion earthlings — had but one single throat to slit. The countermotto of all free and ethical societies — namely, the individual as a holy end in himself — was formulated by Seneca: *"Homo res sacra homini."*

of time prepare ourselves psychologically for the worst. For two kinds of worst:

1. *The best of the worst:* a gallant resistance movement, secreted deep down in the rubble catacombs of our razed cities.

2. *The norm of the worst:* the Katyn-moment. This is the moment when you, too, stand there with your shovel, in that endless impersonal queue, knowing you are listening for the last time to a stray sparrow chirp; speculating for the last time about the quantum theory of physics or about the date of Shakespeare's sonnets; filling your nostrils for the last time with air instead of with gravel and beetles. Your crime? You believe in human liberty; you are a sincere and not lip-service anti-fascist. And that is the one crime Stalinist fascism can never afford to tolerate.

How prepare for the norm of the worst?

The first step is to face emotionally, and not merely cerebrally, the truth that the Katyn queue line may become *the* typical "condition humaine" of the Stalin-Hitler century (even introduced by the Agrarian Reformers into Korea, as the streamlined way of dealing with Americans). Second step: every free spirit, by an exercise of nerve and will, must then school himself ahead to face this experience with composure, love, and a heart sweet and clean, empty of all merely personal bitterness. It may help to read daily a few pages of Boethius's *De Consolatione Philosophiae,* to learn how a kindred spirit found the inner grace to face a Dark Age of the sixth century.

But you will also need to make preparations of a more homely, practical, prosaic nature. For example, every American and European intellectual (especially in exposed France) with the courage to be a "witch-hunter" and "war monger" — that is, the courage to defend civil liberties against communist invasion — should consult his dentist prior to Der Tag. Have your dentist remove all gold teeth, all gold and silver fillings. Have him substitute plastic fillings (or, as a posthumous practical joke on the seventh Five Year Plan, pseudo-gold fillings that turn out to be worthless). Since friends of freedom in our generation do not have the traditional human satisfaction of dying in bed, surrounded by doctors, priests, and grandchildren proffering pillows and orange juice, then let us at least have the "deathbed" (death-ditch) satisfaction of grudging the tiniest grain of extra valuta to *their* foreign exchange.

In case you become an underground worker after the Occupation, you should also (in view of their record of increasingly imitating their Gestapo allies of 1939) take the following precautions. Sweat off excess fat and cut your hair short (diminishing by several rubles the industrial value of your chemical composition). With aid of morphine, remove your fingernails in advance (diminishing the educational possibilities that precede The Confession — and there won't be morphine then). Spoil the commercial market value of your skin (for the modernistic lamps in the smarter dacha salons) by tattooing it with uproariously ribald witticisms about the Politburo.

III

Alternative: here are reliable methods of preserving your gold fillings temporarily, perhaps as long as six months after the introduction of Paradise. Sign the Stockholm "peace" pledge. Urge U.N. membership for the Agrarian Reformers. Let not one day pass without spreading a new rumor against Whittaker Chambers, the less true the better. Every time the government politely chides another "Scientist X" for walking out of an atomic lab with a pocketful of secrets, you must publish a clarion-call against "the police state," in which you defend the right to spy — as a new kind of "civil liberty" — by quoting something Jefferson said to Madison about free minds. Such a clarion call may later turn out to be inexpensive life insurance.

Even the most groveling party members, if they have ever resided in the West, end up in a new Titoist "trial." So the best insurance of all for surviving liberation by Stalinist fascism is simultaneously to join the Ku Klux Klan. There's always a sure job for certain occupations, regardless of their politics. Soviet Rumania and Hungary prove that a well-documented record of fascist or Nazi atrocities is the best prerequisite for a snug job in the M.V.D.

Western intellectuals need suffer no uncertainty about which groups will stifle in the cattle cars. A photostat of Soviet instructions about this is now available in the U.N. Economic and Social Council, obtained by the American Federation of Labor and published, for all to see, by the International Confederation of Free Trade Unions.[1] This secret document lists the categories of victims deported to slave labor when the Soviet armies liberated the Baltic countries. The list includes (to cite from the text):

prominent positions in the civil or communal service; prominent members of the anticommunist parties, Social Democrats, Liberals, small farmers, active members of the Jewish organizations, Bund, Zionist organizations, . . . persons who have been in the diplomatic service, relatives of persons who have escaped abroad.

The same categories would be used for the cattle cars in France, Italy, England, and — never wholly impossible — New York. Therefore, the editors of all those brilliant, nimble weeklies of neutralist liberalism are advised right now to bone up on the exact composition of this list. Note that there was no mention of Nazi collaborators nor even of nonpolitical criminals between such choice items as "Social Democrats" and "Liberals." Lesson: in the long run, the neutralist liberals will end up on the same list as the rest of us; their fawning and fellow-traveling will get them nowhere. If their motive in this is to save their "skins" (literally), let them also go join the Ku Klux Klan. Then, when the post-invasion Soviet ambassador appoints the Reverend Gerald L. K. Smith as Minister of Religion and Public Enlightenment in the American People's Democracy, they will have nothing to worry about . . .

What else is there to say? Merely this: meanwhile reread the "reactionary," classicist, post-1789 critics of Rousseau to see why the romantic idyll[2] of spontaneous self-expression and "natural goodness of man" was switched somehow. The romantic idyll of self-expression could not be bothered with the ethical discipline of a universal value-framework. So the arcadian pastoral was switched — by an almost imperceptible Caligari-tilt of the mirrors — into Belsen-Buchenwald-Kolyma-Katyn. "We didn't know it was loaded."

[1] *Stalin's Slave Camps* (Boston: The Beacon Press, 1952), p. 15.

[2] Is the Florentine's *l'altre-stelle*-moving "love" to be treated today as no *more* than that?

GOOD[1]

"Thou shalt love the Lord thy God with all thy heart, and with all thy soul, and with all thy mind. This is the first and great commandment. And the second is like unto it: Thou shalt love thy neighbor as thyself. On these two commandments hang all the Law and the Prophets." — *New Testament*

"It is better to bear the burden of impracticableness, than to stifle conviction and pare away principle until it becomes hollowness and triviality."   — JOHN MORLEY

We hear a lot about the smartness and earthiness of using four-letter monosyllables to become a best-seller. Read current headlines, contemplate certain "current events" — and you will wonder what has happened to that other, less best-selling four-letter word: "good." What would it feel like to the Secret Police who once lied for Hitler and now for Stalin or to whoever peddles marihuana to children or fake cancer cures to grown-ups — what would it feel like to them, what strange new *frisson* of a thrill would it afford — to be "good"? In such a context, "good" seems the most truly shocking and daring four-letter word of all. And at the same time — so many are the nuances of simplicity — "good" is such an awkward, homely, heavy-footed, lovable word, like "bread" and "kindness."

Not always so, not at Marathon, not on Armada Day, not at El Alamein nor in the anti-Nazi uprising of the Warsaw ghetto — yet today more leaders know the feeling of expediency than of outright, downright, death-defying goodness. Armed communism is obviously the greatest single threat to the world today. The greatest, yes, but not the only one. Let us in addition sometimes think of other evil threats, even if at present subsidiary threats. Can we solve these other threats by mere expediency and short-range self-interest? Here is one example among many: the neo-Nazi threat in Germany. To be sure, it is often exaggerated today. Nevertheless, an unrepentant nazism may yet triumph tomorrow and, by playing for bids from both West and East, pretend to be our "ally against communism." The present loose talk of seeking any ally,

---

[1] From an address delivered to a class of graduating college seniors.

no matter whom, does not prepare us for the moral crisis that will arrive when such or similar shocking offers are made.

In the present crisis we naturally ask of every measure: "Is it or is it not useful for the cold war?" But the present crisis is no more eternal than the present Russian government. And even now there must be moments, in the heat of struggle, when we take time out to see things from a more permanent viewpoint. At such moments we see things in their eternal aspect: *"sub specie aeternitatis."* At such moments in the present, and even more so in the future after the Soviet despotism is overthrown and new challenges confront us, we will desperately need a profounder code of values than we now possess. We will need a code that is not merely negative and suspicious and "good for the cold war" but positive and reconciling and good-in-itself. In some soul-searching hour of the future, the survival of freedom and creativity may depend on having values beyond the ephemeral utilities of ephemeral political crises.

We must live in two worlds at once. We must live in the practical world of the Soviet threat, or it will wipe us out physically. We must meanwhile keep some part of our minds in the idealistic permanent world, seeing the eternal moral aspect of every material triumph, or it will wipe us out culturally and spiritually. The first of these two worlds in us would protest, and rightly so, if we ignored the Soviet danger by escaping to an ivory tower. The second of these worlds would protest, and rightly so, if we ignored the spiritual and cultural danger by stooping to thought-control demagogics at home or to cynical fascist alliances abroad. Only by the maturity of living in both worlds not alternately (as if inwardness were only for Sundays) but simultaneously, can we overcome Soviet aggression on both fronts at once, the military front and the front of the free spirit.

II

The American is neither Galahad nor Machiavelli's "Prince." His politics is necessarily human-all-too-human. It must strike some feasible balance between expediency and morality. Morals in politics may be pushed so far that we become priggishly feckless and have no allies at all. Thereby we would succumb to an evil enemy by trying to be too good. Such exaggerated and pedantic moralism would lead to suicidal pacifism.

However, an exaggerated moralism is not the most imminent danger to the human race, to put it mildly. It is not the danger represented by those leaders in both parties who talk of any kind of ally being welcome and of any means to national or personal success being justified by the end. They and the millions in their climate of thought are in danger of the opposite extreme. That is the danger of the balance going too far toward expediency. I mean the expediency that bartered the Czechs at Munich, and the Poles and Manchurians at Yalta, and that perhaps today pardons atrocious Nazi criminals like Ilse Koch or lionizes General Rommel[1] in a movie.

We have seen the shambles caused by Munich deals with despots. We have seen the stupidity of shrewdness. We have seen the suicide inherent in narrow self-interest. Having seen all these things, let readers consider the following, directly opposite approach. Suppose every responsible citizen in America or Europe (every product of the Christian-Hebrew-Hellenic ethic of the West) had made in the near past, or will make in the near future, the following vow. Suppose he vows never to associate either in personal friendship or in any close political alliance with any individual or group that advocates Nazi-style or communist-style massmurder, or that apologizes for it, or that appeases it, or that calls criticism of it "warmongering," or that — though without supporting it actively — retains a calculating and mean-spirited silence and passivity toward the horror of Soviet slave-labor camps or Nazi concentration camps.

Under the catalyst of such a vow, what would have happened in the Russia of November, 1917, or the Germany of 1933, or the Czechoslovakia of 1948? Would history be different if responsible citizens had vowed to serve at any cost the ethical code that

---

[1] Because Rommel did not commit atrocities personally but was a "gallant" Nazi who broke with Hitler at the daringly early date of July 1944 after serving his aggressions since 1933, the democracies are rewarding such clean-shaven wholesomeness by making an epic saga of his chivalrous resistance in Africa. Concretely, what the chivalrous resistance of his African saga "accomplished" was to keep the pot under the crematories boiling one whole year longer.

lights our darkness? "At any cost" means possibly martyrdom and certainly the cost of friendships, profits, and alliances. Would such quixotic "folly" not have resulted in a better world than the present one? Even if it failed, as "too impractical," could it have resulted in a world very much worse? And if it could have worked in the past, which we cannot change, then what of the future, which we still can change?

Are there non-partisan or bi-partisan individuals or groups who from this day on will live up to such a vow? If so, let them start right now. Let them do so quietly, without exhibitionism. Let them do so first of all on the simplest human level in their private relationships. Let them no longer suffer loose vicious talk in silence. Let them be inelegant enough to show indignation. Let them remonstrate reasonably — and then, if necessary, break off relationships — with anybody who persistently and uninnocently repeats, say, anti-Semitic and fascist lies or pseudoliberal fellow-traveler lies or who displays a "1984" callousness toward suffering or slavery or suppression of the individual. Such details of bad character may seem trivial when they occur in ordinary life all around you. But when they spread far through society by the Gresham's law of unbeatable banality, they can betray civil liberties and civilized values as surely as the more dramatic treason of cloak and dagger. Conversely, the practice of personal and political decencies at the humble grass-roots level can start an ethical chain reaction that saves the soul of a nation despite itself, and despite all the pontifical laws of economic determinism.

It is time to return to that inelegant virtue: righteous indignation. It is never time for that elegant vice: self-righteousness. A new moral emphasis, as a basis for breaking or maintaining political and private relationships, must not become a vindictive fanaticism. Nor must it become holier-than-thou smugness. Nor busybody officiousness. Here my argument seems to take away with one hand what it gave with the other when urging righteous indignation. But moral problems are not always black and white. They are subtle, complex and underground. The way to improve the private or public codes of behavior around you is not by the sanctimonious brand of denunciation. The best way is by friendly persuasion and a sense of humor. By a stress on common interests and on shared values. Often the passive healing power of time helps you overcome those hates that still resist an active love.

In fighting what we rightly or wrongly believe to be evil, force must be only the reluctant last resort after all other alternatives are truly exhausted. A circle of brotherhood, inclusive and not exclusive, must be the first resort. Remember the quatrain of Edwin Markham:

> He drew a circle that shut me out —
> Heretic, rebel, a thing to flout.
> But love and I had the wit to win:
> We drew a circle that took him in!

But here, too, the subtle and complex problem must be qualified. A faith in love, a distrust of the bludgeon as a method of persuasion, must not be oversimplified into appeasement of the unappeasable, surrendering the world to unappeasable Nazis and Communists. Loving peace, we must always be as pacific as possible — but not pacifistic. Loving mutual tolerance, we must always appease the appeasable — but not the unappeasable. How distinguish these alternatives? Where draw the line? Here in the end we must fall back on that quality known as mature judgment. Mature judgment, plus the needed stimulus of righteous indignation, plus the needed counterstimulus of compassionate forgiveness: these three qualities must supplement each other to become effective. It would be an impoverished sensibility and a shallow personality that had only one, or only two, of the three qualities.

The ideal: voluntarily to subordinate the foolish wisdom of cynicism to the wiser folly of universal ethics. Like every universal and abstract ideal, the individual's concrete practice can alone make it a reality. Therefore, let whoever vows to share these aims, practice them quietly. Let him desist from "organizing" them or from writing "letters to the editor" or from any go-getter "rally" or ostentatiously virtuous get-together, as if the practicing of the Christian ethic were nothing but a chummy-hearty clambake, or some ghastly Commencement Day homily, or some philistine "progressive" mass meeting.

Organization (just imagine the pep-talks!) would misdirect the aim of such a vow by sacrificing long-run inner change to short-run successes. Pragmatic programs and outward organizations are indispensable for many fine aims. But not for this one. For this one, they would be too superficial and too subject to partisan exploitation. Only through inwardness — through a change of heart, not of hat or of party — can an increasing number of responsible citizens put such a vow into effect immediately.

America's strength is not the brute militarism of Prussianism and Russianism. Ours is the stronger strength of gentleness and tolerance. This is why our strength is irresistible in its self-defense if aggressed against once too often by totalitarians of left or right. Meanwhile let us answer the clenched fist of Stalinist fascism with the clean hands of liberty. Let them be hands not weakened by the delirium tremens of jittery thought-control bills.

When we dedicate our society to the Christian-Judaic code of values, when we vow to use good means and nothing but good means for whatever political ends, then the key word is humaneness. With a generous, unhypocritical humaneness, many lesser sins of inefficiency can be forgiven a social order, and it will still thrive. Without humaneness, not the best of written constitutions and of economic resources can maintain that free society in which opposing parties defend each other's civil liberties and oppose the unparliamentary extremes of left and right. Inhumanity was the key to those pseudoconservative appeasers and fascist apologists who felt no compassion for the victims of Hitler's camps and who still doubt the documented evidence of Nazi atrocities. Inhumanity is the key to those pseudoliberal appeasers and neutralists who feel no compassion for the victims of Stalin's Belsens in Siberia and whose still influential publications belittle the documented evidence of communist atrocities.

No miracles may be expected. Humaneness alone will still not end the economic problem. Nor the military problem. Nor any number of material problems, distracting us from the lasting aspect of things; from living *sub specie aeternitatis*. There is no easy, patented solution to military and economic problems, least of all in escapist neutralism toward the Soviet threat. But whichever material solution we eventually find for these material problems, we will not find it without one nonmaterial prerequisite also. The prerequisite — and you have heard this too often, and it's still true — is vision. We can consecrate even our crassness: by the vision of ethical self-restraints. We can make reality livable again: by a frankly "unrealistic" vision of the brotherhood of all suffering. We can elude self-corruption: by a frankly soft-boiled rejection of the cult of hard-boiled ruthlessness.

You can never improve politics by being exclusively political. To improve the outward and public life, you must also cultivate a rich and private inwardness.

Our concrete military and economic problems must be (as the phrase goes) coped with. They are part of our present reality; the most obvious part of it; temporarily, perhaps the larger part. But in order to "cope with" them sanely, the present must also build ahead towards a world of peace and kindness in some distant but inevitable future.

Russia and Peace

". . . It is inconceivable that the Soviet Republic should continue to exist for a long period side by side with imperialist states. Ultimately, one or the other must conquer. . . .Co-existence is impossible; conflict is inevitable." — STALIN, *Questions of Leninism,* pp. 170, 261

"To work on Saturday in a capitalist country is exploitation; to work on Saturday in a People's Democracy is a duty and a privilege." — *Praco,* periodical of the Czechoslovak communist worker organizations

CHEWING GUM OR KARAGANDA?

"The peasant with his axe is coming;
Something terrible will happen."
                    — from an old Russian song

Many an American traveling abroad is "hurt," after all his sacrifices for aid to Europe, to find many Europeans speaking sarcastically of an alleged "American obsession with Russia." They assume an alleged American hysteria that "exaggerates" the Soviet danger. For example, here is how one of Europe's most influential novelists, himself an anticommunist, currently describes an American dinner party:

Russia is always weighing on their minds. . . . As soon as the idea of Russia occurred to them, their faces became blood red; they ceased to be human. No one seemed appalled by the display but myself, no one was surprised; and our hostess congratulated herself afterwards on the success of her party.

At this point getting likewise "blood red in the face," though without "ceasing to be human," I feel like asking all loftily non-"hysterical" Europeans how long they would continue to be alive if Americans ceased to let "Russia weigh on their minds." Forty thousand Russian tanks are straining at the leash to race westward and pound European civilization into pulp beneath their treads, the very instant we "obsessed Americans" cease to be "hysterical" about that "exaggerated Soviet menace." Churchill was Europe's wisest statesman when, instead of "baiting" our atom bomb in Stockholm "peace pledge" fashion, he called it the guaranty of peace.

Soviet police documents have been smuggled from Lithuania and elsewhere, showing that Moscow, already before World War II, laid plans for mass-deportations of "liberated" Europeans to Siberia. The most cruel of these documents, ordering the deliberate breaking up of families into separate cattle cars, has the official signature of General Serov, Deputy Minister for Soviet State Security, January 21, 1941. Hundreds of thousands of victims die en route. Those sturdy enough to survive are worked to death as forced labor. This genocide is now depopulating the Baltic states. From this, Englishmen, Frenchmen, and Italians can construct the fate probably *already planned* for them by the M.V.D. It is a fair assumption that plans for the cattle cars from Paris and Rome are drawn up long in advance of occupation, just as we know they were (from documentary evidence) for Eastern Europe. Because Europe's free mentality is intolerable to Stalin, Western Europe would simply have to — cease to be. I mean "cease to be" literally. Just as Russia's Tartar Crimean Republic ceased to be after World War II.

These words sound "alarmist." The facts themselves are alarming.

Since Western Europe is the cradle of parliamentary government (and uniquely honored for that in American culture), it would never fit in with a Genghis-Khan absolutism. The Kremlin would have no choice but to liquidate or deport its inhabitants and then to resettle it. These are measures no more ruthless than their murdering and jailing over twenty million of their own citizens in the Ukraine, the Crimea, and the purges. This would make Europe forever part of Asia, as the Persian absolutism vainly attempted to do against Athenian democracy at the battle of Marathon in 490 B.C. Unless Europe and America stand alertly united in free and equal co-operation today, and unless both can endure stoically the bitter defense taxes needed to deter the aggressor, Marathon will be undone in the 1950's.

As the endless cattle cars from Paris and Rome move to a frozen death in the slave-labor camps of Karaganda and Kolyma, Western Europe would be resettled with millions of indoctrinated slaves from Kazakistan and Uzbekistan, to whom the Sermon on the Mount, the Philippics of Demosthenes against tyranny, the British Bill of Rights, trial by jury, Lincoln's Gettysburg Address — in short, Western civilization — are concepts never allowed to be mentioned at school. "Progress" — modern techniques for mass-killing and mass-deportation — has made easy for Stalin what was impossible for Genghiz and Attila: the complete physical extermination of Western man.

I hold no special brief for "blood red faces," Coca-Cola, or whatever else may fray European sensibilities as "crudely American." Perhaps our architecture in the American war cemeteries in France is also crude in taste. But in order to avoid the total liquidation of the West in Karaganda, "I reckon" (as we are supposed to say in crude Americanese) that Europe might even — all things considered — put up with American chewing gum. Yes, all things considered, including those modern Marathons when England, France, and America stood shoulder to shoulder — twice — for freedom's sake.

DICTATORSHIP OVER THE PROLETARIAT: PORTRAIT OF A FASCIST[1] RULING CLASS

> "There is more that binds us to Bolshevism than separates us from it. . . . I have always made allowance for this circumstance, and given orders that former Communists are to be admitted to the Party at once. . . . The trade-union boss will never make a National Socialist, but the Communist always will." — ADOLF HITLER, *quoted by H. Rauschning*, The Voice of Destruction (*New York: 1940*), p. 131

To characterize the two greatest world powers:

1. Soviet Russia is the extremest plutocracy in history. The most savage and relentless enemy of all workmen all over the globe

---

[1] I use "fascist" to mean a one-party totalitarian ruling class, militarized and nationalistic, ruling its slaves by terror and circuses. The term "Stalinist

is Russia's rich ruling class. The Soviet is the highest fulfilment of the selfish ideals of unlimited monopoly capitalism.

2. America is history's extremest example of the freedom and well-being of the workingman and his trade-unions, the widest spread ever achieved of free consumer choice and high living standards among the large majority of the population. America is the highest fulfilment of the honorable ideals of socialism (though achieved — significantly — not by socialist means but by a democratic capitalism).

American trade-unions are rendering a useful service to freedom in their campaign of telling European trade-unions the truth about Soviet working conditions. As an additional service, it is suggested that American unions distribute translations, without comment, of Russia's incredibly cruel labor laws, with her Simon Legree penalties for petty infractions. "The dictatorship of the proletariat" is the dictatorship over the proletariat.

To understand the Stalinist mind, Westerners must understand not only its innate affinity for fascism (the Hitler-Stalin pact, the present use of Nazis in Hungary and Rumania, the tacit pact with Perón) but also its hate of the workingman. Its hate is logically justified: are not the workers of the West always trying to get higher living standards — that is, to accommodate themselves in the existing capitalist system — when they should instead aim at causing depression and misery so as to cause revolution? Are not American workers, in particular, treacherously indifferent to the drive for funds and circulation of the martyred *Daily Worker?* — leaving it to the humiliation of being financed by mere millionaires. Millionaires are the sole class of unemployed in America which produces communists. (Is this explained less by Marx than by Freud?)

The difference in power and in living standards between the

---

fascist" is used here simply because it is accurate, corresponds to the facts. But use of it should not lend aid and comfort to the non-Stalinist or "true" Bolsheviks, those who prefer Lenin or Trotsky. Although Lenin and Trotsky were more Marxist and internationalist (less fascist in that sense) than the Stalinist bureaucracy, yet they were every whit as terroristic and despotic toward the rest of the country, including the workers, as Stalin or any frankly fascist regime. All were terrorists who believed in bad means to bad ends; down with all of them!

Soviet ruling class and its workers [1] makes the difference between America's "classes" negligible in contrast. On October 2, 1940, fees for higher education were imposed (instead of the free education of Lenin's day and of American public colleges). This encourages class differences to become permanent, owing to the increased educational opportunities of the rich in Soviet Russia. Since 1940, Soviet youth has, in effect, been divided into two groups:

1. Those with rich parents, the families of the bureaucratic and party hierarchy. These youths go on to the universities and can end up as high officials.

2. Those whose parents cannot pay for higher education. By a special mobilization-of-youth law, these are sent to learn various trades wherever the state decrees.

Except for those who earn special university scholarships, Group 2 tends to produce the hereditary lackeys and employees of Group 1, for the class gap in Soviet power and living standards is so much greater than the admitted gap in America.

When a capitalist employer pays his workers too little or himself too much, he can often be halted by strikes, pickets, unions, and a critical public opinion. But what is there to halt or even faintly restrain the enslavement of the workers by the employer when the employer is also the "state" and the secret police and the judicial system and when no opposition movement may even be dreamt of?

In no other country, can the "capitalist employer" (in this case the "state," meaning the Soviet ruling class) tie the workers to their jobs like medieval serfs. Workers need passports and special permission to move even from town to town. They are told what jobs to work at. Of course, all strikes against the employer are forbidden as treason.

American trade-unions rightly point out that a sales tax falls hardest on the working class. The Soviet ruling class raises over half of its state budget by a sales tax on the masses. It then pays

---

[1] On the misery of the Soviet working class, and on the higher living standards of the tsarist period and of the early NEP era, see Manya Gordon, *Workers Before and After Lenin* (1941). Also Harry Schwartz, *Russia's Soviet Economy* (1950); M. Yvon, *What Has Become of the Russian Revolution* (1937); Freda Utley, *The Dream We Lost* (1940).

itself proportionately far higher salaries (in effect "profits," with plenty of what Marx called "surplus value") than the average employer in the West. Refugees to the West, whether simple workers or high Communist officials, join in expressing their dismay at the contrast in Russia between the working-class misery and the feudal privileges of the new slave-owner class in their *dachas*.

Sixty per cent of the Soviet national budget has usually come from the sales tax (or turnover tax).[1] It falls heavily on all significant consumer goods, including the indispensable food items. It does not fall on capital goods (favored over consumer goods). Thereby it becomes not only a tax but a ruthless weapon. The weapon achieves three purposes:

1. It prevents the Russian consumer — the worker and peasant — from ever rising beyond his near-starvation level.

2. It diverts national income from consumer goods (high standards of living) to capital goods (machinery and high armament production).

3. It protects the power and class distinctions of the new feudal ruling class. As follows.

By putting the main tax on the masses (consumer goods), the sales tax makes it possible to keep the income tax very low indeed. And the income tax is what concerns employers in all countries, meaning the high Communists and bureaucrats in the case of statist Russia. In recent years, Soviet income of over 1,000 rubles monthly has been receiving a flat 13 per cent tax, instead of a progressively rising tax as in capitalist America. This means that technicians, industrial directors, and officials in "socialist" Russia — that is, the ruling class — pay a much tinier income tax than they do in capitalist America. In America a millionaire would

---

[1] H. Schwartz, *Russia's Soviet Economy*, pp. 414-416:

"It is essentially a differentiated sales tax imposed heavily . . . upon commodities at the time of fabrication and upon government purchases at low requisition prices of peasant obligatory deliveries. The tax must be included in the price of the commodity thereafter, so that is *passed on fully to the consumer.* . . . Soviet budgetary statistics list it as revenue from socialized production, though ultimately it is paid in full by consumers and is clearly a sales tax. . . . The trend over the past two decades has been toward freeing non-consumer goods from the tax. . . . Food items and consumer goods were the sources of almost 90% of all turnover tax receipts in 1939."

create a national scandal if he could hire fiendishly clever lawyers to outwit our progressive income tax and get off with paying a mere 13 per cent.

American consumers — the working population — can ultimately protect their own interests by means of the ballot and of democratic economic legislation. So we see the two biggest powers moving in opposite directions: class and wealth distinctions diminishing in America as fast as they are increasing in Russia. When I say "wealth," I am in addition implying that power is the chief form that "wealth" takes in any communazi totalitarian society. To be rich in power is also the most intoxicating variety of wealth. And intoxication decreases inhibitions and restraints; hence, the Politburo's "absolute power corrupts absolutely."

II

If you are lucky enough to belong to communism's slave-owner class instead of her slave-labor class, why shouldn't you overpay yourself and underpay your proletarians and slap 60 per cent of the national budget on their consumer goods and keep at a minimum any taxes on your income and inheritance? What's to prevent you? — so long as you have twenty divisions of armed secret police to prevent criticism, strikes, free trade-unions, free press, and any opposition party.

What's to stop you, as history's largest slave-owning corporation, from framing up nine million opponents in the "Trotskyite" purges, butchering over five million peasants by a horrible deliberate famine, and working to death over ten million of your slaves as the personal chattel of the MVD's camps in Siberia? What moral, legal, or physical force remains to stop you? World conscience perhaps? This moral power did help force the nineteenth-century tsars to mitigate their treatment of their serfs. But world conscience cannot rally against the new serfdom so long as any intellectual in the West who expresses humane compassion for the victims of your Himmlerisms gets baited as a "Red-baiter."

Then, when the mass discontent of your slaves gets too unbearable, you can always divert it. You simply use your state-kept newspaper prostitutes and state-kept radio prostitutes to whip up an anti-Semitic campaign at home (the Soviet anti-"cosmopoli-

tanism"[1] and the anti-Semitic purges in Hungary[2] and Czechoslovakia[3]) and to create an imaginary monster abroad (the South
Koreans, "American imperialism," "Wall Street fascism"). And
those old pie-in-the-sky promises ("the state will wither away"),
though threadbare by now, can always be hauled out just once
more for the yokels back in Uzbekistan.

No wonder a Soviet peasant, on being asked if his village contained many Communists, replied: "Good heaven, no! We are all
poor here."

The essentially Nazi mentality of the Soviet slave-owner class is
no longer in doubt among the terrorized masses of Occupied
Europe. Nor was it in doubt among the Russian D.P.'s and P.W.'s
in 1945 who slit their own throats with razor blades when American officers tried to force them to return to Russia, in one of
America's most shocking violations of human rights. But it is still
in doubt among the duped workers of Unoccupied Europe and the
fellow-traveler "liberals" of France and Italy. For them, the Communist Fuehrers must keep up the moldy old Potemkin-Village
façade and — between yawns — the old "democratic" battle cries.

Marxism, not religion, is "the opiate of the people." Under its
infallible Kremlin pontiff, the Marxist church provides the other-
worldly "pie in the sky" to distract the opiated people from changing the sorrows and realities of Russia's "this world."

This double-speak and double-think has interesting psychiatric
results on its own manipulators inside Russia. What makes the

[1] For anti-Semitic insinuations in the Soviet-Russian press, with full names
and dates, see P. Viereck, *Conservatism Revisited* (New York: Scribner,
1949), pp. 157-187. Two-thirds of the "cosmopolitans" purged in 1949
were Jews, with the original non-Russian, Jewish names often supplied in
parentheses by the Soviet press.

[2] Bela Fabian, "Hungary's Jewry Faces Liquidation," in *Commentary*
magazine, October 1951. *The American Jewish Year Book,* released January
1, 1952, published by the American Jewish Committee and the Jewish
Publication Society, includes a documented account of the Soviet reign of
terror (and of deportation to slave-labor camps) raging against Hungarian
Jews.

[3] The purge of 1950-52 included an "extremely high percentage" of Jews,
such as the former Communist party secretary Rudolf Slansky. The Prague
Communist newspaper *Rude Pravo,* December 19, 1951, published an anti-
Semitic speech by Czech Premier Antonin Zapotocky. He attacked "inter-
ference from Jerusalem" and "Jewish capitalism" (*sic*). New York *Herald
Tribune,* December 20, 1951; p. 16.

Communist hate and contempt for the working class almost frenzied in its slave-driving brutality is the fact that the hate can never be expressed verbally. It must be suppressed[1] and sublimated. It must remain on the mere reality level of Soviet practice instead of on that grander slogan level of Marxist theory. The attitude of many Western "progressives" toward this discrepancy between the actual and the theoretical position of the enslaved Soviet workers, is summed up by a witty old Russian proverb:

If it is written on the cage, "this is a lion," but your eyes see an ass in the cage, do not trust — your eyes.

III

The Soviet hate and distrust of its workers is reflected in its stricter-than-tsarist penal laws. You can read for yourself in the official Soviet law code the needlessly cruel and excessive penalties for minor infractions (often ignored in America) like dawdling during the lunch hour or a tardiness of 20 minutes. If you run through the various labor-discipline decrees from 1938 on, you will note the steadily increasing severity towards "a worker or employee who is late in coming back from dinner or idles during working hours."

Two Soviet decrees of 1940, still valid, read: "Workers and employees who arbitrarily leave state, co-operative, and social enterprises and institutions shall be prosecuted, and on the sentence of a People's Court shall be subjected to imprisonment of two to four month's duration. . . . We order: workers and employees who without valid reasons are more than 20 minutes late after the dinner interval or leave work without permission earlier than 20 minutes before the dinner interval or before the end of the working day, shall be prosecuted as for absence without permission." For this the penalty is set as "corrective labor" (euphemism for forced slave labor) of "up to six months" plus "a cut in wages of up to 25 per cent." Six months for 20 minutes! — one would like to hear a comment on this from all those Western fellow-travelers

---

[1] Suppressed by the new feudal barons even *from themselves*. They are not mere charlatans and by no means deliberate hypocrites. They are double-think, newspeak schizoids.

whose heart professionally and almost haemophilially "bleeds for the working class."[1]

Even more severe than these decrees of 1940, are some of those listed in the 1947 Soviet publication, *Legislation Concerning Labor,* providing sentences of up to eight years in "corrective labor camps" for workers who endeavor to quit their jobs!

In connection with sentencing workers to "corrective labor," there is one key Soviet law that makes all other laws unnecessary. It crushes all concepts whatever of personal rights and fair trial. It makes all American "ordeals by slander" utterly trivial in contrast, for it facilitates incomparably wilder accusations and incomparably sterner punishments. It puts the entire Soviet populace legally at the mercy and whim of its slave owners, thereby legalizing lawlessness. It enables the slave owners to sentence to forced labor (in practice, usually death from cold and hunger) anybody who they *admit* is innocent of any "specific crime" but whom they may vaguely suspect, or pretend to suspect, of being "socially dangerous." A decree of the Central Executive Committee of 1934 gives the secret police "the right to apply against people who are regarded as socially dangerous" (even when no crime is committed) "confinement in corrective labor camps for a period of up to five years." Article 22 of the basic criminal code allows the broadest leeway to punishment where there is admittedly no crime:

Punishment in the form of exile [Siberia, etc.] can be applied by a sentence of the state prosecutor against persons recognized as being socially dangerous, without any criminal proceedings being taken against these persons on charges of committing a specific crime or of a specific offence and also, even in those cases where these persons are *acquitted* by a court of the accusation of committing a specific crime.[2]

Under so loose a law, no Soviet citizen is safe or dares talk back to his wildest accusers. Definition of Soviet reality: the McCarthyite's dream of paradise.

---

[1] The labor-discipline quotations in this and the preceding paragraph occur in the following official Soviet sources: *Spravochnik Po Zakonodatyelstvu Dlya Sudyebno-Prokurorskikh Rabotnikov,* volume 1, 1949 edition, pp. 431, 503; *Trudovoye Zakonodatyelstvo S.S.R.,* 1941, p. 236.

[2] Italics mine. *Stalin's Slave Camps* (Boston: Beacon Press, 1952), pp. 10, 14, 15. Further documents in David Rousset's *The Decay of Liberty and Justice in the Soviet Union,* translated and edited by Charles R. Joy (Boston: The Beacon Press, 1953).

Western capitalism at its nastiest never degraded any proletariat so ruthlessly into beasts of burden. You can hear from the Soviet officials themselves why they prefer to keep the Russian proletariat at starvation level *even when* the economy would permit food increases. Aside from the natural desire of any ruling class to widen class lines, there is another reason for keeping Russian workers at near-starvation on principle. After being in Russia, a Communist deputy of the German Politburo has testified:

> A high Soviet officer confessed to me, "We are starving people into Communism. Not only because we are building more and more canning factories and hoarding food for use in case of war. No, only hungry people work as hard as our gigantic efforts require. Only someone who suffers is prepared to work like a slave for something better, and, if necessary, to die." Hunger is a part of the system; I have seen a thousand times how prisoners worked to the point of exhaustion to earn an additional seven ounces of bread of the worst quality. Only people who never get quite enough to eat, allow themselves to be ruled with the whip; at the same time they believe the doctrine promising them salvation, and are prepared to fight for it. Well-fed humans are dangerous to the Soviet system.[1]

According to the official Soviet Law Code, no Soviet worker is allowed to negotiate for higher wages, although happily he has the right, if in the coal industry, to demand "steam baths." The Spanish Communist leader Enrique Castro Delgado (better known under his famous pseudonym, Luis Garcia) represented the Spanish Communist party in Moscow in the Comintern during the war and was particularly interested in the condition of Soviet workers. Indeed his sympathy for the hardships of workers under capitalism had made him an ardent communist in the first place. During six years in the "workers' paradise," he visited any number of Soviet industrial plants and familiarized himself with working conditions. Here is his report in his recently-published book, *I Have Lost Faith in Moscow* (Paris, 1950):

> If I had to choose between the gallows and work in a Soviet plant, I would unhesitatingly choose the former. A few hours of anxiety and an instant of pain are preferable to months and years of frightful agony: fourteen hours of work each day, meals consisting of a plate of warm water with a few leaves of cabbage, a production tempo that

---

[1] *Partisan Review,* New York, January-February, 1952, p. 47.

makes Ford and Citroën seem like splendid philanthropists; a ten-ruble daily wage, of which 30 per cent is withheld on various pretexts; constant surveillance by the party, the trade union and the NKVD; for billets, a hovel that an animal would scorn; the sight of one's fellow-workers' agony without the right to protest, to fight or to escape; the obligation to repeat constantly amid one's misery, "I am a citizen of a land of happiness."

No! The life of a worker is tolerable anywhere but in the "land of socialism." To be a worker here means hell.

IV

Marx's prophecies about the future of capitalism have been almost 100 per cent wrong. He prophesied increasing rigidity, poverty, and misery, with the rich getting richer, the poor poorer, class lines widening, and democracy being replaced by class dictatorship. On the contrary, Western capitalism has adjusted itself with remarkable flexibility. Far from abolishing democracy, it has extended democracy, the franchise, trade unions, living standards, and civil liberties beyond anything dreamt of by Marx.

Capitalism has benefited from democracy's capacity for peaceful self-correction, a capacity ignored by Marx. This capacity has resulted in democracy's political reforms of capitalism's economic abuses. In the West, capitalism is a tool of democracy instead of vice versa; this is why both have survived and thrived. Marx's and Lenin's prophecies that capitalist "surplus value" would lead to an ever more aggressive form of "imperialism," are today likewise erroneous. While the Western capitalist nations have freed half a billion colonial peoples since World War II, it is Soviet imperialism that has conquered a half billion of its neighbors and turned them into exploited colonials.

Because history has refuted the Marxist "surplus value" theories of capitalist poverty and doom, most capitalist economists assume these theories are valueless today. On the contrary, the Marxist theories of widening class lines and economic imperialism work beautifully today when applied to — Soviet Russia. Marx can still be valuable. He can even be an accurate prophet after all. But you must apply his prophecies not to the increasingly democratic capitalist West but to the increasingly undemocratic ruling class of the country that claims to worship him. Here is how we may apply

to Soviet Russia the Marxist theories of "surplus value," excess
profits, class lines, "business cycle," recurring "capitalist crisis,"
and the resultant imperialism and war. The application is such a
complete reversal of the usual picture held by anticapitalist Western
liberals that it merits a long quotation: [1]

The Kremlin houses neither mere adventurers, nor men propelled
by passionate devotion to the idea of "world revolution" or "world
Communism." On the contrary: they are prisoners of basic maladjust-
ments in their own economic system, which drives them inexorably to
seek an escape in external conquest. . . .

The underlying reason for the periodic crises of the Soviet system
is the disproportionate rise of non-productive expenditures. The totalitarian state is a huge parasitic body. Besides the ordinary administration, there are swollen armies of supervisors to supervise the bureaucracy, and a large military machine with its own personnel. These are
the new high-income groups whose economic demands are steadily rising — to leave them unsatisfied would be to undermine the classes that
form the social foundations of the entire system. The "take" of this
top strata of the state is quite apart from what are normally considered
the "fixed costs" of an economy (administration, accounting, etc.); the
tribute paid by all producers to the holders of political power far exceeds the practices of a private, capitalistic social order, and only an
authoritarian ruling group — backed to the hilt by a secret police —
is able to extract it.

A few figures may be quoted to throw some light on the inflated
size of these unproductive overhead costs. In 1937 the number of
"bookkeepers, accountants, etc." was 1,617,000 in addition to 822,000
"economists, statisticians." In the United States in 1940 only 447,000
persons were employed as "bookkeepers, accountants, cashiers, ticket
agents, etc." Thus the American economy required one "bookkeeper"
for each 54 workers, the Russian one for each 20 workers. In all
branches of the economy, inflated bureaucratic staffs have come into
existence. In 1940 about 20 percent of all kolkhoz (collective farm)
members were engaged in administrative or office work.

*The wage differentials that these officials enjoy are far higher than in
capitalistic countries.* The salaries of chief engineers, directors, and top
administrative personnel are often one hundred times greater than
the average worker's wage. In the Soviet Army the ratio of a private's
pay to a colonel's is 1:240, against 1:5 in the American Army.

Yet, at the same time that these new "fixed costs" are far greater than
in any capitalist country, the level of productivity in Russia is much

---

[1] From the economist Dr. Guenter Reimann, "The Economic Crisis Behind Soviet Expansion: Does Russia's 'Business Cycle' Compel Foreign
Aggression?," in *Commentary,* September, 1948. Italics mine.

lower; a vicious circle begins to squeeze the regime like a vise. The state must seek to bolster the economic system by ever more stringent controls or "planning," but, in turn, centralized controls, national monopolies, and the upkeep of a secret police, result in tremendous economic costs. The more the state seeks to increase its share in the national wealth, the more it contributes to waste and unproductive expenditures: that is the "business cycle" of Soviet economy. . . .

To flee the permanent economic crisis that looms before it, the Soviet economy must seek to transfer its deficits to the shoulders of satellite countries. That is the dynamic behind Soviet expansion.

It is not a "socialistic" dynamic, or even a "collectivist" one. It is, in the old-fashioned sense of the term, a "class" dynamic — an expedition for plunder on the part of a ruling class whose very existence throttles the workings of its own economic system. The main purpose of the Soviet occupation of the countries of Eastern Europe was not to hasten the advent of world socialism; all policies of reconstruction and reorganization in Poland, Rumania, Hungary, etc., have been subordinated to the needs of the Russian government — needs filled by the dismantling and transfer of factories, highly advantageous and one-sided trade treaties, and the like. . . . New transfusions become ever more necessary, and they are sought for, grimly, at the point of a bayonet.

Using the Marxist phraseology, it is the "contradictions" of the Soviet statist economy that lead irresistibly to imperialist expansion — and possibly war.

Nevertheless, America still has a real chance of preventing this almost inevitable war — provided that this time not Karl Marx but our democratized capitalism tells the Soviet proletariat: "Unite; you have nothing to lose but your chains!"

THE TROJAN DOVE: "PEACE" VERSUS PEACE[1]

"It would be absolutely wrong, theoretically, to forget that war is the continuation of politics by other means. . . . Disarmament is not an international program of the revolutionary proletariat. . . . Only after we have completely forced down and expropriated the bourgeoisie of the whole world and not of one country alone . . . only after the disarmament of the bourgeoisie by the proletariat can the latter, without betraying its world-historical task, throw armaments on the scrap heap. . . . The victory of socialism in one country . . . implies

[1] Much of this and the following chapter is addressed especially to the book's neutralist readers in Europe.

wars." — *Article by* LENIN *on "Disarmament"* (*in* Sbornik
Sotsial-Demokratia, *1915, two years before launching in Petro-
grad the Soviet thirty-year war against the globe*)

"[Despite] enormous increases of power and territory,
[the Soviets] show no sign of being in any way satiated or
even contented, and we can perceive no limits at present to
their aims. . . . Nothing stands between Europe today and
complete subjugation to Communist tyranny but the atomic
bomb in American possession. . . . A peaceful settlement may
be reached with the Soviet government if a resolute effort is
made on the basis not of our present weakness but of American atomic strength. This is the policy which gives the best
chance of preventing a frightful war. . . ."
— *from speeches of* WINSTON CHURCHILL, 1948-50

Soviet propaganda has taken as its symbol the dove of peace,[1]
designed by Picasso. The Trojan dove has replaced the Trojan
horse.

That the Soviet peace dove is Trojan in purpose, was admitted
at a conference of Communist party officials at Limoges, October
1950, by the authoritative French Communist leader, Waldeck-
Rochet. This key speech frankly stressed that the "peace" movement has as its purpose "the destruction of our enemies" and the
"rearmament" of Russia, so that "the Soviet Union will choose the
right moment" to start World War III:

You will say: "Why doesn't the Soviet Union intervene in Korea?"
It would throw the Americans into the sea — that is true. But it
would start a world war, *which for the time being* is contrary to the
peace policy of the Soviet Union. . . . A year of peace *is a year
utilized to the utmost by the Soviet Union to reinforce its army and the
armies of the popular democracies.* It is to permit this rearmament, this
development of the Soviet Union's strength, as well as the strength of
the popular democracies, that we must actively continue our propaganda in favor of peace. It is this movement for peace that will
undermine the imperialist armies and delay the outbreak of war [and]

---

[1] Sometimes with peculiar results. In 1951 a fellow-traveler Indian magazine published the following effusion, a poem to the Soviet peace dove:

My Dove, after her bath of freedom
In Volga's streaming waters,
Carrying the pitcher of Peace
Betwixt rosy lips,
Sprinkles the twentieth century.

Needless to say, the sprinkling Soviet dove is rhapsodically contrasted
with that warmonger of the bird family, the American eagle.

assure destruction of our enemies. *The Soviet Union will choose the right moment* and the imperialists will have no say in the matter.[1]

This speech cannot be brushed aside as unauthoritative or as not representing the official Soviet viewpoint. It has been reprinted in the Soviet press without denial from Waldeck-Rochet or the French Communist party, and without Soviet disavowal.

The Moscow war pledge, falsely named "the Stockholm peace pledge," has been sufficiently exposed in America. Most Americans saw through its crude trick of trying to abolish solely the weapon in which America has a lead (the bomb) and not Russia's chief weapon (the Red Army). But owing to the usual failure of American peace propaganda, Moscow's "Stockholm" pledge has not been sufficiently discredited in Western Europe. There even prominent anticommunists have been duped into joining the countless signatories. The antipeace "peace"-lovers of the West would coax a Soviet Pearl Harbor against Paris or New York by ending our defensive alliances and armaments.

Ostrich isolationism prevents the peace it seeks. The right-wing isolationism of the Chicago *Tribune* and of the Europe-abandoning Asia Firsters is as suicidal as the left-wing isolationism of the fight-home-oppression-first liberals.

There are no more influential isolationists in America and England. But what we may call the "semis" are still influential: semi-isolationist, semi-interventionist. They do not yet see that our existence depends on recognizing the "Thirty Year War" of communazism against America. The distinction between the semi-isolationists and the world-minded interventionists counts for more today than the anachronistic distinction between left and right. In foreign policy, what is the difference between such semis as the leftist socialist Bevan and the rightist capitalist Taft? Both would snip that seamless web of world-wide collective security which could have stopped Hitler peacefully in 1936 and which can preserve peace from the Soviet.

The stale charge of "imperialist expansion" is loosely used against the West today not merely by Marxists but by most confused liberals everywhere. Especially in Asia. Who today is the

---

[1] Italics mine. *Manchester Guardian Weekly,* November 16, 1950, p. 15.

THE SOVIET RECORD

TERRITORIES ANNEXED	AREA (km²)	POPULATION (before annexation)
1. Rumanian Provinces August 2, 1940	50,200	3,700,000
2. Estonia 1939	47,400	1,122,000
3. Latvia 1939	65,800	1,951,000
4. Lithuania 1939	55,700	2,958,000
5. Northern East Prussia during World War II	14,000	1,187,000
6. Eastern Czechoslovakia June, 1945	12,700	731,000
7. Eastern Poland September, 1939	181,000	11,800,000
8. Finnish Provinces after November, 1939	45,600	450,000
9. Tannu Tuva October, 1944	165,800	65,000
10. Japanese Possessions	46,100	433,000
Total	684,300	24,396,000
SATELLITES CONTROLLED		
11. Albania	28,700	1,186,000
12. Bulgaria	110,900	7,160,000
13. Czechoslovakia*	127,700	12,463,000
14. Eastern Germany	111,100	18,807,000
15. Hungary	93,000	9,224,000
16. Poland*	311,800	24,500,000
17. Rumania*	237,200	16,007,000
18. China	9,700,300	450,000,000
19. Outer Mongolia	1,621,100	2,000,000
20. North Korea	125,600	9,100,000
Total	12,467,400	550,447,000
Total Soviet-Dominated	13,151,700	574,843,000

* Parts not annexed.

big imperialist expander, Soviet Russia or the West? Let us familiar-
ize ourselves thoroughly with the exact figures. Then Americans
abroad will know how to answer European and Asiatic intellectuals, liberals and democratic socialists, who should all be, for
their own survival, America's enthusiastic allies instead of baiters.

While Soviet imperialism has been subverting and swallowing
country after country, the West has been liberating country after
country and giving them economic and political aid. Since World
War II, whether gladly or grudgingly, the West has peacefully
relinquished rule over the same number of human beings as the
number annexed by Soviet imperialism. Namely, half a billion.
These are the newly independent countries:

	AREA (km²)	POPULATION
India	3,131,300	347,300,000
Pakistan	874,200	73,300,000
Indonesia	1,511,200	79,300,000
Ceylon	65,600	7,300,000
Philippines	296,300	19,200,000
Burma	677,900	18,000,000
Israel	20,200	1,000,000
Total	6,576,700	545,400,000

II

The enemy is not Russia nor any other particular ethnic group.
The enemy is totalitarianism. Human rights are *absolute* for lovers
of freedom. This holds true whether you base these rights on
supernatural religious sanctions or on non-supernatural humanistic
traditions. (The controversy within the human-rights camp, about
whether these absolutes are supernaturally or naturally sanctioned,
must not be allowed to divide us in the face of the Soviet threat
to both sides.) Since human rights are absolute, and since the
dignity of man is sacred to freedom lovers, it is utterly abhorrent
to take so *relativistic* a position toward totalitarianism as "peaceful
coexistence." Not in theory but in practice, peaceful coexistence
with so dynamic an aggressor means a "big deal" with it, a super-
Munich, to divvy the world's loot with it.

Suppose, for the sake of the argument, we accept this relativist attitude toward communist imperialism, which has conquered half a billion foreign peoples in a decade. Even then, we shall find peaceful coexistence pragmatically impossible. For totalitarianism means war. First of all, it means the certainty of an Iron Curtain cold war. Secondly, and in consequence, it means the possibility — very likely the probability — of hot war. No totalitarian police machine can afford the risk of peace. Peace means the risk of being overthrown by demands from below for a return to normalcy and decency. Totalitarianism needs foreign enemies, needs to change even former allies into enemies, in order to make its slaves put up with lack of freedom and lack of basic living standards. Because this war risk is innate in all communazi dynamism, peaceful coexistence with it is too risky an aim.

Like philosophical anarchists, pacifists are the salt of the earth. The presence of anyone with such stubborn — almost I said belligerent — integrity is a moral asset to our society, which needs to encourage its statist-threatened individualism. Nor is our present defense effort impaired in the slightest by a group inherently so tiny and so nonconspiratorial as genuine pacifists. The rest of us have no right to suppress what, with them, is a matter of conscience. What we do have a right to ask of them is: join genuine pacifist groups, not front organizations infiltrated and subtly guided by peace-hating communists, like the Hotel Waldorf "peace" conference of 1949. Let pacifists continue to be pacifists, and God bless them. But let them be open-eyed about it; let them not plunge blindly into "antiwar" without examining the credentials of their associates; let our good Quakers, in short, look before they quake.

Every Quaker ought to post the following warning over his desk. It is by a prominent pacifist minister on discovering he had been hoodwinked. The Reverend Donald Harrington of New York, when he withdrew as a sponsor of the Midcentury Conference for Peace, a communist front, held in Chicago on May 29 and 30, 1950, made this public statement:

The stark fact is that the American Communist movement not only is willing to resort to any method or subterfuge to accomplish its purposes, but also it takes orders directly from Moscow and functions as an

American arm of the Soviet Foreign Office. At this moment, though the international Communist movement is waging war, both cold and hot, and engaged in violence in many parts of the world, the American Communists have launched an exceedingly widespread and well-financed campaign for "peace."

The Communist Party line seems for a brief period to be running parallel with the point of view of pacifists and liberals. Communists, operating through a wide variety of "front" organizations, are seeking support of liberal and peace leaders and seeking to give them their support. They are not really interested in peace, but in appeasement. Their support will be turned to *sabotage* the moment it serves Soviet policy for this to occur.[1]

Well-meaners who have never in their life read a Soviet newspaper or the text of any Soviet anticosmopolitan decree are saying America could create a "peace atmosphere" by "conducting free discussions" between Soviet and Western intellectuals. Fine idea; but it takes two to discuss. Here is what the official Soviet party magazine, *Bolshevik,* No. 11, June 1950, commands on this subject:

Soviet scientists do not conduct discussions with obscurantism, with the representatives of bourgeois pseudo science, but expose them relentlessly and extirpate rotten bourgeois philosophy.

Such a scientist as the eminent physicist Peter Kapitsa of Cambridge University went from the West on invitation to Russia to "conduct discussions" fraternally with Soviet colleagues — and was not allowed out again. His "rottenness" was speedily "extirpated" by the Soviet police. Siberia likewise awaits Soviet scientists who discuss with "rotten bourgeois" Western scientists; for example, the pitiful fate of the late N. I. Vavilov, who — after disagreeing with Lysenko's genetics and exchanging intellectual ideas with Westerners — suddenly disappeared to do what was tactfully reported as "research on Arctic problems."

Accompanied by wringing of hands, the escapist voices continue to plead, with an undoubtedly sincere whine: "Why cannot we somehow, by some new concession, some super-Yalta at the expense of those who trust us, or by some new direct conversation, improve Russian-American relations? Oh somehow, somehow!"

---

[1] Reverend Donald Harrington, quoted in New York *Times,* May 22, 1950; p. 19.

The answer continues to be: the Russian ruling class cannot risk improving relations, lest it lose the imaginary plotting enemy who keeps it in power. Suppose America did decide to become a People's Democracy under the Progressive party and destroyed every atom bomb and turned all Europe and half our resources over to Stalin. Not one word about our "pacific gesture" would appear in the censored Soviet press. The only result of such a gesture of good will and trust would be to make certain, instead of merely likely, a victorious Soviet Pearl Harbor against New York.

Yet if the Soviet rulers can never afford friendly foreign relations, they probably cannot afford war either. Whenever possible, they will seek their objectives by means short of a world war. Their aim, in which they have succeeded up to a point, is a middle stage that equally avoids peace and a major hot war. They will perpetrate a Pearl Harbor, as a matter of course, the instant they can do so without being themselves destroyed. But not before then, and that instant need never be reached; can be deterred by a free world both armed and united.

Our present international troubles might never have happened, or would have happened less seriously, had it not been for the key blunder, from which all else flowed. I refer, of course, to our unilateral evacuation of liberated Europe and our unilateral demobilization of 1945-46. It is not wrong in itself to disarm or to quit foreign shores; on the contrary; but it was wrong to do so unilaterally. "We didn't demobilize," said Bernard Baruch, commenting on 1945; "we scuttled and ran." On the fateful day of June 24, 1950, America had only ten and a half divisions all over the globe. The Soviet army had almost twenty times as many to draw on. Americans hate militarism and almost unanimously crave peace. Our policy therefore must be bilateral pacifism. But it should not be unilateral pacifism, so long as Soviet policy is to pounce instantly upon the disarmed. The Soviet pounce upon Korea, and upon its European neighbors, shows that unilateral pacifism brings war.

The present costly and dangerous atomic race would have been entirely avoided by America's Baruch plan for atomic disarmament and inspection. This fair and workable plan was backed by almost all the countries of the world, including neutrals, except for the Soviet bloc. For propaganda purposes, Russia periodically offers atomic counterproposals; none is sincere or feasible because none allows a truly thorough atomic inspection.

It is no use hoping they ever will agree — except perhaps in vague lip service — to full inspection in the future. They cannot afford to. They cannot let the outside world see the truth of what is happening behind the Iron Curtain. The truth, as countless escapees have confirmed beyond cavil, is that communist Russia is one big slum. It is a slum with an average of eight to ten people — two families — starving in each slummy room. Not in each apartment but in each room. This is the average; yet the American press was rightly shocked when it discovered cases, admittedly exceptional, of five in a room in the ghastly slums of Chicago. These horrors, which disgrace American culture, would seem paradise to the Soviet slaves. Can such a regime allow the outside world to see it freely? Not if it would survive.

Or can such a regime ever permit friendly relations with the West? Again the answer is no. Its survival depends on playing up "the capitalist menace" to its own people. The real rage of the Soviet rulers against America is that we were so friendly to it during and after the war. Lend-lease was in our interest; the war was still on. But even *after* Germany was defeated, we poured a quarter of a billion dollars of UNRRA into the Soviet Ukraine, saving it from certain starvation and permitting the rebuilding of this area of grain and of military industries. Even the Marshall Plan aid was offered to the communist world; the communists of Poland and Czechoslovakia were frantic to join it; only Stalin's veto prevented their joining that same Marshall Plan which they now pretend to regard as harmful to the European economy.

This shows that a friendly, normal relationship with the West is the one thing the Soviet government cannot afford, no matter what we offer. If a hostile world did not exist, Stalin would need to invent it. No matter how many concessions we give them, no matter how many future UNRRA's and Lend-leases and Yaltas we shower upon them, even if we appease them with the rest of Asia and the rest of Europe, they will still need to create new war crises constantly for home consumption. Americans are Stalin's non-Aryans. He needs Wall Street as a scapegoat to hate and to blame for all home ills, for the same reason that Hitler needed the Jews for his own home propaganda.

This policy does not mean the Politburo wants an all-out world war. Such is presumably not their intention. They want not war but war crises, always just short of war. It means a continual playing with fire. One war crisis too many will get out of control, sooner or later. Such a blunder, rather than an outright immediate war wish, is what may cause World War III if we passively let things continue to drift. Peace formula: whatever leads to the overthrow of Russia's present fascist dictatorship leads to peace; whatever strengthens or appeases it or tolerates passive coexistence with it as "normal" is an automatic threat to peace.

III

Let Europe's and India's neutralists, who imagine they can remain as an independent "third solution," take warning from Stalin's essay on "Marxism and the National and Colonial Question":

The party of the proletariat decisively rejects what is known as "National Cultural Autonomy." When a life-and-death struggle is being waged, and is spreading, between proletarian Russia and the imperialist Entente, only two alternatives confront the border regions: 1. Either they join forces with Russia . . . *Or* they join forces with the Entente. . . . There is *no third solution*. So-called independence of a so-called independent . . . Poland, Finland, etc., is only an illusion.[1]

Ah, but Lenin, at least Lenin, we are told, was "against war and imperialism." In order to get the most authoritative statement of the Soviet war policy, let us not listen to its propaganda "peace" drives; let us go to the top primary source of all, the works of Lenin himself. Here are his four basic war statements, and they are not being "taken out of context." Note his use of the words "holy" and "inevitable" to describe the war against the non-Soviet world. (Italics mine.)

If war is waged by the exploiting class with the object of strengthening its class rule, such a war is a criminal war, and "defencism" in *such* a war is a base betrayal of socialism. If war is waged by the proletariat after it has conquered the bourgeoisie in its own country, and is waged

[1] New York, International Publishers, p. 79.

with the object of strengthening and extending socialism, such a war is legitimate and *"holy."*[1]

We are living not merely in a state, but in a *system of states,* and the existence of the Soviet Republic side by side with imperialist states for a long time is unthinkable. One or the other must triumph in the end. And before that end supervenes, a series of *frightful collisions* between the Soviet Republic and the bourgeois states will be *inevitable.*[2]

As soon as we are strong enough to defeat capitalism as a whole, we shall immediately take it by the scuff of the neck.[3]

As long as capitalism and socialism exist, we cannot live in peace: in the end, *one or the other* will triumph — a funeral dirge will be sung either over the Soviet Republic or over world capitalism.[4]

Let nobody repeat unchallenged the stale half-truth that the battle between Russia and the West is one of ideologies only, or else one of economic systems, but not one of military force. According to this illusion, there is no battlefield involved; the differences can be settled in a big debating hall, with the best debater winning. That might suit our parliamentary tradition. But it is utterly ruled out both by the theory and practice of communism. This was shown by direct quotations from Lenin and Stalin, staking the issue not on ideological debate but on what they call an "inevitable" and "holy" war. Their conquest of half a billion people proves that here at least they practice what they preach. Our main enemy is not the communist ideology nor their "socialist" economics but the Red army, the Red air force, the Red spies and saboteurs.

A non-risky foreign policy is impossible in a world where freedom must either "live dangerously" or not at all. Also risky, but less risky than either appeasement or war, would be a Western foreign policy of liberating the East.

For the millions of slaves behind the Iron Curtain, "peaceful" coexistence means not peace but a continuation of torture and murder. For them, such coexistence between governments is not a "lesser evil" than war, but indistinguishable from war. According

---

[1] Lenin, *Selected Works,* Moscow, official English translation issued by Marx-Engels-Lenin Institute, VII, 357.

[2] *Ibid.,* VIII, 33.

[3] *Ibid.,* VIII, 282.

[4] *Ibid.,* VIII, 297.

to the most convincing estimate,[1] nine million Soviet citizens —
5.5 per cent of the country — were arrested, deported, or killed
during the political purge of 1936-39 against alleged Trotskyites.

Prior to that and even grimmer, was the economic purge against
free peasants and alleged kulaks during Stalin's collective-farm
program. Numerically this was the most murderous single peacetime crime in all history. According to several different and independent accounts of reliable ex-officials of Soviet collectivization,
between five and ten million peasants were *deliberately* starved to
death. At least an equal number of peasants were worked to
death in forced labor camps. During all this time, Soviet Russia
was "coexisting" with the West. This is the warlike hell which
Western peace policies toward the Soviet dictator have inflicted
upon Soviet citizens, ever since the abandonment of our much
too inadequate intervention of 1918. To denounce the Churchill-
sponsored intervention of 1918 as imperialism, instead of hailing
it as an attempt to liberate our Russian allies of World War I, is
still another of the parrot-clichés of liberal intellectuals.

In its peacetime political and economic purges, the Kremlin
dictatorship has murdered in cold blood a larger number of Soviet
citizens than the number of Red Army soldiers (about seven
million) killed by the cruel Nazi invasion in World War II. Add
to this the Katyn massacre of Polish officers, the genocide against
the three Baltic states, the postwar liquidation of the Crimean
Tartars and Volga Germans, and the current liquidation in labor
camps of the Jewish population of Hungary and of Russian border
areas. Such a Soviet "peace" is indistinguishable from a foreign
war for its victims. No wonder millions of Czechs, Poles, and
Hungarians hope for a liberating foreign war — mistakenly, from
our own antiwar viewpoint — in preference to the endless murders
and tortures of a Soviet "peace."

Heartless indeed (or at best ignorant) are those who praise such
a Soviet "peace" as a goal. Heartless are those who prefer "containment" to liberation.[2]

---

[1] Alexander Weissberg, *The Accused* (New York, 1952).

[2] In connection with our policy toward Soviet-occupied nations, American
officials should read the article, "Beyond Containment to Liberation," *Commentary,* September, 1951, by the able Yugoslav political analyst, Professor
Bogdan Raditsa.

The Quakers of the eighteenth and nineteenth centuries did not compromise their opposition to southern slavery. They bluntly called it an evil. They refused to regard "coexisting" with it as peace. What a shock and disappointment, therefore, to read the widely-hailed Quaker "peace" plan of 1949. It advocates appeasement and coexistence and concessions for the far worse slavery of Stalin. It rejects, as fomenters of bad Russo-American relations, those who would expose, denounce, and terminate this Soviet war against its own Russian people. It warns against the "temptation" of "promoting the overthrow of the Soviet regime," even though Quakers had never hesitated to work for the "overthrow" of American slavery. It warns America against "proposing in the UN measures sharply divisive in effect" (the proposals for investigating Soviet slave labor), even though Christian ethics itself is "divisive" from evil and even though the Quakers rightly felt "divisive" against Hitler's slave camps.

If Quakers are still Christians, if they still prefer human rights to slavery, if they still seek to prevent World War III instead of causing it by substituting appeasement for liberation, then their next "report" will be an indictment of Soviet slave camps. As an admirer of their great past and of their pacifist objectives, I hope we shall not have to wait too long for such a report. I hope it will point out that the very existence, or "coexistence," of the Soviet dictatorship is a perpetual aggressive war, with more Russian victims than World War II.

It is time for sincere pacifists to abandon "coexistence" and to work for peace by working for the political weakening and eventual overthrow of the Soviet terror. I say this not out of any reactionary or militarist mockery of Christian pacifism. I say it out of bitter sorrow because this celebrated "peace report" is such a mockery of the Sermon on the Mount, such a mockery of peace, such a betrayal of the Quaker antislavery crusade of the nineteenth century. The goal of the West should be no tough-minded cynical militarism but the peace-loving decencies of civilization. The route to this goal is still the Biblical one of liberation. Liberation from the dictatorship of the Big Lie: "Ye shall know the truth, and the truth shall make you free."

IV

Fortunately America's alternatives are neither Scylla nor Charybdis. Scylla would be: an insane preventive war against Russia. This might unite the Russian people against us and destroy both our nations. Charybdis would be: to buy "peaceful coexistence" from the Politburo by callously ignoring the suffering Soviet peoples and by paying the ever increasing blackmail of surrendering our last defenses in Europe, Asia, and South America.

The third alternative: avoid military war by aiming at the political weakening (overthrow may be too optimistic at present) of the communist dictatorship and the political wooing of the Russian people. We must recall to them their own free Duma tradition of 1905-17. We must evoke their own nineteenth-century prophets of freedom and their more individualistic, less statist days of ancient Kiev. Since freedom grows organically in its native soil and cannot be transplanted in "liberal" fashion, this approach seems wiser than schoolmasterishly telling them to adopt our foreign democratic constitution wholesale.

This misery of the proletarians behind the Iron Curtain caused several million during the past decade to risk lives and families in order to desert. From the land of proletarian dictatorship they fled to the lands of democratic capitalism or of social democracy. In 1952, despite death penalties, reprisals against families, and electrically-charged barbed wire, 20,000 a month were still fleeing westward from East Germany alone, and at least 1,600 monthly from the adjoining Iron Curtain countries.[1]

What is the West doing about this? Almost nothing. What can it do about the suffering working classes of the East? Almost everything, for we have hardly begun to try. The Soviet is spending 1.5 billion dollars[2] a year for revolutionary activities abroad, trying to turn non-Soviet workers against their governments. By the close of 1951, the United States for the first time voted funds for counter-action. But only 100 million dollars. Without attempting to equal the vast Soviet figure of 1.5 billions (15 times our own), why not spend at least an *effectively* large sum on wooing the Soviet work-

[1] New York *Herald Tribune,* January 9, 1952; editorial page, "Freedom's Two Faces."

[2] New York *Herald Tribune,* January 30, 1952; page 13, columns 2-3.

ers and peasants? It may save us the same sum many times over in military expense. More important: it alone can still save the human race from World War III.

This all-out wooing of the Iron Curtain peoples may make the Politburo too unsure of its Red Army to embark on large-scale foreign invasions. The Politburo never will forget, and we ought not to forget, that the invading German armies of 1941 were greeted with cheers and flowers. Only because they soon revealed themselves as merely a brown-shirted version of Bolshevik oppression, did the Russian peoples wage their brave "fatherland war" against Germany. They fought Germany not for communism but despite communism.

The Politburo never will forget, and we ought not to forget, what happened among officials in Moscow in October, 1941. Moscow seemed about to fall. High officials were ordered to transfer to Kuibyshev. At this point, the secret police, the very pillar of the regime, broke down. It burnt its own files, while many party officials fled to remote spots of Russia, along with party funds.

Many able authorities call it hopeless to woo the Russian masses politically. Difficult certainly: the secret police are in full control; talk of anti-Soviet guerilla bands is at present a romantic exaggeration (although in case we are attacked, we ought to drop guns and commandos over slave-labor camps and over disaffected minorities). Yet even today, political wooing of the Russian people is not hopelessly hopeless. This is shown by the external desertions from Russia today and the internal desertions in Moscow in 1941. After a year of intimate experience with Russians, General Richard Hilton declared (italics his):

Among the vast non-official masses, there is absolutely *no* crusading zeal for the spread of communism over the world, *no* xenophobia, *no* genuine belief that foreigners of any kind are plotting dark deeds against Russia, and *no* desire whatever for another war.

V

Too bad there is no truth in the adage that "it takes two to make a fight." It takes only one if the one is insatiable. The communist aim continues to be world conquest. They say so in their theories (read them!). They behave so in their practice (list the countries conquered!). Optimists who hopefully quote Lenin's repudiation of "imperialist war" fail to quote his equally firm approval of "progressive war." The distinction between "imperialist" and "progressive" would be defined by the Politburo, not by American Quakers. Therefore, "progressive war" may be defined as any aggression the Politburo chooses to wage, and "imperialist war" would be any defense made by the West. Any treacherous Pearl Harbor against America would be justified as "progressive" both by Leninist theory and by Stalinist practice.

All the more reason for reaching the Russian people. We must plan new means to reach that vast majority who lack short-wave radio sets. The use of wind-borne balloons by "Crusade for Freedom," bearing gifts and messages, seems effective. It is helped by a symbolic coincidence of meteorology: the winds of Europe blow mainly from the free West to the East, not vice versa. It is merely one of many methods of piercing the Iron Curtain which Yankee ingenuity will have to devise. All this will involve changes in our foreign policy and our broadcasts. We must start treating the thousands of monthly deserters from the Iron Curtain as cherished allies, not as unwanted D.P.'s. We must let them broadcast, as Russians to Russians. More conviction-carrying than our American voices will be these Russian voices to their countrymen, telling them of American friendship and good treatment and debunking the lies about our "capitalist oppression" or our "plots" to bomb Russia.

Since the Soviet dictatorship rejects the Baruch plan and all enforceable disarmament plans, peace still depends on the collective security of the Atlantic Pact. The H.Q. of the Atlantic Pact in France (SHAPE) is one of the most fervently peace-dedicated, war-loathing atmospheres that can be found anywhere in the world today. The American statement at SHAPE in late 1951 made this crystal-clear: "We seek only to deter the Russians from some act of aggression, which could ignite the world. Our mission here is to avoid war, to give the world time to find the road to peace."

Nothing can be gained at the moment from disarmament conferences, aside from the propaganda gains of both sides trying to put the blame on the other for the *inevitable* failure of all such conferences. Inevitable because disarmament and a stable peace requires an end of the Iron Curtain, which Russia has no intention of ending. What is gained by making a scapegoat of armaments? They are an effect, not a cause. It is not armaments that are creating the war danger. It is the war danger that is creating more armaments. The chief war danger, which must be removed before armaments can be removed, is the Soviet dictatorship itself.

SERMONS OF SELF-DESTRUCTION:
A FINAL APPEAL TO THE *NATION*-ITE MENTALITIES

> "I returned from Spain more optimistic than ever. One month later, President Truman's dramatic announcement that Russia had the atom bomb served to strengthen my confidence." — ALVAREZ DEL VAYO, *foreign editor of* The Nation, *in 1950*

> "How long, O Catiline, wilt thou abuse our patience?"
> —CICERO, *in 63* B.C.

I

The Soviet threat to the West is the most important political fact of our day. Yet many hearts — and even heads — in America, Europe, and India are still crammed with neutralist or even fellow-traveler sentiments. Why? And with what arguments can an American abroad or at home answer them? In that connection, I should like to propose and attempt to answer four questions.

1. How can fellow-traveling and neutralism still be so influential today? Because the United States is pictured as the land of lynchings and "hysteria."

2. What motivates such noncommunist dupes of communism? Not love of Soviet despotism, but hate of fascist despotism and of American babbittry.

3. What are the chief organs of "softness" towards the Soviet among American and European noncommunist intellectuals? *The*

Nation in New York and *The New Statesman* in London.[1]

4. What current literary explosion is a catalyst forcing waverers finally to choose between all-out anti-Stalinism and a new "treason of the clerks"? *The Nation* libel suit against its own former art editor, Clement Greenberg, for protesting its alleged pro-Soviet bias.

Let us consider these four theses in detail.

For any *serious* crusader against the neutralist opiate and the fellow-traveler poison, America's anticommunism must logically be accompanied by its democratic correlative: a rebirth of the anti-fascist spirit. A *serious* anticommunism (as opposed to a merely demagogic headline-hunting pseudo-anticommunism) means no coddling by our drugstore Machiavellis of those Nazi collaborationists who now have the impertinence to offer themselves to our great democratic Atlantic union as "allies against communism." Self-interest and ethics unite to say: only those who resisted the

---

[1] Instead of repeating here an overwhelming evidence more ably presented elsewhere and readily accessible in libraries, I urge the reader to consult the following current articles. They cite at length the concrete evidence of persistent fellow-traveler bias in both *The Nation* and *The New Statesman:*

(1) *New Republic,* March 5 and 19, 1951; articles by R. Strout. They cite a wealth of examples of pro-Soviet distortion from the *New Statesman.*

(2) *Commentary,* April, May, July, 1951; articles and letters by Granville Hicks and others, charging "pro-Soviet bias" in *The Nation* and documenting it with quotations from the recent *Nation* 85th-anniversary number. March, 1952; Irving Kristol, " 'Civil Liberties,' 1952—A Study In Confusion."

(3) *The New Leader,* August 27, 1951, indispensable detailed study by Daniel James of pro-Soviet bias in *Nation* foreign policy; April 2, 1951 (long list of pro-Soviet quotations from Del Vayo's column in *The Nation*); May 21 and 28, 1951 (articles by N. Muhlen); July 14, 1952, Richard Rovere, "How Free Is *The Nation?*" perhaps the best psychological study of the *Nation* fellow-traveler bias.

(4) *Partisan Review,* May-June, 1951; editorial on "the Stalinists and their 'liberal' collaborators" in *The Nation.* From analysis of a recent article by A. Werth, it concludes: "only pro-Soviet bias can account for a magazine like *The Nation* publishing Mr. Werth's calumny."

It is obviously essential to listen to the other side. Readers must also consult and weigh objectively the long protest letter in May *Commentary* of 1951 by Freda Kirchwey, editor of *The Nation.* Of all her defenses of *Nation* policies on Russia, this is the longest and ablest. Having read it, next pick up at random a dozen back numbers of the *Nation* and *New Statesman* of 1936-52; read the regular contributions by Werth, Del Vayo, Carey McWilliams, Kirchwey, "Carolus," and Kingsley Martin; then judge for yourself.

Hitlerite murderers, not those who appeased them, have the spunk and spirit to smash the communist murderers today.

Thoughtful Americans rightly abhor the McCarthyism[1] and intolerance of our yellow journalists. Freedom requires two fronts, at home and abroad. But freedom also requires a sense of proportion. The America-baiters in India, Paris, Rome, London, and at home equate the disproportionate misdeeds of America and Russia and then let them cancel out, thus insidiously conditioning their readers to semi-neutrality. The conditioned results are even *physical,* at least as metaphors: the evasively cynical eyebrow, the glibly defeatist shrug of the shoulder. But more far-sighted antifascists cannot evade the battle against communism; they will never equate the many flaws of the capitalist West with the unequaled malignancy of bolshevism, or with the unequaled menace of its Red Army.

Or are Stalin's raging mass-murders and slave-labor camps not fascist but "progressive"? Two dozen years ago America had one single Sacco and Vanzetti case. Ever since, millions of Americans have hung their heads in remorse. Rightly so. Yet what is one such case compared to the ten million martyred Saccos and Vanzettis today toiling in the Siberian terror camps? May my country never cease its promising advance against the horrors of Jim Crow bigotry. May we never cease to fight the lynchings, averaging perhaps one a year, wreaked by uncontrolled mobs at home. Yet shall liberals at home, and America-baiters abroad, concentrate

---

[1] For scholarly documentation of the errors in Senator McCarthy's charges, see the study by the anti-communist Professor Hornell Hart: *McCarthy Versus the State Department,* available directly from Professor Hart, 4653 Duke Station, Durham, N. C., revised edition of March 1, 1952. Such evidence suggests that "McCarthyism" is what I have called "pseudo (or demagogic) anti-communism" in the preceding paragraph of this chapter, as opposed to "serious anti-communism." Such pseudo-anti-communism, by discrediting a sound and genuine anti-communism, plays into communist hands, a fact which should be the final closing word on the overpublicized subject of "McCarthyism." The instinctive tendency of many liberals to distrust as "McCarthyism" even a seriously-documented charge of communist infiltration (for example, the key role of the communist Frederick Vanderbilt Field in the Institute of Pacific Relations) plays into communist hands likewise. Downright monstrous is the growing notion that Americans must "choose between" the two evils threatening our civil liberties: the McCarthyite exaggeration of communist infiltrations and the *Nation*-ite apathy or indulgence toward them.

on this so exclusively that they stand silent before the thousands of annual government-controlled lynchings in the Soviet satellites?

As a specific example of this false equating and its incalculable damage to the democratic cause, consider the widely-read London *New Statesman*. This is the most maliciously, subtly, and obsessively anti-American organ in the world today. This is the "Great Liberal Magazine" that had editorially urged surrender of the Sudetenland to Hitler long before Chamberlain's Munich Pact. Today it slanders and profanes the young Americans dying for U.N. collective security and for refusing to make another Munich Pact. For example, its issue of January 20, 1951, featured some Pravdoid fiction by A. Baron, describing Americans in Korea as murderers, fascist-style racists, and aggressive imperialists. Why is the influence of such articles and magazines a real menace to peace and unity and not merely a minor nuisance? Because in the words of an editorial of August 1952 in the liberal *New Republic:*

> The Moscow Radio is charging Americans in peacetime with acts as bad or worse than anything charged to Germans or Japanese in time of war. . . . The *New Statesmans* of Europe and the *Blitzes* of Asia have conditioned thousands of noncommunists to respond to these atrocity stories with a shrug and a "Well, who knows?"

If we go down, if 1984 is permitted to triumph in the 1950's, then let us at least *know where the guilt lies.* It lies not only in the aggressions of the Hitlers and Stalins. To some degree perhaps the fatal guilt lies also in the appeasement and in the exaggerations about "American imperialism" spread about by the influential *New Statesman* and by its New York ally, *The Nation.* Their tuggings at the pillars of their own temple are not true liberalism but the liberalism of suicide.

Recently *The New Statesman* unliberally refused to print a letter from Richard Strout refuting their anti-American slanders. At the same time it did print the following letter from that knight-errant of all East-West "peace" congresses, Konni Zilliacus. The Zilliacus document (May 26, 1951) is part of a broader European neutralist campaign. The campaign is directed against "choosing sides" between Russia, and the West (as if the victims of Russian aggression have any "choice") and against the "aggressive" Atlantic Pact (a purely defensive pact). Zilliacus's letter, in space denied to

Atlantic Pact liberals like Strout, urged appeasement via a Labor Party revolt against its anti-Soviet leadership. Zilliacus concluded:

> We must . . . be prepared to go to the lengths of withdrawing our forces from the Far East, getting out of the Atlantic Pact, and sending the American air force home, if the U. S. will not agree with us on how to make peace.

In effect, here is what this letter in *The New Statesman* is shouting to Kremlin policy-makers:

> Step forward — hurry, hurry — you Red aggressors and bomb my own beloved democratic England to death. We peace-loving noncommunist liberals are sending you our unmistakable invitation to invasion by removing that Atlantic Pact and that American air force which alone protect England and the West from certain total annihilation.

II

Socialists use the German word "Lumpen-proletariat" ("bum" proletariat) to describe the fascist lowbrows at the bottom dregs of the masses. Let us coin a new American word, "Lumpen-intellectuals," for the Stalinoid upper-middlebrows near the top of the literary and journalistic world. Here belong the self-pitying and overeager yearners of literature's fringe, the shabby-genteels of kultcher. For the not-quite-first-rate intellectual, note the immense therapeutic value of blaming all personal inadequacies upon capitalist persecutions. This dilettante fellow-traveling of the irresponsibles is not logical but psychological. So it is hard to budge by rational arguments. It is not a case of being converted by logic to being a Lumpen-intellectual but of being rich enough, idle enough, and sick enough for it. "The physician says 'incurable,' the philologian says 'fraud.' " The flirtations with fellow-traveling, like all fashionable neuroses and expensive Fifth-Avenue-doctor allergies, are mainly found in the upper-income brackets: the Sophisticated Rich Man, insistently "open-minded."

Here are eight earmarks of the true Lumpen-intellectual (habitat: the United States, Western Europe, and India; never found in the Soviet, since there he is either shot or joins the Party):

1. He is too pretentiously intellectual to be a Stalinist or read the unrespectable *Daily Worker*. Instead he is a Stalinoid and reads the respectable Red Dean of Canterbury or *The Nation*.

2. Being -oid, not -ist, he calls himself neither anticommunist nor procommunist but "noncommunist." Thereby he commits the *trahison des clercs,* evading deliberately the basic moral choice of this decade. Dante reserved a special circle of Inferno for the luke-warm indifferent ones. There belong those who still defend neutral-ism and lukewarm noncommunism when the blood-soaked stones of Magadan, the Lubyanka, and Korea cry out for passionate moral commitment.

3. Like neurotics whose nervous tics prevent them from looking at certain real objects, so the Lumpen-intellectual obsessively avoids certain real subjects: the vast Russian aid eagerly rendered to Germany during the Hitler-Stalin pact; the purge of all Lenin's internationalist Marxist associates; the postwar Soviet anti-Semitic drive; the slave-labor camps; the increasing class-lines and pay differentials between Soviet rich and poor, so much greater than in capitalist America.

4. He signs Soviet "peace" petitions against atomic war and flocks to fake "peace" conferences. Thereupon he calls any frank free discussion of this ruse "an attempt to suppress free discussion" and self-righteously baits "Red-baiters."

5. For the future or for his bad conscience, he puts himself on record as criticizing Russia — and then always adds "but." For example: "The trouble with Uncle Joe, just between us, is that occasionally he uses bad means, mighty bad means, for his wise, idealistic ends — *but* what about all those constant American lynchings?"

6. Being a power-worshiper, he won't vote for the insignificant American Communist party. Often he never votes at all — are not "both warmonger parties really the same?" What he would like to vote for, he says, is a "healthy, grass-roots, Real American party of the Common Man." By that he means such independent grass-roots as the American "Labor" party or back in 1948 the "Pro-gressive" party.

7. Lumpen-diction can be spotted immediately, not only by the paranoid-conspiratorial "it is no accident that" for the acci-dental, and by "as is well known" for the unknown, but by what I call the Anyburg Umpteen technique. The lumpen-intellectual's conversation is dramatized by ominous references to the Holly-

wood Ten, the Trenton Six, the Martinsville Seven. In Lumpen-intellectual terminology, the slightest attempt to stop a communist spy from destroying democracy is defined as "the garrison state" or "rushing headlong into fascism." In the lumpen's number game, every latest Oshkosh Eight becomes the greatest crime since the Crucifixion. To test if he is really sincerely concerned with civil liberties, ask him how he feels about the oppression of the Muscovite Two Hundred Million.

8. Finally, as the last resort of the noncommunist who defends Communists against anticommunists, there is the "you can't draw the line" obsession. One can fill volumes by just listing examples of this obsession from current pages of the *Nation,* the *Compass,* the *National Guardian,* and also some genuinely liberal periodicals that ought to know better. This obsession says: you cannot draw the line between criticizing Communists and suppressing the free speech of everybody else, including honest dissenters and those independent radicals who are the salt of the earth. This lumpen-earmark has been best described by Lewis Berry (*The Workmen's Circle Call,* January-February, 1951):

The You're-Next technique: we are persuaded that if we attack a Communist or allow him to be attacked, we will be the next to be victimized. This has worked so astoundingly well on liberals who are members of minority groups or who hold minority opinions, that its use gives Communists sure-fire immunization from critical examination. Lie number one — that to describe honestly and critically what a Communist is, is to deprive him of his civil rights. Lie number two — that because Communism has the allegiance of only a minority it is necessarily good and worth insulating from criticism. Would you be afraid that Jews were next or Socialists next, if the minority that centers around Gerald Smith or the German-American Bund were made the target of a national campaign of enlightenment? If you think that the Communists are *different,* you have *stopped* arguing their minority position and are arguing their virtuousness. That's not a You're-Next position; that's a *pro-communist position.*

III

This is the era of New and Fair Deals, whose full social gains Eisenhower has sworn to maintain. In such an era, *The Nation, The New Statesman,* and the Lumpen-intellectuals have a hard time finding an American reactionary menace to cancel out the Russian radical menace. Sometimes just when they have an American menace built up, it collapses. Then the merry chase resumes: to find a bigger American menace. Two examples:

1. The dismissal of General MacArthur (whether justified or unjustified) was in one way a blow to the fellow-traveler world. *The New Statesman* depended desperately on MacArthur for its increasing circulation and influence. It had just built him up for British readers as the real ruler of America, a menace to equate with Stalin. Then suddenly MacArthur and his strategy were dismissed by the President and the Joint Chiefs of Staff in a Great Debate such as is only possible in a very, very free country.

2. Another menace, built up to cancel out Soviet thought control, was the California Teachers' Oath. Unfortunately for "exposers" of American "hysteria," this law was quite properly thrown out by the courts.

But no complacency! Anticommunists must continue their "ceaseless vigilance" for civil liberties against thought control. Let us continue to resist hysteria. But let us also resist hysteria about hysteria. Let the splendidly self-critical conscience of American intellectuals become as critical of suicide as of Red-baiting. Let this American conscience turn its cleansing scorn at full blast upon those self-baiters who ignore the ten million Saccos in the neo-Belsens of the Kremlin.

Many sincere democrats in Europe, India, and America applaud the neutralist baitings of our foreign policy as if these were attacks on irrational militarism or McCarthyism. The exact opposite is the case. They are often really attacks upon American democracy itself and upon the collective security indispensable for peace. Thereby they are attacks upon international democratic civilization, whose righteously armed American fist in Korea and Europe is not irrational militarism but reason exasperated, the last hope of peace against Soviet world conquest.

What about *The Nation* and *New Statesman* side of the case? In their defense they raise two arguments. Both are unjustly ignored by the professional Red-baiter and must in fairness be here presented. First, they rightly warn against making anticommunism a pretext for Nazi revivals abroad or for suppression of independent native radicals at home. Second, they rightly point out anticom-

munists among their contributors. But these are outweighed by
the Del Vayos and the appeasers, a fact which raises the separate
question of respectable window dressing.

Even though no anticommunist liberal weekly has the influence
of *The Nation* and *The New Statesman,* yet it would be too pessimistic to call antineutralism a lost cause among literary intellectuals.
Also in Paris it does not lack defenders. What it lacks is a world
unity among anticommunist intellectuals as close as that among
fellow-travelers. The most promising attempt at such unity is the
Congress for Cultural Freedom. This was ably organized in Berlin
by Melvin J. Lasky. Later it also met in India. It achieved
wonders in challenging and rebutting neutralists. Its global range
and diversity is shown by its honorary chairmen: Benedetto Croce,
John Dewey, Karl Jaspers, Salvador de Madariaga, Jacques Maritain, Bertrand Russell. Its American branch is the newly-founded
"American Committee for Cultural Freedom." [1]

What about the argument that *The Nation* and *New Statesman*
are too uninfluential to jeopardize our national security or to
justify attacking them? The influence of intellectual journals can
never be measured by quantitative circulation. In any great
historic decision, such as our 1945 appeasement, one factor is
that amorphous thing known as "climate of opinion." This is
created not by mass circulation of unread yellow-press editorials
and other popular comic books but by small qualitative circulation among those who "count." In the Yalta era, is it more likely
that such honorable but confused noncommunists as Harry Hopkins
were reading a large-circulation Hearst paper or a small-circulation
Nation? Circulation figures are no yardstick for measuring the
influence of our false prophets.

In *The Nation* of June 28, 1952, the key editorial has this message: Soviet expansion, though deplorable, expresses not the
brutal conquests of the Red Army but the "emerging forces of

---

[1] Address of the American Committee: 35 West 53rd St., New York 19,
N.Y. By writing there, you may obtain its pamphlet *We Put Freedom First*
and other publications exposing tyranny as well as its recommendations of
anticommunist lecturers for college audiences. Though a member of its executive, I must emphasize that I speak solely for myself in this book; my
heresies and *faux pas* are strictly my own and not to be blamed on any innocent bystander.

popular revolt" against capitalist reaction. We must not oppose this "popular revolt" lest we thereby shoulder the

thankless, hopeless job of sweeping back the great tide of change. . . . What has happened is that the United States, together with its allies in so far as they can be held in line, is engaged in heading up the new counter-revolution.

But though the editor thereby places almost the entire blame on America rather than Russia, it cannot be alleged that she fails to attack communism also. Her use of the word *"may"* (italics mine) suffices to differentiate her from the unquestioning party liner: the Russian communists (she says) have "a brutal energy which *may* defeat the very purposes they proclaim." "May" leaves it open (doesn't it?), one way or another, utopia or not utopia. But nothing is left open about America, which, by committing the crime of resisting Soviet world conquest, seems to be going "fascist" (her word). The obvious implication of this is that the Soviet, despite all its deplorable faults of "brutal energy," is the bulwark of democracy against American fascism.

If I were a young student, reading this magazine and drawing this implication, I would wish to take part in this "great tide of change" and to frustrate this American "counter-revolution." In such a dream world, my first allegiance would be to the "democracy" represented by Russia, not to the "fascist" American government. This, in turn, might also make pro-Soviet espionage and sabotage not merely legitimate but a sacred moral duty to democracy. I don't know what periodicals in the Barnard library molded the mentality of a Judith Coplon, nor what molded the outlook toward his own country of Alger Hiss. But it was certainly nothing so crude and explicit as the *Daily Worker*.

Since it goes without saying that the disagreement between freedom-loving "professors" and the "bloody-minded professors" must be settled in the arena of free debate and *not of censorship,* the answer to *The Nation* is not to discourage the college student from reading it, but to encourage him (I am thinking of the many classrooms that assign it) to read it with a more critical open mind and side by side with periodicals intelligently giving freedom's side also. Of these there is almost none — amid our overwhelmingly anticommunist press — that has the same cultural and psychological appeal to potential Judith Coplons as *The Nation* or *The New Statesman*. This appeal will have to be analyzed and met. No intellectual ever became pro-communist from reading the *Daily Worker*: it is too stupidly transparent. No, it is these non-communist but West-baiting and East-appeasing journals, with their "charming" belletristic snobbery and their "cultivated" artistic veneer, that entice the wavering intellectual by flattering — and then misapplying — his or her justified distrust of babbittry and American commercialism.

The Nation and *The New Statesman* sincerely detest communist treason and all such logical, disciplined aspects of Stalinism. The serious intellectual level of the present controversy must not be lowered to demagogy by anybody questioning their undoubted loyalty to America and England. Never was it their intention to help mold this self-destructive generation of Alger Hiss or Burgess and MacLean. But results, not intentions, may perhaps help us lose World War III through the intellectual defection of key atom scientists or through misrepresenting abroad America's peaceful intentions. Both magazines have a Sacred Cow prestige in the academic and literary world. Their prestige intimidates (it seems incredible, but I have personally observed it) many an intellectual from criticizing the fellow-travelers, lest the anti-anticommunist lynch mob of upper-middlebrows assassinate his character with false accusations of "McCarthyite," or "menace to civil liberties," or just plain "name caller."

IV

Apologists for Del Vayo, finding nothing to defend in his present peculiar role, have to go back to the day of Loyalist Spain. At least then, they say, he was against dictatorship; was he not fighting against Franco? According to the following open letter by Lewis Corey (an ardent supporter of Loyalist Spain and for thirteen years a *Nation* contributor), the del-Vayo-supported Stalinist terror in Loyalist Spain is what helped the Franco tyranny to win:

So the *Nation* is suing *The New Leader* for libel! Good! Let the defense use this opportunity to tell people the truth about the *Nation's* anti-liberal and anti-American promotion of the reactionary objectives of Soviet Communism. From 1928 to 1941, I was a fairly regular contributor to the *Nation*. I have not written for it during the past ten years because of its pro-Communist, pro-Soviet policies. The complete identification of Freda Kirchwey with Soviet imperialism appears clearly in her article in the *Nation's* anniversary issue, in which she justifies the use by Communist governments of aggression and armed force to spread Communism. I quote from her article: "That the North's attack (on South Korea) was an 'aggression' is disputed only by Communists and their backers. . . . But to say this and nothing more is again to blur meanings. For the attack was more than an aggression; it was also an act of civil war and revolution."

The devil in the piece of the *Nation's* degeneration is Alvarez del Vayo and his fatal influence on Freda Kirchwey. This man . . . promotes every twist and turn of Soviet Communism and imperialism. In his autobiography, *The Last Optimist,* published in 1950, del Vayo writes in the third from final paragraph of the book: "I returned from Spain more optimistic than ever. One month later President Truman's dramatic announcement that Russia had the atom bomb served to strengthen my confidence." And in this same autobiography, del Vayo, by half-truths and silence, covers up the reign of terror let loose during the Spanish Civil War by Soviet agents and their local Communist allies against Socialists, trade unionists and the non-Communist Left generally. This terror was as much responsible for destroying the Spanish Republic as were Franco's troops.

Professor Arthur Schlesinger, Jr., a leader of the New Dealish and anti-McCarthyite "Americans for Democratic Action," wrote *The Nation* this letter, which it typically refused to print:

March 26, 1951

Dear Miss Kirchwey:

As an occasional contributor to *The Nation* I would like to associate myself with the general sentiments expressed by Clement Greenberg in his letter to *The Nation,* published in a recent issue of *The New Leader*. I know that many readers feel these days that *The Nation* is betraying its finest traditions — traditions which you yourself have courageously sustained in times past — when it prints, week after week, *these wretched apologies for Soviet despotism.*

I am equally troubled, however, by a separate issue — that is, by *The Nation's* refusal to give space in its correspondence columns to Mr. Greenberg's good-tempered and sensible letter. Quite apart from the discourtesy to an old *Nation* writer, this action deprives *Nation* readers of knowledge — to which they are surely entitled — of the reaction in liberal circles to Del Vayo and to *The Nation* editorials. I suppose it would be too much to hope that you would publish this brief letter from me, so that *Nation* readers might at least know of the existence of the Greenberg letter and of this controversy.

Sincerely yours,

ARTHUR SCHLESINGER, JR.

Note Schlesinger's agreement with the Greenberg letter, whose actual text is still concealed from *Nation* readers. On this issue every waverer must at last take a clear-cut stand. Either he will support free speech for anticommunist letters like those of Schlesinger and Greenberg. Or he will be smoked out, despite indignant virtuous denials, as a dupe of Stalinist fascism.

The Nation appealed to "free speech" when excluded (I believe, unjustly) from certain public school libraries. No word in these pages should be twisted as condoning curtailment of the free speech of the fellow-travelers here attacked. But today the shoe of free speech is on the other foot. Today *The Nation* refuses to print the protests of Schlesinger and of its former editor Greenberg, and even sues the latter for libel.

A decade from now, this refusal and this libel suit may be famous as a turning-point: the final self-discrediting of the Lumpen-intellectuals. The Greenberg letter cited detailed evidence to allege that Alvarez del Vayo, foreign editor of *The Nation,* is a Soviet apologist. With this we may agree or disagree. In either case it is the sort of important intellectual document that a democratic magazine throws open to free public debate.

The Nation also refused to print letters from Richard Chase and countless other leading liberals backing the Greenberg or Schlesinger stand on Del Vayo. *The Nation* also failed to announce and discuss the crucial fact that Reinhold Niebuhr and Robert Bendiner have quit its staff to protest its foreign policy toward Russia and its libel suit. *The Nation* still prints the work of such anti-Soviet liberals as its distinguished literary and drama editors, Margaret Marshall and Joseph Wood Krutch. Unfortunately its foreign editor represents its more dominant political tone.

Meanwhile is there no reader who will *do something* about the following alarming fact? In capitalist, anticommunist America *The Daily Worker* has Field and other millionaires to aid it. *The Nation* has its "angels." But the consistently anticommunist *New Leader* is in financial crisis! Its function is to provide unique sources of

necessary information about Soviet Russia by these leading experts:
Bertram Wolfe, W. H. Chamberlin, David Shub, Michael Karpo-
vich, Hans Kohn, Melvin Lasky, Norbert Muhlen, Harry Schwartz,
David Dallin, and Dwight Macdonald. Yet, while *The Daily
Worker* gets its capitalist subsidies, *The New Leader* and the liberal
Catholic *Commonweal* still lack the slight funds to expand their
exposures of both communism and Nazism.

V

Why the present writer's insistence on calling *The Nation* and
other noncommunist waverers "well-intentioned"? Communists
and Fascists are motivated by power; their success would feather
their own nest. But the fellow-traveler intellectual, who for fifteen
years bulldozed American cultural life, would be destroyed by his
success. His motives often are not power, not self-interest, but anti-
fascism abroad and anti-babbittry at home.

As an anti-fascist abroad, he still thinks in terms of the accidental
World War II alliance of Russia with the democracies (after the
failure of the more basic, less accidental Stalin-Hitler pact). As
an anti-babbitt at home, he correctly notes that the forces of mean-
spirited bigotry are denouncing "Reds" who sometimes are not
Reds at all but honest democratic reformers. Therefore, abroad
he calls anticommunism pro-fascist. And at home he calls it a
mere trick to persecute honest democratic reformers. In this —
let us do him full justice! — he is partly (perhaps 10 per cent)
right: insofar as our right-wing extremists have indulged fascists
abroad and smeared innocents at home, they are often to blame
for turning intellectuals into fellow-travelers.

But fascists and right-wing extremists are not in power, are not
Truman nor Ike, a crucial fact minimized by our sermonizers
of self-destruction. Let us herewith challenge *The New Statesman*
to stop concealing from its readers the true statistics: less than
half of 1 per cent of America's three and a quarter million Government workers were even subjected to loyalty investigations; and
after long legal hearings a mere 308 (.009 of 1 per cent) were
dismissed.

Or is even .009 excessive? Is even that a fascist panic, a terrorization of the entire working-class? Would *The New Statesman* or *The Nation* wish in the name of "free speech" that Fuchs and Hiss and Coplon had not been dismissed and should now be reinstated in high secret posts in order to end "American witch-hunts and anti-Red hysteria"? Does "democratic tolerance" mean self-murder? And if so, why are they not equally tolerant to fascist spies? Or is tolerant "liberal" ethics a double bookkeeping, somehow distinguishing between fascist and communist traitors?

Meanwhile *The New Statesman* tells its influential British readers the following damnable lie (let us use the blunt word "lie") about America's supposed reign of terror:

> The drive for conformity in "true Americanism" is intensified: properly to qualify the citizen would need a purity certificate from the Un-American Affairs Committee, the National Association of Manufacturers, and the Hearst newspapers. Among those unable to qualify fear of the informer strikes restraint even into private conversation. There are few Americans apart from the residents of some big cities and the comparatively small group of college teachers and intellectuals — the kind of people who read *The Nation* or *New Republic* — who today have much chance to read or hear dissenting opinions.

For the authors of the above hysterical paragraph and for all Bevanites and European neutralists, Senator McCarthy has been a heaven-sent opportunity. He has become their rhetorical device for discrediting in gullible foreign eyes the fair-mindedness and democratic idealism basic to most American anticommunism. He is so indispensable to their profession of America-baiting that, even if McCarthy did not exist, they would find it necessary to invent him. This last fact at times makes one doubt (in Kafka fancifulness) whether he really does "exist" or is merely a pipe dream, smoked up in a séance by Sartre, Kingsley Martin, and the I.P.R. conscience of Owen Lattimore — and then nourished from smoky specter into beefy reality by that liberal panic which did so much to overpublicize the word "McCarthyism" and to inflate it into a balloon ogre.

Every balloon ogre looks terrifyingly enormous until the right person pops it. The right person to pop McCarthy by public refutation must be a fellow Republican so beyond suspicion in the eyes of America that no slander can stick to him. The person who best meets that specification is Dwight Eisenhower. Unless the new Republican administration restrains or pops this specter, it will be guilty of flagrant moral evasion. One qualification: the actual power of the McCarthy specter has been overrated by leftists seeking a pretext to avoid facing the far greater overseas danger on the left. But this qualification does not relieve the Republicans of the moral duty to repudiate manfully that kind of political indecency. So basic a moral duty becomes an imperative absolute, not to be evaded by pragmatic party unity or by even the most correct pragmatic reassurance that the power of the indecency happens indeed to be overrated.

The Nation mentality and the McCarthy mentality need each other, feed on each other, and are both wrong. Though their noise sounds deafening to Europe, both these hysterical extremes are unrepresentative (Europe, please note!) of American public opinion.

Some of our present preachers of self-destruction were once sincere anti-fascists and anti-appeasers in the 1930's. For that all honor to the editors and disciples of *The Nation* and *The New Statesman*. It would sacrifice fair-mindedness to oversimplification if in the heat of this debate we deny this link between them and us anti-appeasers, the link of a common free culture despite ourselves. Does not 1688 unite us psychologically as much as 1917 divides us politically? Then let us appeal affectionately and understandingly, in the name of our common bond of anti-fascism, to our wavering anti-fascist colleagues in the literary and academic world. Let it be a last appeal to join with the forces of global freedom in an all-out drive against the Red terror abroad and against the infamous disingenuousness of the fellow-travelers at home. Before being ethically forced to a final break with them, let the free, Stalin-loathing portion of American and European intellectuals appeal this once more to the slave and neutralist parts, in the words of Cromwell: "I beseech you in the bowels of Christ, think it possible that you may be mistaken."

Lest We Forget: Fascism Revisited

"Went out around three this morning to be present at a large-scale gassing of deportees for the first time. In comparison, Dante's Inferno seems almost a comedy. It's not for nothing that Auschwitz is called an annihilation camp! . . . At eight in the evening, dinner with Obergruppenführer Pohl in the Führerheim, a real banquet. We had pie — as much as one wanted — real coffee, excellent beer . . . and wonderful vanilla ice cream." — *from the captured diary for September, 1942, of* DR. KRAMER, *resident physician at Auschwitz*

PUT UP OR SHUT UP

"The thing to do is to let South Korea fall, but not let it look as if we pushed it." — OWEN LATTIMORE in the New York *Compass,* July 17, 1949

"Why die for Danzig?" — MARCEL DÉAT, a leading French appeaser of Hitler, 1939

War in the atomic age is more dreadful than ever before in history. I am confident war can be and will be avoided by such peace measures as those analyzed in the section on "Russia and Peace," measures building peace and brotherhood with the overwhelming mass of Eastern Europeans (rather than with their unappeasable, warlike oppressors). But if ever the choice should be between war and liberty (and fortunately this will probably never be the case), then I hope my country will commit itself to the dreadful word "war." I hope it will commit itself not with blind jingoism, never with easy self-righteousness, but open-eyed and with bitter calm, just as it did unanimously in 1941.

World War II killed millions of the world's finest, including the person closest to the author. Yet if it put a stop to Dachau in at least the Western half of the world, then not one died too many. The moral fiber of America could not long have survived the degradation of idling and enjoying a life of comfort while human beings were sent by other human beings into gas chambers. How long today can the Christian-Judaic moral basis of American freedom survive our tolerating by "containment" — as opposed to liberation — the comparable horrors of the Soviet slave camps?

It is said, very likely correctly, that a third world war would become — if our hopes of Red Army mutiny fail — the most destructive in history, so that supposedly it is wiser to surrender our liberties to the Kremlin than to fight for them. Because of this dreadfulness of World War III, we hope by liberation of the East to avoid World War III completely. Yet if the decision should ever be between freedom and war, then the Christian view of freedom must tragically choose rather a physical crucifixion by war than a moral surrender to the most evil of slaveries.

These words sound naïve, Sunday-school-ish, rhetorical. Well, these are the words — freedom, morality, Christianity — that Western man has been mouthing for a number of centuries. Either he really lives these words and is ready to put up or shut up for them, when challenged by their opposites; or else, these sacred words have become mere eloquence for him, hollow and devitalized. It will be fascinating to find out in the next ten years which of these two alternatives more closely describes the complex and pluralist American reality.

THIS MORNING IS SAINT CRISPIN'S DAY

In 1945 General Patton forced undemocratic Germans to see with their own eyes the skeletons in a local concentration camp. Today democratic but forgetful Americans ought to force themselves to think again of these skeletons of fascism. When American soldiers put a stop to such infamies, so that Western Europe today is free, did they "die in vain" for "stupid idealism"? So says the new school that blames today's Soviet menace on our war with Germany.

But our costly delay in blocking Soviet expansion was not the result of our necessary war with Germany. It was the result of two other factors:

1. Our bungling the peace that followed the war. This bungling was no necessary consequence of waging and winning the war

itself. Churchill, despite his mistake in Yugoslavia, might have won the peace as well as the war.

2. The Hitler-Stalin Pact. Not American interventionists but the Nazis in 1939 let Stalin into Poland, Finland, the Baltic states, and the Balkans.

Only our learning the price of isolationism and appeasement the hard way against Hitler has educated our country into our timely Atlantic Pact and our defense of collective security in Korea. If America ever minimizes its anti-Hitler war, it minimizes one of the wisest and most decent acts in its history.

"Who," to echo the chant of the new "revisionist" school, "got us into war?" As an historian, and also as one of a million enlisted men in the Italian campaign of 1944, I wish the answer were:

"It is we, the American people, who 'got' ourselves in. We got in because we happen to be human beings and, therefore, prejudiced against tyrants and torturers. Because we are the product of two thousand years of Christian and Hellenic traditions, making us indeed our brother's keeper."

Unfortunately for America's claim to greatness, the above is not a sufficient answer to why we "got in." We had no choice but to fight because Japan attacked us and Germany declared war. . . . Suppose Japan had not attacked. Further, suppose our isolationists had won our elections and had accepted their humble niche in a Hitler-ruled world, as some revisionists may now prefer. Our nation would have disintegrated, morally and materially. Evidence of this is the partial disintegration that was already taking place before Pearl Harbor restored American unity. The issue of 1939-41 was how to halt, before too late, the *Mein Kampf* program of "Germany, mistress of the globe by the victorious sword of a master race." How did America react to this issue?

On the one hand, America's anti-fascist majority guarded the light in those three dark years. But let us unflinchingly recall the other, more embarrassing aspect of our own country. During 1936-41, the yellow press, the "America First" mentalities, and Senator Taft heckled so relentlessly for isolation and neutralism that America was unable to build its alliance with France and England in time. Such an alliance of the free could have deterred the inevitable communazi alliance from attacking Poland and from unleashing World War II. It could also have at least narrowed the postwar Soviet expansion by standing firm on the pledges of the Atlantic Charter. Hindsight? Admittedly yes, but useful also as a future program of Atlantic unity. World War II and Korea, Munich and Yalta, Hitler's expansion and Stalin's expansion, were partly the result of the Trojan "peace" dove of our "trust Hitler" pseudo-conservatives and our "trust Stalin" pseudo-liberals. Today, unless we continue to feel the shared emotional experience of the anti-Nazi war, our hearts will never be sufficiently atune with our Hitler-ravaged partners in the Atlantic community, the free community that America must foster to deter the Red Army and to transcend nationalism.

Europe's neutralists and anti-anticommunists are libelously mistaken when they suspect America of abandoning democracy and moving toward fascism. Yet their suspicion does reflect the existence of a very real — though different — American sin. That sin is not pro-fascism nor those much-denounced and exaggerated "witch hunts against communists and nonconformists." No, it is the subtler sin of thickskinned forgetfulness about fascism, the sin of a sluggish indifference to the moral — as distinguished from material — threat of both fascism and communism. (A similar moral sluggishness characterizes those sincere but undynamic anticommunists in Washington whom I'd call containment-mongers and coexistence-relativists.) In our vast antifascist majority, this postwar forgetting of fascism stems not from lack of democracy, which America practices sincerely, but from moral sloth.

Moral sloth is hardly an auspicious atmosphere for effective anticommunism. Only the spirit that stopped Hitler can stop Stalin. Antifascism (exactly as much as anticommunism) is creative humaneness, the answer of human dignity to brute force. A rebirth of the anti-fascist spirit will be the salvation of the West, the answer to Spengler's pessimism. The sacrament of 1939-45, its exaltation and dedication, must not become mere lip service to freedom; it must again, in Wordsworth phrase, be "felt along the heart." Without it, we can preach our anticommunism to Europe and Asia "with the tongues of men and angels" and yet have no effect.

April 30, 1945, is a day for Americans to remember annually: the anniversary of the death of one of the two monsters. Concerning the other monster, you may — if you choose — quote from Shakespeare: "That I may live to say the dog is dead!"

It is easy, but insufficient, to denounce self-righteously a dead monster's past crimes. It is harder, but necessary, to anticipate and prevent future crimes. For this, you need to prevent the lulling in yourself of that deepened conscience for whose creation we must remain ironically grateful to the dead monster: I refer to what can only be called the anti-fascist conscience. This conscience cuts across the merely secular lines of liberal and conservative, socialist and capitalist. Far from being a monopoly of the left, anti-fascism includes all men of decency and *aretê* regardless of politics.

Almost every single family on the globe was affected, directly or indirectly, by the atrocities and aggressions of the Rome-Berlin-Tokyo Axis of 1936-45. This fact has made the anti-fascist conscience a world-wide conscience, shared by all classes and races.

In the very thick of their anticommunist struggle, this world-wide conscience should make most Americans pause soberly and reflect a minute on every April 30. The pause makes us recall that America's enemy is still fascism, the same old fascism, even though this time concealed under democratic-progressive patter. Only this pause and only this recall will enable us to continue our battle against Soviet fascism and its appeasers with redoubled zeal. For it is a zeal inspired by no mere power politics, and not solely by material interests, but by the sacred anti-fascist conscience of mankind.

So when a Spanish Falangist or a domestic Nazi like Gerald K. Smith, a "charming" Vichy diplomat or an "efficient" Nazi general step forward with an expectant smile to offer us their services against communism, impressarioed with a knowing wink by those patriots of the yellow press who were isolationist toward Hitler and interventionist toward Stalin, then let public opinion — no longer amused — thunder back at the whole crew of them: "Crawl under your stones again; we do not want you!" Memories of the battle against nazism and appeasement by America's bi-partisan interventionists in 1939-41, must today reunite conservative and liberal America against Communist infiltration and new appeasement, in exactly the same way that the battle of Agincourt united Englishmen of all diverse views on Saint Crispin's Day:

> He, that shall live this day, and see old age,
> Will yearly on the vigil feast his friends . . .
> And gentlemen in England, now a-bed,
> Shall think themselves accursed they were not here;
> And hold their manhoods cheap, while any speaks
> That fought with us upon Saint Crispin's Day.

For is not the life of man an unending Saint Crispin's Day, no meaningless vanity of ego and mean-spirited self-interest, but a battle where every slightest political act may become an unshirkable responsibility of infinite moral significance?

SECTION SEVEN

The Nature of Freedom

"Ends pre-exist in the means." — RALPH WALDO EMERSON

"I then realized . . . there are certain standards of moral behavior which are in you and that you cannot disregard." — KLAUS FUCHS's *explanation, in his espionage confession, of why he lost faith in communism*

FREEDOM IS A SEMI-CLOSED SOCIETY

"Love is not in gazing at each other, but outward together in the same direction." — ST. EXUPÉRY

In some ways the nineteenth century of Mill and Gladstone is, unfortunately, more remote from us than the fifth century of Attila. Here is the attractive goal of the confident, seemingly triumphant liberalism of the nineteenth century: an Elysian Field of carefree, spontaneous individuality, with as many different "values" to pick by caprice as there are wild flowers. Most of us are emotionally committed to Millsian liberalism, even when we criticize its innocent optimism about reasoning away and educating away Evil. Therefore, we share in our hearts its nostalgia for this nineteenth-century diversity. But how much of it can be safely preserved in an age that must "close its ranks" to survive?

Just as much as *can* be preserved, ought to be preserved, with the benefit of the doubt always in favor of the individual, not the state. Nevertheless, ranks must close. Simply must. No use cheering Justice William Douglas's well-intentioned but indiscriminate protest against "the new orthodoxy"; it's no go "anything goes."

The West is too innately pluralist to be a closed society (in the sense of the medieval Catholic church or any other "infallible authority"). The West is not an open society either (in the sense of total liberal relativism). "Semi-closed" is the term I would propose.

190

This problem — open or closed society? — most liberal men-of-good-will fail to face. Not merely theocracies but every viable, post-caveman society has its indispensable code of thou-shalt-nots. Our semi-closed society must be sufficiently intolerant of physical and of ethical atrocities to avoid the liberalism of suicide, *trahison des* lumpen-intellectuals.

"Intolerant" — are you afraid of that word (even when properly used as intolerant of intolerance) because it sounds un-avant-garde or conservative? It is the liberalism of suicide when you tolerate a communazi military conspiracy as a political "party," whose "civil liberties" are double-think for the purpose of murdering civil liberties. Liberal suicide: Germany 1933, Czechoslovakia 1948, maybe France and Italy tomorrow. Guarantee full civil liberties to all who will share a round robin guaranteeing the civil liberties of others; guarantee full parliamentary rights to all genuinely parliamentary parties; but not to criminal communazi conspiracies involving not political words but military deeds. All parliamentarians (parliamentary capitalists, parliamentary socialists, parliamentary Catholics, parliamentary monarchists) must at last close ranks, voluntarily and for the sake of peace and love, in order to survive the Katyn of those who close ranks coercively and for the sake of war and hate.

In our semi-closed society, with its common denominator of shared values, our free democracy and our precious civil liberties rest on the statement: "These truths we hold to be self-evident." They do not rest on the statement: "These outworn medieval hypotheses we hold to be the operational tools of economics or of the libido."

THE NONECONOMIC NATURE OF FREEDOM

"A man is rich in proportion to the things he can do without." —THOREAU

"Isn't it a fine excuse for the Devil," asked the Renaissance scientist and magician Paracelsus, "to shield himself behind astrology and to blame the stars for what he has done?" This question can be paraphrased in twentieth-century terms. Isn't it a fine thing for your personal conscience to shield itself behind economic determinism and to blame impersonal capitalism for what it has done? War, imperialism, fascism — these are an ethical default older and deeper than capitalism; don't try to shift this personal responsibility to any impersonal statist or economic force.

We know, if anything we know too well, Anatole France's sarcasm about the "equality" which imprisons the rich man as well as the poor man for stealing bread. Obviously no free society can remain free, or is free for all its citizens, unless it eliminates an unbearable poverty that makes a sham of civil liberties and invites dictatorship.

True enough. However, American capitalism, continuously raising the mass standard of living year after year, needs no lecture on *this* from Marxists eager to prove our genuine liberties ungenuine. On the contrary, the fault of the American capitalist outlook is that it shares with Marxism — more than most European socialists do — an almost corybantic devotion to economic production figures. Thereby both are inclined to overlook those psychological, moral, and traditionalist shields of freedom against tyranny with which this book is concerned.

The motive for tyranny is not economics but will to power. Behind power, such motives as vanity, inferiority complex, sadism, fear, frustration, and just plain cussedness must also be considered. Economic gain is sought as a means toward power; not power as a means toward economic gain. This distinction must be remembered when confronted by a capitalist tyranny and by injustices committed by capitalists. The economic structure of capitalism is being used as a means toward power and tyranny but is not the cause of it. In the same way, socialism, feudalism, and other -isms can be used as a means toward tyranny without being the cause of it.

Lenin (via Hobson) "explained" imperialism, war, and fascism as the inevitable results of capitalist economics. *Imperialism, A Study,* published in 1902 by the British economist John A. Hobson, founded the modern devil-theory of capitalist imperialism, culminating in Lenin's *Imperialism: the Highest Stage of Capitalism,* 1917. The Hobson-Lenin half-truths have been so widely and glibly parroted that Babbitt Junior repeats them as a conditioned reflex at any mention of the British Empire or "Western imperialism," without reflecting as to the source and soundness of these clichés.

Today all the ills of Asia are blamed on the past sins of capitalist imperialists. Their imprisonment of a Gandhi and a Nehru excited Western liberals to more indignation than all the mutual butchery of half a million Hindus and Moslems in a "free" India. When imperialism actually did lead to those pre-1914 "war crises," such as the German-French rivalry over Morocco, it was the bankers and capitalists who hesitated and preferred peaceful trade; it was the militarists and political leaders who preferred to risk war.

That much-denounced "exploitation" of colonies usually paid mere chicken feed in profits. Hardly a major motive for those much-denounced bankers. In the case of pre-1914 Germany and Italy, colonial imperialism was economically a dead loss. It served only psychologically: a boost to the national inferiority complexes of the two latecomers in the race. Imperialism, war, and fascism are a case of power motive using economics as a pretext, not of economic motive using political power as a pretext. Bertrand Russell's materialistic, nineteenth-century "modernism," which flogs the dead horses of Victorianism and Puritanism while the living dangers escape, usually symbolizes everything I disagree with.[1] But on this issue of over-estimating economic motive, he says exactly what needs to be said:[2]

The fight for freedom is not to be won by any mere change in our economic system. It is to be won only by a constant resistance to the tyranny of officials. . . . To suppose that irresponsible power, just because it is called Socialist or Communist, will be freed miraculously from the bad qualities of all arbitrary power in the past, is mere childish nursery psychology.

---

[1] For example, Mr. Russell writes in *New Hopes for a Changing World* (New York: 1952): "Propagandists have acquired a habit of talking about 'western values,' and it must be confessed that a great deal of what they say is rubbish. I am inclined to think that the most important of western values is the habit of a low birth-rate." If this is meant merely as a sarcastic *bon mot,* the matter need not be pursued further. If meant as serious philosophy, at a moment when western values are so lethally menaced, then would Mr. Russell explain whatever happened to values in the corrupt, materialism-corroded Third Republic of France? With its low birth-rate, it should be, for him, tops in values.

[2] *The Wit and Wisdom of Bertrand Russell* (Boston: Beacon Press, 1951), pp. 68, 94, 122.

Will economic change — specifically the abolition of capitalism — "solve" the psychological cause of tyranny, fascism, imperialism, and war? Old-fashioned socialists believe so. So do those liberals who still parrot a fashionable Marxist jargon without themselves being Marxists. To fight tyranny by abolishing capitalism and abolishing the profit motive may increase, not decrease that power motive which does more than mere money to cause tyranny. The success of any society's restraint on power-motive and on tyranny depends on the past traditional framework of that society. It depends not only on the economic realities of the society but on the political methods of change. So every discussion of economic freedom ends up in noneconomic problems of politics. In turn, every discussion of political freedom ends up in the nonpolitical problem of ethics, the problem of the chapter that follows.

THE ETHICAL NATURE OF FREEDOM

> "A book on employee counseling laws down as a rule of procedure, 'Remain impartial and never make moral judgments.' A psychoanalyst declares, 'A scientific psychology is absolutely free of moral valuation. For it, there is no good or evil, no moral or immoral.' " — SEBASTIAN DE GRAZIA, *Errors of Psychotherapy*, 1952

> "There is no truth; everything is permitted." — Secret motto of Syria's medieval "Order of Assassins"

The false antithesis of bread versus ethical values, with a feet-on-the-ground preference for the former, is often used as a debating point to justify police states that destroy ethical values but supposedly give bread. "But bread comes first," says the materialist; "when stomachs are full, and not until then, the values will follow after." Wrong! — true only if you are alone on a South Sea island, picking your "bread," your material sustenance, from trees. As soon as you are in society, where bread is achieved by the organized co-operation of many men, values come first. Organization implies the prior presence of values.

To organize society for economic production means to organize it according to some system or other, some credo, whether just or unjust, rational or irrational; and this means some kind of values. These values, according to their degree of justice and rationality, determine the economics and the material prosperity of their society. Not vice versa.

For example, why is the ordinary Soviet citizen so exceptionally miserable, so oppressed, so lacking in the material necessities which are a matter of course in other countries? Why will misery continue to remain basic to the Soviet system? Because this is the economic result of the lack of ethical values on which that particular society is organized. Organize a society on police-state values of terrorism and of privileged bureaucracy, and what else can you get?

You can only achieve economic gains by a credo that subordinates economic gains. Subordinates them to individual freedom. If you base society solely on the idea of economic gains, scrapping freedom and justice for the sake of the total tyranny needed to organize total planning, then you lose not only your freedom to your planners but also those economic gains for which you sacrificed freedom in the first place.

Totalitarianism is not the opposite of naturalistic relativism, as many liberals believe, but its consequence. Totalitarianism is not rule by law but dictatorship by Fuehrer whim, that most relative of all concepts. Being relativists themselves, many liberals call Hitler an "absolutist" in values because they do not care to admit he was produced by the same amoral scientific relativism that (on a far nobler plane) produced them. Let us hear Hitler's own words on the question of whether he regarded laws as relative or absolute. During the mass-killings of June, 1934, the Bavarian Minister of Justice became squeamish about so many shootings without trial. He protested to Hitler (feebly no doubt) against this violation of all established general laws of humanity. Hitler replied:

Now everything depends on my authority. The laws are valid only because they bear my name! . . . You and your legality. Don't forget that every revolution demands its sacrifices! Why, if one had to ask you lawyers beforehand for permission, then there would never have been a revolution in all the thousands of years of history. Revolutions are the great forward thrusts which create upheaval and force things forward. Many must break and bleed in the process! From the viewpoint of law every revolution is illegal, and you lawyers are only annoyed because you must learn new law when the old is overthrown![1]

[1] G. M. Gilbert, *The Psychology of Dictatorship* (New York, 1950), p. 76.

Whereas the traditional moralist stresses conscience, the arch-relativist Hitler denounced conscience as strongly as he denounced all universals of either human or divine law. Hermann Rauschning, the former Nazi President of Danzig, has recorded the following typical remarks of Hitler:

> We must regain our clear conscience as to ruthlessness. . . . The word "crime" comes from a world of the past. Conscience is a Jewish invention. It is a blemish like circumcision. Brutality is respected. . . . The people . . . want someone to frighten them and make them shudderingly submissive. . . . They need something that will give them a thrill of horror.

In 1904 Mussolini took the courses of Vilfredo Pareto at the University of Lausanne. Four years later, the future fascist, then still a Marxist, referred to Pareto's theory of morally-relative power politics by élites as "probably the most extraordinary conception of modern times." This does not mean that Pareto intended all the immoral consequences to which his theories were warped by his student. The distinction between intentions and outcomes is obvious. In any case, Mussolini saw fit to appoint his Lausanne professor of 1904 to the Senate of fascist Italy in 1923.

Lenin was just as outspokenly relativist and antilegalist as Hitler and Mussolini. In *Left-Wing Communism, An Infantile Disorder,* Lenin wrote:

> It is necessary to agree to any and every sacrifice. . . . To resort to all sorts of devices, maneuvers and illegal methods, to evasion and subterfuge. . . .[1]

In short, any means whatever to seize power; no restraint by any universals of ethics.

In the well-chosen words of Harry Gideonse:

> Freedom is *not the absence of restraint.* Historically, freedom emerges when internal checks can be substituted for external constraint. Conversely, freedom is endangered if a free society's shared values are no longer sufficiently vigorous to preserve the moral cohesion on which the discipline of free men rests.

The good liberals who help originate these codes of codelessness are too decent to practice the ultimate implications — the commu-

---

[1] New York: International Publishers, 1934, p. 38.

nazi implications — of what they preach. Still living on the past capital of the Western value code, the good liberals smuggle in the decent, democratic values, whose moral basis they undermine, by conveniently "discovering" for them a new pragmatic basis. Unfortunately the communazis, more logical and less decent than the liberals, feel no need to make this convenient discovery:

"Bad" people like Hitler and Goering simply carried out more or less consistently many of the ideas long held by respectable, "good" people. . . . How do "good" people deny morality? In many ways: "I believe in morals, but all morals are relative"; "I have my own private code"; "morals are entirely a matter of opinion"; "there are no absolutes in morals that can rationally be discovered." A Hitler or a Mussolini could accept every one of these statements.[1]

However, it would be much clearer terminology to say "universals" instead of "absolutes" as the tenable alternative to relativism. Nothing mortal is absolutely absolute. Universals are those rediscovered values, transcending national, class, and individual differences, which are relatively absolute.

Suppose it were some day proved — as today alleged but unproved — that these universals ("relative absolutes") of right and wrong are indeed mere bourgeois prejudices. Suppose it were proved that right and wrong do not exist. Our instinctive comment would be: so much the worse for right and wrong. But our more reflective comment would be: so much the worse for existence. For we would then learn soon enough, through bitter experience, that man can only maintain his individual and material existence through guiding it by the nonexistent: by the moral universals of the spirit. If to logic this sounds like paradox and untruth, then it is of such paradoxes that human truth is made.

One boast made of science by one kind of pragmatic liberal is that it is "ethically neutral." This is supposed to be science's greatest achievement. The supposition illustrates the value-denying, standard-destroying, and therefore freedom-destroying character of one kind of relativistic liberalism. (I am not attacking and never intend to attack liberalism in general.)

It is easy to figure out the political consequences if "scientific

---

[1] Oliver Martin, *Two Educators* (Hinsdale, Illinois, Regnery Pamphlet No. 29), April, 1948; pp. 6-7.

mind" means "ethical neutrality." According to one scientific, sophisticated, and "knowing" liberal, justice and liberty and ethics are mere symbols of "ego insecurity." According to another, they are just "fancy rationalizations" of economic self-interest; according to still another, of sex; or of inferiority complex. The explanations of what the values of civilization mask and rationalize, are varied and endless; the important thing in this "explaining" game is that the explanation must sound sordid enough to sap away the social effectiveness of the value or virtue in question.

Such political science involuntarily makes fascism and communism triumph by trampling down the moral will to resist it. By the rules of this game, you can talk about "power" and be scientific; but if you talk about "justice," you are sentimental. You can talk about "pressure groups" and "class interests" and be scientific; but if you talk about "freedom" and "ethical restraints," you are sentimental. You can talk about values and virtues as "tools" but never as "truths." In short: you can talk about "empiric facts" but never about ideal aspirations, even though the latter happen to be just as real a half of human nature.

Here is the appropriate comment on this ruinously dominant trend in our political science. Gertrude Himmelfarb:

> Science, we are often told, is willing to sacrifice all of the amenities of civilization — sentiment, style, and moral indignation — upon the altar of truth. Truth is indeed worthy of the greatest sacrifices; but it would be tragic were the sacrifice to be in vain, were it to prove that what is sacrificed is truth itself. Consider the dilemma of the political scientist who has engaged to analyze the most important phenomenon of our time, the concentration camp. Presumably, he would have to refrain from such obvious expressions of judgment as cruelty, inhumanity, barbarousness, savagery, horror, atrocity, ignominy, degradation. Yet not to use these words, or their moral equivalents, would be to ignore the most important facts in human history. To think of them in the judicial manner prescribed by political science is to think of them as the Nazis did.

II

The first function of the intellectual, as guardian of values, is moral and educational, not — except in consequence — political. This function is well described in a book by Eliseo Vivas, *The Moral Life and the Ethical Life:*

Let us reiterate that, as against belief in the primacy of the political, the truly humanist teacher — and properly viewed the teacher must share with the statesman, the priest, and the poet the ultimate responsibility for the success or failure of his people and culture — must conceive the fundamental problem today, yesterday, and always to be the need to stave off the snarling beasts of barbarism that are always and everywhere on the alert to get out of their inward cages into which culture drives them.[1]

It is heartening to see a somewhat similar conclusion reached by someone far to the "left" of Vivas in his attitude toward all established churches. The great Italian liberal and hero of the anti-Mussolini movement, Gaetano Salvemini, after years of stormiest political strife, reached a conclusion likewise subordinating politics to morals:

Our civilization will break down if the school fails to teach the incoming generation that there are some things that are not done.

The directly opposite educational view, which subordinates morality to politics and to alleged social progress, was best expressed by Lenin:

In our opinion morality is entirely subordinate to the interests of class war. Everything is moral which is necessary for the annihilation of the old exploiting social order. . . .

The fascist has the same anything-goes morality, substituting "national war" for "class war" in the Lenin quotation.

To the general laws of ethics, civilization subordinates the ego of any individual and the ego of Lenin's "class" or of the fascist's "nation." This view is permanently innate in the experience of man. But it must be newly learnt by every generation. Our generation learned it from the class wars of modern communism and the national wars of nazism. Thucydides learned the same lesson from the radical class wars of Corinth and Corcyra and the reactionary "patriotic" wars of Athens and Sparta. His comment five centuries before Christ:

Men too often, in their revenge, set the example of doing away with those general laws to which all alike can look for salvation in adversity.

_____
[1] Chicago: University of Chicago Press, 1950, p. 132.

Be not ungrateful to the achievements of scientific materialism and to the insights of many pragmatists. In practice you are living every day on the benefits of those achievements and those insights, even if you greet them with an affectation of pseudomedieval scorn. No church is going to rip out its telephones and electric lights because they are a product of scientific materialism. But though gratitude is overdue, yet enough is enough. Civilization depends today on conserving, against the nihilistic brand of scientific relativism, this Thucydides principle of a central common law. It alone protects all against the centrifugal special laws of class ego, nation ego, and individual ego.

Powerful psychological safeguards are needed to prop up this common law in a time of toppling values. But not all safeguards are compatible with the human dignity that alone justifies their use. The safeguard most compatible with human dignity is not external brute force but a deeply-entrenched inner check. About this check, there are two tenable views:

1. According to the humanistic non-supernatural view, this inner check comes from that solid universal ethical tradition which most great religions and philosophies share. Examples range from the lofty Hellenic Stoics to Harvard's Irving Babbitt.

2. According to the religious view, this inner check comes from God. God, in turn, is defined by several conflictingly different definitions. These range from anthropological concreteness to mathematical abstraction. Every one of these definitions is partly inadequate, and necessarily so, because formulated by mere humans, wading beyond their depth. If we could adequately define God, we would be gods ourselves, instead of mortals aspiring toward God.

Though both are equally within the fold of Western civilization, these two schools disagree as to the natural or supernatural origin of this ethical inner check. I am not minimizing nor evading the obvious importance of their disagreement. But at this moment of history, confronted by the anti-ethics of class egotism and national egotism, I prefer to see the upholders of universal ethics stressing the code they both agree on, instead of stressing their disagreement about the unknowable (natural or supernatural) origins of that code. By itself, the fact that the author is undecided between these two alternatives is not of the slightest interest to anybody else. But it is no merely private matter — it is an objective generalization — that today most of those who reject relativism and who return to values, are likewise undecided between these alternatives. Does not such a situation call for less hostility between related groups of value affirmers?

The most effective, most automatic way to enforce the ethical check is to formalize and institutionalize it, even at the painful but unavoidable price of sacrificing a certain amount of inspiration to institution. Some of the spirit must always be sacrificed to some of the letter of the law. The price must be paid. For society's sake. Whether grudgingly or with eager faith, you can never get around paying it — unless you take the anarchist position that civilization does not depend on organized society but can survive with no more framework than the natural goodness of man.

Because every human being is a cave man by nature, capable of every insanity and atrocity, you must prefer art and artifice, classicism and formalized social convention, to the cults of natural goodness, progressive education, and instinctive self-expression. For the same reason you must prefer the "conservatism" symbolized by the pruned and patterned gardens of Versailles to the "anarchism" symbolized by the romantic barbarous jungle. But if you can disprove this view of social stability, then you are entitled to be a philosophical anarchist. An idealistic pacifist anarchism (Thoreau, Kropotkin, Gandhi, George Orwell), rather than liberalism or socialism, would be the most logical and most attractive alternative to conservatism, in case the latter's pessimistic premises about human nature were proved wrong.

To make people live the ethical check instead of only theorizing it, the best sanction is the community's experience of having lived it for centuries, the feeling of it "always" being so and being there: just as "so" and just as "there" as the sky and earth that form the roof and stage of the innately ethical drama of man. Whether your source for your ethical code is natural or supernatural or that blurred borderline to which both science and religion tend, only this conservative experience of communal tradition will turn it from abstraction into a way of life.

Liberals favor universal suffrage horizontally in time. Conservatives favor it also vertically. If you have become convinced that freedom depends on the unbroken continuity of a communal ethical tradition, then you must give the vote also to your ancestors.

THE ANTIREVOLUTIONARY NATURE OF FREEDOM

"Jefferson believes in the perfectibility of man, the wisdom of mobs, and the moderation of Jacobins."

— GOUVERNEUR MORRIS

The success of parliamentary restraints in America, England, and sometimes Western Europe and their failure in the rest of the world suggest a lesson. The lesson is that parliamentary restraints only work when democracy has ceased to be revolutionary. They only work when it has become traditional, conservative, well-rooted. Therefore, American liberals, who demand that our democracy today must "defy all traditions" at home and outbid Russia in "leading the revolution sweeping Asia," are cutting off the limb on which they repose. The strength of that democratic limb is its deep roots below, its traditionalism, nurtured by a slow organic evolution. Democracy can no more be transplanted today by Jacobin methods than it could when the French Revolution was replacing the monarchist King Logs of Europe with the Robespierrian King Storks.

What actually keeps a free society free? Society is kept free by the traffic lights of law, not by the revolutionary lawlessness of well-meaning radicals and hasty innovators. In the complex structure of life today, revolution means not romantic barricades, as in a simpler age. It means the total economic and psychological disruption of the social mechanism, with disaster, starvation, and new tyranny as revolution's inevitable fruits.

In most liberal books and magazines, we hear America has "a great revolutionary tradition," to which we should "again" be "faithful." It is time to counterassert that this talk of America's "revolutionary tradition of '76" is mostly or partly a myth. This myth hampers and embarrasses our necessarily antirevolutionary foreign policy today. (Of course, "antirevolutionary" does not mean pro-reactionary but evolutionary; the alternative to revolution is not an equally extremist right-wing but peaceful reform.)

For the sake of accuracy, let us speak less of the so-called "American Revolution of 1776." Let us speak more of what ought to be called "the American Conservation of 1776." George Washington and most of his colleagues were great conservatives. They were conserving the traditional established rights of all free-born Englishmen and the by-then-traditional heritage of 1688. It is George III who was the revolutionist against the status quo. George III, this alien Hanover despot unsteeped in Britain's free past, was the real radical. He was upsetting the time-honored existing rights which Burke in England and Washington overseas were trying to conserve.

A new school of American historians should do research in such neglected conservative statesmen of our past as Rufus Choate, Gouverneur Morris, and John Randolph of Roanoke,[1] with their stress on minority rights, on decentralization, and on the Burkean view of freedom as an organic evolution within a closed value-framework. There has been too much stress on our revolutionary Tom Paine tradition and on the absolute dictatorship of majoritarianism. Majority rule, as thoughtful liberals like John Stuart Mill have recognized as much as any conservative, must sometimes be restricted (which is not the same thing as saying it must ever be destroyed). It must be restricted by such factors as reverence for tradition, rights of the individual, rights of economic and racial minorities, and the lasting value-framework of the West, which must not be wrecked by ephemeral and transient majorities. The failure of radical illusions about Russia should send Americans back to the great Conservation of Washington, Hamilton, Gouverneur Morris, and (except for his indefensible pro-slavery) Calhoun, not the shallow revolutionary slogans of Tom Paine, Patrick Henry, and Henry Wallace.

In the words of the poet Goethe, "Only law can give us liberty." In the words of the poet Baudelaire: "Je hais le mouvement qui

---

[1] Since these words were written, Professor Russell Kirk has published his brilliant research in conservative Americana — *Randolph of Roanoke* (Chicago: University of Chicago Press, 1951). See also his extraordinarily perceptive article on "Burke and the Principle of Order" in *Sewanee Review*, April, 1952.

déplace les lignes." Society depends on antirevolutionary legalities. They need to be widely accepted as objective, not as mere operational tools of power and self-interest. These unifying common traditions must be more than mere rationalizations of disunifying private greeds. Freedom must have roots deeper than the eighteenth century, though including that enlightened century. Freedom must have roots not restricted to such thin top-soil as utilitarianism and eighteenth-century "social contracts." Its roots must be more deeply anchored. They must anchor in the moral (originally religious) doctrine of the infinite preciousness of each individual soul.

Not revolution but "law can give us liberty." What revolution can give — temporarily, so long as the guillotine acts as bed-of-Procrustes — is equality. Equality is desirable. A lot of things on earth are desirable. But equality is not the same as freedom.

Some may prefer equality to freedom, in the context of a social misery that makes freedom seem meaningless. But they soon find out that an enforced equality, without free individualism to temper it, becomes an Orwellian nightmare version of the workers' paradise, in which "all are equal, but some are more equal than others."

THAT "MASS FERMENT":
DOES FREEDOM NEED A MORE REVOLUTIONARY
FOREIGN POLICY?

> "Those who have given themselves the most concern about the happiness of peoples have made their neighbors miserable."   — ANATOLE FRANCE

Not lack of social reform (which actually America is promoting by peaceful evolutionary measures in much of the world) — not lack of social reform but bloody conquest by the Red Army and by well-armed communist parties is what has spread communism over Eastern Europe and over Asia. The Czechoslovakia of 1948 had some of the most advanced social reforms in the world and lacked completely these bogeymen of liberalism, the "feudal reactionary landlords," on whom we are supposed to blame communism instead of on Stalin's and Mao's gunmen.

Every liberal who repeats the romantic myth of "revolutionary ferment" in Asia (rather than communist military conquest) must read — for example — the scholarly booklet by Paul Kattenburg, *A Central Javanese Village in 1950*.[1] It is vouched for by such Far East authorities as Professor Richard L. Walker of Yale University. This conscientious study of the *reality* of unstirring peasant traditionalism explodes the *myth* about "stirring peasant masses," a myth for which several unpeasant-like Asia experts would like to wreck our foreign policy.

The two leading upholders of the revolutionary myth are Aneurin Bevan in regard to Europe, William O. Douglas in regard to Asia. Both these honest anticommunists ignore the conservative, anti-revolutionary nature of liberty and would, so to speak, "ferment" their way to utopia. To illustrate their view and its opposite, let us quote a key passage from each of these men and then quote a rebuttal to it.

Recently Aneurin Bevan proclaimed at Jarrow:

> The dangers from Communism, if dangers there are, come not from military plans but from the failure to redress wrongs that exist in Western society. One of the reasons that the Tories can think only in terms of guns is because the only answer to Soviet Communism is an alteration of social practices and social principles they are reluctant to swallow.

Rebutted by Salvador de Madariaga, the Spanish anti-Franco political philosopher:

> Really, Mr. Bevan, do you believe that the only answer to Soviet Communism is an alteration of social practices and principles? Do you believe that there is one single country in Europe which went over to Communism because its social practices and principles were not good enough? Do you believe that had it not been for the ruthless intervention of the Red Army — actual or potential — a single European nation would have adopted a system that abolishes trade union freedom, the right to strike, freedom of press, party, religion, and association and which keeps its Opposition in concentration camps little better than ante-rooms for cemeteries?[2]

---

[1] Data Paper: Number 2, Southeast Asia Program, Department of Far Eastern Studies, Cornell University, June, 1951.

[2] From Madariaga, "Open Letter to Mr. Bevan," *World Liberalism*, London, Spring, 1952, p. 9.

Similarly Justice Douglas has written in *Strange Lands and Friendly People:*

America is fitted by tradition for directing and guiding revolutions. We won our freedom by revolution and set the example which today inspires the peasants of Asia. We cannot remake the world in our image, but we can help those who are seeking an escape from squalor to find alternatives to Communism. We cannot do it by talking democracy and peace. We can do it only by making our foreign policy understandable in terms of the aspirations of these people. Our foreign policy must be specifically related to the land problem. . . . If that were our announced policy, if that were the word that went out from all our embassies and legations, the masses of Asia would soon be on a basis of understanding with us. . . . It would mean that in every capital of Asia American sympathy and understanding would be behind the liberal, progressive groups, whose mission it is to break the hold of the feudal system. Groups who enjoyed the prestige of that kind of American support would be in a strong political position.

Rebutted by G. F. Hudson, Fellow of All Souls College, Oxford, and regular contributor to *The Economist,* London:

Such a program must be attractive at first sight to all men of good will; it seems to offer the prospect of accomplishing something intrinsically desirable and at the same time forestalling the Communists. Unfortunately, Justice Douglas fails to draw any line between that discreet exercise of influence behind the scenes which is proper to diplomacy, and public, demagogic, political activity. . . .

Such methods might be very effective in humiliating, weakening, and discrediting established governments that Justice Douglas did not regard as sufficiently progressive, but it is very unlikely that they would produce better and equally stable governments. . . . "Directing and guiding" revolutions is not so simple a matter as Justice Douglas supposes. American policy has no such instruments either for subversion or indirect rule as Moscow and Peking possess in the local Communist parties of Asian countries. Communists everywhere serve the international Communist power because of their Marxist-Leninist faith, but there are no organized parties in Asia that are pro-American in a corresponding sense. If American diplomats or visiting politicians were to try to go over the heads of existing governments and play popular politics on the Asian stage, this would only result in a disintegration of authority in which not they, but the Communists, would reap the advantage.

The lesson Justice Douglas draws from the Chinese disaster is that America ought never to support any government like the Kuomintang's. But, historically, it is *not* a fact that America consistently supported the Kuomintang. During the three crucial years 1944-46, the main aim of American policy was to compel Chiang Kai-shek to compromise with the Chinese Communists. . . . Those were the days when nearly all the experts in London and Washington were endlessly repeating the line that the men of Yenan were not "real" Communists, but just "agrarian reformers." This confidence trick was worked at the highest level; Stettinius has related in his book *Roosevelt and the Russians* how on one occasion the President read out to Gromyko "a wire from General Patrick Hurley in which Hurley had said that Molotov had told him that the Soviet Union was not interested in the Chinese Communists, that they were not really Communists anyway." Chiang, of course, knew better.

Realization of the antirevolutionary nature of freedom does not exclude revolution in all circumstances; it excludes it under normal circumstances. In the special circumstance of being ruled by a monster like Stalin-Hitler, revolution is the only way out from the intolerable. But a monster like Hitler or Stalin is rarer than Halley's comet and does not justify generalizing about revolution for societies not so uniquely terrorized and uprooted. Besides, it is not inside Russia that the Bevans and Douglases urge us to foster revolution but inside the countries of our allies. This is a perverse reversal; for if history does force us to use the distasteful method of inciting insurrection, then Russia is the place to use it in.

It is the Politburo, not our "feudal" allies, that threatens peace; among our allies, timely reform, not revolution, is called for.

Even the most anticommunist liberals and intellectuals are sometimes misdirected by the myth that freedom is served by always backing the more revolutionary side everywhere, "on principle," regardless of the special local context. This myth makes them the disruptive Katzenjammer Kids of world politics: harmless fun in a stabler context; a game of Russian roulette in the present context. The semi-Stalinization of many European and Asian intellectuals is really an unconscious process of cliché addiction; never has it been better analyzed than in these words of William Phillips:

"The current anti-Americanism is neither profound nor consistent. Why then should it have arisen? The causes are many and complex, but I can only touch on the primary ones here. Perhaps the most important factor is what might be called *the 'Stalinization' of European thinking and of much of our native liberalism,* by which I do not mean that all the intellectuals affected are Stalinized, but rather than Stalinism has managed to impose many of its assumptions and attitudes on them. The image of America as a political and cultural menace, here as well as abroad, is something that has been propagated by the incessant efforts of the Communists; and many of the Europeans who question this image do so only in terms of size — that is, they believe that America may be the lesser evil by contrast to Russia.

"But there is a larger sense in which Europe — and *'advanced' thinking throughout the world* — *has been Stalinized:* it has been infiltrated by the Marxist ideology of progress and socialism to the point where it is ready to accept as historically inevitable the doom of Western civilization and the messianic role of the proletariat in the creation of a new world. As a result, the 'progressive' mind here and abroad, confined in the past to liberal ideas and reforms, has acquired a new faith in the forces of revolution. And to contain the ambiguities of such a position there has arisen *a 'progressive' myth,* joining 19th-century liberalism with elements of the Communist philosophy, that has radically affected the thinking of many people who do not follow the Marxist line in every respect and in many cases even regard themselves as anti-Marxist. On the whole, identification in one way or another with this myth has come to be synonymous with enlightenment, with the triumph of humanism — with simple decency. That such a force as Stalinism has not only won a monopoly on socialism but is also the beneficiary of our zealous humanitarianism is a final irony.

"An essential feature of the 'progressive myth' is that it carries the determinism and libertarian spirit of the Marxist tradition without being directly committed, at least on the surface, to the specific theories of Marx and Lenin or to the distinct aims of Stalinism — at the same time that it does have *a soft spot for any movement that presents itself as 'revolutionary,'* especially if led by the Communists. This is why, it seems to me, most sympathizers with Stalinism both here and abroad connect themselves with the ideals of justice proclaimed by the Marxist system rather than with the totalitarian state in Russia.

"The question remains why the mythology of history and progress, that has grown up around the Communist movement and is so shrewdly exploited by it, should have become so potent just now, thirty-five years after the Russian Revolution. The chief reasons, I think, lie in the economic and physical exhaustion of Europe, and a *blundering American policy that permitted Russia* to become so powerful. Caught between its own moral defeatism and fear of the Red Army, the Continent has naturally been attracted to a revolutionary ideology that promises everything — peace, progress, economic improvement, Russian friendship, and above all a resurgence of national energies. And if the millions of Europeans who seem to be under the sway of Stalinism have not been affected by the terror of the Russian regime, it is because they are moved by a vision of an equalitarian and creative society, which they imagine the Communists will help them to achieve.

"Even non-Communists, who have only the vaguest idea of goals and policies, have dedicated themselves to being *revolutionary at all costs, competing with each other in their 'radicalism' and their opposition to 'reaction.'* "

II

Let us consider further how Western intellectuals compete with each other and with the communists to bait any kind of status quo. They compete (Judge Douglas, Bevan, the earlier Henry Wallace) to spearhead that "revolutionary fervor in Asia" which allegedly represents the Common Man. Meanwhile the Common Man continues fervently to flee from that "fervor" by the millions, always from North to South in Korea and from East to West in Europe. Not vice versa.

If you recall that China has had no feudalism since 200 B.C., you will not be impressed by tales of how an alleged communist "abolition of feudalism" won the love of this "revolutionary mass ferment." Undoubtedly such details as Russian aid, the captured Japanese arms, and the Russian "liberation" of industrial Manchuria at Yalta helped this mass to ferment a bit faster. Its fermentation was gently prodded by the officially-boasted execution of a million and a half Chinese "Common Men" as unfermenting slackers. Where "reactionary landlord feudalism" really did exist, and oppressively so, was not China but Japan. And there, without a single cheer from the American and European adorers of antifeudal ferment, landlord tyranny was abolished and the peasants endowed with land by the "reactionary American Military Government." Of course, this was under certain auspices that have meanwhile "faded away."

So much for American actions. In actions (economic aid to Japanese peasants) we obviously outdo the Communists in helping the masses. Promises of utopia are another matter. In promises the Communists will always outdo us. This is because we fortunately are partly inhibited by a bourgeois prejudice against lies. If we follow the super-progressive strategy of trying vainly to compete with the Communists in revolutionary rhetoric, they will not only unscrupulously outbid us. They will also scare us out of using (for fear of seeming unprogressive) the tremendous conservative appeal that tradition, custom, religion, and stability still have all over the globe. This conservative appeal becomes irresistible when accompanied by the higher living standards for the masses which American policy has already brought to Japan and Western Europe and would bring to a free Korea.

Under the agrarian law of October 1946, the American-directed government of Japan bought 27,000,000 plots of land and divided them on easy-payment terms among the poor tenant farmers. In 1946 these were tilling only 46 per cent of the land. By 1950 they tilled and privately owned 89 per cent; they were no longer feudal peasants but free men. This is perhaps the greatest and most beneficial agrarian advance in the history of Asia.

In contrast, the Chinese peasants have, in effect, lost their land completely to the small neo-feudal clique of the Chinese communist Quislings of Russian imperialism. These Chinese Quislings in 1950 got half their government revenue by collecting rice at bayonet point from their terrorized serfs and by openly threatening to execute the families of all who hid their rice crops. So far as there is any valid "mass revolution" in China today, it is neither the communists nor the Formosa government. It is the revolution represented by that majority of Chinese prisoners in Korea who prefer death to repatriation under Mao.

Earlier, it was represented by the two million anticommunist peasants who had flocked to the hills as guerillas before Mao had ruled the mainland even a year. Unfortunately these guerillas, left without American aid to equal Mao's Soviet aid, were subsequently mopped up in the greatest reign of terror in the history of Asia. They are now far fewer than that number; we must have no illusions and premature hopes on that score. Nevertheless, the anti-repatriation vote in Spring, 1952, by our Chinese prisoners — supposedly enthusiastic, undrafted "volunteers" — shows that the Red dictatorship is still opposed by most Chinese.

Before World War II, only 400,000 Japanese workers managed to belong to trade-unions. The capitalistic American Military Government arranged for seven million to belong and also brought them immense improvements in economic conditions and individual rights. Thus can American foreign policy improve life for the workers of Asia. It does so legally and peacefully, by evolution and never revolution. Meanwhile revolutionary communism enslaves the workers of Asia. It liquidates their free trade-unions. It decreases their real wages. It increases their working hours, as in the horrible stretch-out factory system introduced by Russia's Quislings in North Korea. Here death sentences are imposed on workers failing to produce the communist-prescribed quotas.

With the second largest army in the world, consisting of millions of troops, Red China cannot prevent constant guerilla revolts. In contrast, during the Korean War of 1950, a mere handful of unseasoned U.S. troops were left to rule all Japan, a nation of 83 million only recently at war with us. This suggests that revolution and communism, not "reactionary America," are hated by the supposedly revolutionary masses of Asia. But the communist neofeudal lords, despite the guerilla resistance to them by the Asian masses, can conquer them by military force so long as America parcels out less aid to Asian anticommunists than it lavished on Soviet Russia during World War II.

Despite all this, one typical liberal analysis concludes: "America is hated all over Asia because it is antirevolutionary." Yet it is usually not the starving and uneducated masses of Asia who hate America. It is the well-fed and half-educated classes who hate America. It is the uprooted semi-intellectuals. These parrot the half-baked Stalinoid clichés about the "starving masses," with whom they have scant contact and of whom they know little more than would some bumbling, patronizing American tourist.

These unstarving, un-mass-like *déracinés* of Asia have lost their ancient home culture. Yet they have been only half-Westernized, only on the surface. They feel at home in neither culture. That is why they welcome communism, first in China and now in India, and become its natural leaders, journalists, and politicians. Communism gives these homeless ones the chance to express their double resentment:

First, their resentment of the old, patriarchal, agricultural culture of their parents (whom they are encouraged to betray to the communist secret police);

Second, their resentment of the scars of humiliation suffered during their misleading contacts with the West.

From these superficial and humiliating contacts, they misunderstand the Western democracies. They see them only as an "exploiting capitalism" and as racial discrimination. They do not see them as the home of the greatest amount of tolerance and political and economic freedom ever achieved. Being only half-acquainted with the West, they are often not even aware that the West, and not Russia, has achieved the greatest social welfare for the workers. They are not aware that American racial discrimination, though inexcusable, is less than the discrimination between high-caste and low-caste Hindus and less than the Soviet genocide against its Crimean Tartars and its Baltic minorities. Such left-wing Asian intellectuals would never even have heard of the fact that New York, Massachusetts, and other states have FEPC laws and that Walter White recently commented that anti-Negro discrimination, though still nasty, is steadily and rapidly diminishing.

In Iran, according to foreign correspondent Ray Alan, the words "communist" and "intellectual" have become almost synonymous in practice. The same used to be true to some extent in China. But today Chinese intellectuals, unlike those of Iran, Syria, Indonesia, Egypt, or India, know at first hand the reality of life under a Red terror; it is the intellectuals outside, never inside, the communist empire whom communism attracts. In India not the poor but "the educated" — really meaning the rich and half-educated — are the communist sympathizers. A perusal of India's noncommunist but anti-American press reveals incredible ignorance of the social welfare, humanitarianism, and civil liberties of the West, plus an incredible suspiciousness of American motives in foreign policy, plus the old cracked record about daily lynchings and ubiquitous gangsters. This is an ignorance that Ambassador Bowles is ably rectifying in India. It is high time to rectify it, not only in India and China but in every part of Asia and Africa. Up to now, we have lost the propaganda battle to communism by default.

Not that America and its capitalists are free from crimes and blunders in foreign policy. But not *that* kind of blunder. For at least the first two years after World War II, while communism was expanding over Eastern Europe and Asia, the crime and blunder of America, including Wall Street America, was our smug, over-confident indifference to revolution. We were not counterrevolutionary and "imperialistic" *enough*. Not "capitalist plots" but dullness is the crime of the American business mind in foreign affairs. The crime has serious consequences: a lack of ideas, lack of imagination, lack of élan. This lack causes America's business-as-usual response to those who want passionate moral leadership. If the imaginative and exciting Marshall Plan is a capitalistic plot, as charged, then I wish my country would perpetrate more capitalistic plots. If the Atlantic Pact and the defense of bulwarks of collective security like Greece, Turkey, Formosa, and Indochina are adventurous Wall Street imperialism, then I wish there were still more Wall Street imperialism.

Whether we like it or not, history has cast America in the role of the great conserver, the key bulwark against Soviet world conquest. If our republic perishes, it will not be from international "meddling" and "adventurous" imperialism (which, as the Japanese farmers know, brings greater civil liberties and higher living standards). If we perish, it will be from pettiness, from some new retreat into isolationism, from unadventurous lack of vision, from failing to rise to the grandeur of our historic role.

III

Mr. Del Vayo mutters ominously in *The Nation* that our intervention for collective security in Korea uses U.N. "as an instrument of counterrevolution." Would that, from 1933 on, America had risen to its historic responsibility by a lot more "fomenting of counterrevolution" against Nazi and communist revolts wherever they occurred. This would have saved mankind from World War II and a possible World War III. Out of the French Revolution, Burke hammered home the lesson still valid today: no society with a stake in stability can afford to be indifferent to a fire in the house of its neighbors.

Freda Kirchwey, that brave and able editor, wrote in the "Peace With Russia" issue of *The Nation*:

We must accept revolution as the dominant, inescapable fact of our time. . . . We must become, and *quickly,* the new *sponsor of revolution,* helping the people of the world to win all that Communism promises or provides — plus liberty. . . . We must, if we are to seize a chance which may indeed be the last, rediscover our democratic beliefs, lost somewhere in the compromises of these years of shifting expediencies. . . . We ditch our professed principles, and along with them goes our security.[1]

These fine words illustrate perfectly the fallacy of trying to outrevolt the revolutionists. Her words sound as if they were written expressly to illustrate and justify the warning quoted earlier from William Phillips. Why this lemming-like compulsion of suicidal liberals to outrace each other in baiting any kind of traditional status quo? When Miss Kirchwey advises America to "sponsor revolution" ("and quickly"), she adds: "— plus liberty." To overlook this afterthought would be unfair; at least it differentiates her viewpoint emphatically from the communist viewpoint. Nevertheless, her "revolution plus liberty" contains an illogicality basic to this whole area of liberal thought. Logically her sentence should have ended "minus liberty," in view of the inherent antirevolutionary nature of freedom.

So much for the Douglas-Bevan-Kirchwey view that freedom

---

[1] *The Nation,* 85th Anniversary Issue, New York, Dec. 16, 1950. Italics mine.

depends on an alleged American mission, today allegedly betrayed, of being revolutionary abroad.

In a review of that fascinating book *White Collar* by C. Wright Mills, Granville Hicks — no longer a revolutionary and now one of America's keenest social thinkers — makes a moving and unanswerable appeal to precisely the type of leftist mentality analyzed above:

Mills's unimplemented revolutionary zeal involves him in some strange paradoxes. He finds himself, for instance, in the position of *deploring the prosperity* that the United States has enjoyed in greater degree than any other country: "People experiencing such a history of increasing and uninterrupted material contentment," he writes, "are not likely to develop economic resentments that would turn their political institutions into means of ideological conflict, or turn their minds into political forums." *What a catastrophe!*

What is radicalism today? To assume the radical air without answering that question is a form of irresponsibility, a *way of escape*. The question to be raised is whether *the radical stereotype* isn't preventing good men, Mills among them, from contributing as much as they are able to contribute to the understanding and control of social processes. The broad tendencies of our society are fairly clear and altogether terrifying. If someone has a practical plan by which the evils of a mass society can be abolished or avoided, let him, by all means, announce it. But in the absence of such a plan, hadn't we better *make the most* of the advantages, the adaptations, the resistances, the loopholes, that have been found to exist or can be discovered? Why not drop the radical pose and get down to work?

Or — to put it more impatiently (re-invoking the title of the favorite leftist "proletarian drama" by Odets in the 1930's) — isn't it about time to stop "waiting for Lefty"?

MONARCHY, FRIEND OF LIBERTY

"America rejoice! America rejoice! The Bourbons have returned to France." — GOUVERNEUR MORRIS, *a framer of the U. S. Constitution and leader of the American Conservation of 1776, commenting thus on the restoration of the French monarchy in 1815*

"I have always considered the Republic an ill-balanced form
of government, which always *promised* more but *gave* less liberty than the Constitutional Monarchy."
                              — ALEXIS DE TOCQUEVILLE, 1848

Many liberals of the Harry Hopkins vintage believe that America,
whose own republicanism is organic and traditional, must forcibly
.establish an untraditional and inorganic republicanism everywhere
in Europe and Asia. Like most Americans, such leaders believe
that parliamentary freedom flourishes better under republics than
under monarchies. This illusion made many Americans indifferent
to the forcible replacement, against the will of the inhabitants, of
the East European King Logs by the Soviet King Storks.

The only East European country today with parliamentary
liberties, is also the only one fortunate enough to retain its monarchy: Greece. Why "fortunate"? Not because monarchy is any
more "divine" than republicanism. The answer is: monarchy
(constitutional, not absolute) provides the stability and unity
that most European republics disastrously lack. No Balkan country
has ever scored particularly high on civil liberties and parliamentary
procedures. But the Balkan country that at least scores highest, is
also the one remaining Balkan monarchy. While this one Balkan
democracy is called a monarchy, all the Balkan states that today
officially call themselves "democracies" are terrorist dictatorships.
They are even worse than the imperfect monarchies that preceded
them.

The adjective "monarcho-fascist," that stereotyped linkage, is
to be expected in Stalinoid propaganda. For example, in the
mendacious guerilla propaganda against Greece. But that adjective
and that linkage are inexcusable in the mouth of American liberals.
In World War II, the *majority* of the anti-fascist coalition were
parliamentary monarchies. They included England, Norway, Denmark, Holland, Belgium, Yugoslavia. Also Italy — after it got
rid of its unparliamentary plebeian usurper. On the other hand, the
two worst despotisms, Nazi Germany and communist Russia, were
led by "men of the people." The most effective opposition to the
Nazi dictatorship came from the monarchists and aristocrats hanged
by Hitler in 1944.

A tolerant, constitutional monarchy under the anti-fascist Don

Juan is the only solution for Spain that can preserve freedom from communists as well as restore it from Franco. Neither of the other two alternatives, a republic or a continuance of Franco, can heal the wounds of the civil war, after the atrocities committed by both sides. Though suitable for countries with a stabler past, any republic in Spain is rootless, unhistorical, a prelude to new civil wars. And the Franco dictatorship is simply too oppressive toward personal liberties (even though less streamlined-totalitarian than old-hat, pre-fascist South American) and is tainted by its Axis origins.

When our crusading American neo-regicides cannot call a monarchy "fascist" — except in the dishonorable, opportunistic House of Savoy, that adjective is usually too crude to swallow — then they do the next best thing. They dismiss it as "corrupt." When speaking of monarchies, "feudal lords," and Chiang Kai-shek, they use the epithet "corrupt" with a puritanical fervor that sounds charming coming from the party of — Boss Hague, Tammany Hall, and the Kefauver revelations.

II

A republic is (in Freudian metaphors) the rebellious son unrestrained. Hence it is in most countries doomed: by an excess of violence and anarchy. A dictatorship (or absolute monarchy) is the tyrannic father unrestrained. Hence it is equally doomed: by an excess of resented authority. A constitutional parliamentary monarchy is a happy balance between father-image and son-image, between restrained legitimate authority and restrained lawful liberty.

Hence, limited monarchy and not republicanism or dictatorship is the normal framework for human politics. Monarchy, as Metternich would say, is the most "legitimate" form of Western government. Its overthrow in 1917-18 in central and Eastern Europe has helped cause the present world instabilities. Its retention has greatly facilitated peaceful social reform — whether socialist or capitalist — in the parliamentary monarchies of Scandinavia and England.

America is not really an exception. Fortunately our government is no Jacobin-style democracy, no majoritarian democracy of mobs.

It is a constitutional government of laws, enforced by the sub-limated monarchy of the father-image of the "nine old men." Yet it avoids the static and revolution-provoking authoritarianism of the rigid tsardoms of Europe by its flexibility, its constant adjustments to popular will, and its outlet of passions through the ballot. The American compromise between republican and monarchic virtues enables the son-image to achieve his necessary self-assertions peacefully and constructively.

Our schoolbooks may give the misleading impression that the American Revolution was against monarchy. Actually George Washington and the founding fathers had no quarrel with constitutional, lawful monarchy. They had served it loyally in the French and Indian War. Their quarrel was with the abuses of monarchy, not with the institution. They rightly rebelled against a tyranny, an unrepresentative dictatorship. They rightly rebelled against a monarchy that violated its own constitutional checks. Such a self-violated monarchy forgot the crucial principle of lawfulness that distinguishes monarchy from mere dictatorship: *Princeps ipse est incarnata lex* (Aquinas).

III

Their organic function justifies European monarchy and aristocracy, especially the British monarchy. At their best, they represent not divisive, short-run pressure groups; they represent society lastingly and as a whole. (When they fail to do so, they become quite properly discredited and overthrown.) Their function is a needed one, the function of unification, social cement, moderation, mediation. Instead of sneering at the valuable function of European constitutional monarchies and aristocracies as if they were mere snobbery and luxury, American liberals should try to insure that this same mediating, non-partisan, non-election-bound function is also achieved in our own country. In our case it can be, and has to be, achieved democratically and without hereditary aristocracies: by means of the Constitution and the Supreme Court.

Asked by President Teddy Roosevelt what was the justification of Austria's supposedly outdated and reactionary monarchy, the old Hapsburg emperor Francis Joseph replied, "to protect my people from their governments." Thus excesses of the various intolerant nationalities, excesses of various class groups and economic pressure groups of right or left, could be moderated by the throne. The Czechs, for example — who overthrew the Hapsburg *monarchy-of-mediation* only to get the Nazi and communist *dictatorships-of-persecution* — have learnt this lesson now; Benes on his deathbed learnt it; so have millions of living Europeans after Hitler and Stalin.

In America, anything approaching monarchy or hereditary power is out of the question, despite Hamilton's hopes. Here the same purpose is served by the Supreme Court, as guardian and interpreter of the Constitution, standing at least partly above parties, above the momentary excesses of heated elections, above momentary mob whims. "To protect my people from their governments": within such a framework, be it European monarchy or American Supreme Court and Constitution, the rivalry of the conservative and liberal halves of truth will mean not civil war or chaos, as in most of the rootless and traditionless democratic republics of Europe's continent, but gradual evolutionary progress, the synthesis of freedom and lawful order.

THE ARISTOCRATIC ORIGIN OF AMERICAN FREEDOM

The palaces of Thomas Jefferson and the founding fathers — examine them yourself any day at the Williamsburg restoration — hardly look like log cabins. Not even to the disciples of Turner. Let us have no Rousseauistic myths, no noble savages. American freedom, the Conservation of 1776, did not spring from the Wholesome Plebeian Poverty of any westward-facing man-with-the-hoe.

Whether for better or for worse, American freedom was founded in the Europe-styled, lackey-tended, varlet-scrubbed châteaux of noblemen like Jefferson. For he, too, was one of Hamilton's "well-born"; today our folksy-progressive prejudices would call them "un-American," "the idle rich," "effete easterners," and, worst of all, "lacking the common touch."

For the crucial first six decades, from the 1770's till the Jacksonian revolution that followed 1828, the American government was not only extremely conservative. It was a closed, hierarchical "government by gentlemen." Power alternated between two rival groups of almost equally conservative gentlemen: Hamilton's élite of northern merchants versus Jefferson's élite of intellectual lawyers and southern planters. Yet neither group neglected our Bill of Rights; they managed to increase, and not only preserve, the liberties bequeathed by our founders.

By 1828 the foundations of American liberty had already been laid, without benefit either of Turner's westward movement or of the A.D.A. The western log cabins and Jackson's proto-New-Deal did indeed contribute to American freedom by diffusing it: from aristocratic republic to — or, rather, toward — mass democracy. An exciting gain. But also a depressing potential danger to liberty; reread Ortega y Gasset on "the mass-man."

The concept of civil liberties is aristocratic. It bravely defies democratic majority rule. If you insist on civil liberties, and there are few things more worthy of insistence, then you must be prepared to say: "Even if a fairly elected, democratic majority of 99 per cent wants to lynch all Negroes, Jews, Catholics, labor leaders, or bankers, it is our moral and legal duty to resist the majority, though we die in the attempt." Guarding the Bill of Rights even against majorities and even *against the people's will,* the American Constitution performs an aristocratic function.

The familiar contribution to freedom made by the log cabin and by the human Grass Roots of the West was valuable and necessary. Yet secondary. It merely broadened the primary impulse of freedom bequeathed by the palaces of our aristocratic Conservers of 1776.

Today Americans will be better and not worse democrats if they reject not entirely our original aristocratic heritage and if they reflect occasionally upon the subtle disadvantages as well as the obvious advantages of majoritarianism. Democracy, yes. In Sandburg's phrase, "the people, yes." But not an egalitarianism in which "bricklayers lord it over architects."[1]

---

[1] Every variation on this theme is examined in one of the most challenging books of our era: Erik von Kuehnelt-Leddihn, *Liberty or Equality* (Caldwell, Idaho: Caxton Printers, 1952). For originality of approach to an old theme, it is equaled only by the very different and equally brilliant book by Eric Hoffer, *The True Believer* (New York: Harpers, 1951).

The inner aristocrat may be defined as the man who enforces his civilized standards from within, by cultural and ethical self-discipline. The inner plebeian, the mass-man, is he who only obeys standards physically forced upon him from without. To the plebeian, be he a millionaire or pauper, life is not a challenge to transcend himself and to carry a great heritage forward. It is a vast garbage pile in which he is ceaselessly rooting — like a wart-hog — for more swill. Economics, which Ruskin called "the gospel of Mammon," is the Good Tidings of the plebeian. It is this latter view of "life" that a great aristocratic artist meant when he said, "As for *living,* our servants can do that for us." The inner plebeian is ruled only by his snout. And therefore only by the knout. And therefore the mass-man is a totalitarian, tending toward a communazi dictatorship of lynch law, whereas to the inner aristocrat the civil liberties of his opponents are sacred, even against a mass majority of 99.9 per cent.

Because the American context is unique in all recorded history, aristocracy must take a unique form in America today. It must abandon the analogies with Old World class lines. I am prepared undemocratically to defend aristocratic class lines as performing necessary functions, beneficial to society as a whole, in certain European historical contexts of the past. But the American context is universal suffrage, fluid class lines, a "new" country without a Middle Ages, without hereditary nobility, and without any élite trained in *noblesse oblige,* as opposed to a plebeian money-bags "élite."

In this very exceptional, very American context, there is only one cure for the quantitative, antiqualitative vulgarism that endangers all democracy. The cure is not to retreat into un-American class lines in order to make *some* men aristocrats. The cure is to subordinate economics to cultural values and to subordinate external coercion to internal self-discipline, in order to make all men aristocrats.

Bait the Baiters

"Two men arrested for trying to buy gold from a supposed black-marketeer, who turned out to be a police inspector, have been released after proving that they too were police inspectors, masquerading as black-market operators."
— News item in *Edinburgh Evening Dispatch*

SNUB THE SNOBS

When in the 1930's and 1940's the literary and political stereotypes of Greenwich Village began to replace those of Main Street, it merely illustrated Talleyrand's observation after the failure of the French Revolution: "The more things change, the more they are the same." America is where intellectual movements are born after they die of senility in Europe. America's twentieth-century game of Babbitt-baiting is a stale rebirth of Europe's nineteenth-century game of flabbergasting the middleclass: *épater les bourgeois*. Historically this was a by-product of the romantic movement. It was reacting against the norms of classicism and traditionalism; it was provoked and *justified* by the dull freezing of these living norms into a lifeless neo-classicism.

The future? In politics and thought, the future will swing back to rediscovering the living norms of the American heritage and *this time* conserving them better. In the arts, the future will swing back to a lucid, intellectually responsible classicism.

Snub the snobs. Bait the baiters. Be the gadfly's gadfly. In art; in political thought. This is more than a whim. Historically the time is overdue for replacing *épater les bourgeois* by *épater les épatants*. Today much of the fresh and nonconformist thinking in the serious quarterlies is coming from various rival brands of the new conservatism. Nothing is deader than the type of The Old Revolutionary after 1815. Or after 1953.

222

The scene is 1815 (or the 1950's). Picture your Old Jacobin at his favorite bistro. Picture his folksy snorts of indignation against those restored Bourbon fripperies. Savor with him his touching beer-nostalgia for those "good old days" when mass-murder and the guillotine were still the chic accessories of Social Welfare. Join his little throng of open-mouthed village gapers, marveling toothily whenever he displays his Honorable Scars, won in many a forgotten "unforgettable stand" against those Witch-Hunters, those Medievalists, those Bigots who preferred tradition and social reconciliation to the Terror of Robespierre's original "people's democracy." If his ever smaller audience buys him ever bigger drinks, our Old Jacobin may consent to amuse them by standing on the table and quavering and creaking forth a few bars of *La Marseillaise* — until grandson comes back (from saying Mass, of course) to lead grandpa off to bed.

In poetry or art or politics, nothing is more arthritic than the mental handsprings of a left-over "trail blazer" from adolescent revolutions long outgrown. Behold the plucked and moulting mocking-bird of gardens gone weedy and gone Middletown.

STOP BAITING BUSINESS

"Be not puffed up for that thou art an intellectual."— From *Proverbs of Ptah-Hetep,* found on an Egyptian papyrus (now at the Louvre) of 2500 B.C.

I

Why cannot free spirits on both sides, as opposed to doctrinaires on both sides, pacify the war that splits American culture? The war between literary introverts and commercial extroverts. There are reasons why this debate must go on: economic tensions, psychological tensions, even physiological tensions (cerebrotonic versus endomorph). But why not transfer the debate to a more dignified and serious level than either business-baiting or New-Deal-baiting?

America stands at an historical crossroads uniquely opportune for such a reconciliation. This is not only because a common danger forces us to "hang together or hang separately." Even more, it is because certain disillusionments make reconciliation possible today. In the 1930's, certain illusions made it impossible. Today the two chief aspects of the intellectual's alienation are losing their glamor: "infantile leftism" in politics, avant-garde preciosity in literature. They no longer are the liberating influences they once may have been.

Reconciliation does not mean relativism in cultural values. It does not mean relaxing your serious literary and political standards. An hour of television is never to be equated with an hour of reading Yeats. Despite Bentham's misquoted remark, pushpins are not so profound a source of fun as Shakespeare. This obvious truth continues to be an obvious truth. But it need not continue to be a pretext for business-baiting.

Nor need you, if an intellectual, assume you have a patented monopoly on Shakespeare or Yeats. People who wear vests and even garters have also been taught how to read. On occasion they even have truer tastes than you do. Moreover, an unpretentious Babbitt Senior outlook, while culturally inferior to the genuine lover of art, is culturally superior to the affected "appreciator" of artiness.

Reconciliation with business does not mean overlooking our political and cultural disagreements with business. We are still not going to treat the very recent, late-nineteenth-century laissez-faire economics of Sumner and McKinley as the "old traditional" values of the American way of life. But these problems can be met if we disagree reasonably with business. Nothing is gained by unreasonably slandering it and diabolizing it, in old-style progressive fashion, as if it were a fascist conspiracy against civil liberties.

Typical of unreasonable business-baiting and Republican-baiting were Truman's election speeches,[1] applauded by many liberal intellectuals, during September-October 1948:

They don't want unity. They want . . . the kind of unity that benefits the National Association of Manufacturers, the private power lobbies,

---

[1] Still more shocking was Truman's fascist-baiting version of McCarthy's Red-baiting in the 1952 campaign. For example, on October 17 Truman wrongly implied the Republican candidate Eisenhower was "willing to accept the very practices that identified the [Nazi] 'master race'" (according to the New York *Times* interpretation of that debated accusation).

the real estate lobbies, and selfish interests. . . . Powerful forces, like
those that created European fascists, are working through the Republican party. . . .

The implication that Republican businessmen and "Wall Street"
are fascists is paralled by Senator McCarthy's cheap remark that
the Democrats are "the "Commiecratic party." Intellectuals and
businessmen alike ought to show a sincerer indignation about *both*
Truman's fascist-baiting of business in the above speech and Mc-
Carthy's indiscriminate Red-baiting of intellectuals. Both sides will
have to trust each other more, in the context of the world emergency.

II

There is much that capitalism has failed to achieve. I wish businessmen made more effort to criticize and reform its weaknesses. I
wish intellectuals made more effort to comprehend and preserve
its accomplishments. Intellectuals might note the philosophical
points made about capitalism by the British economist, George
Winder:

Capitalism's greatest achievement is that it has taken primitive, savage and uncultured man, and diverted his selfish energies from war,
plunder, and food-gathering into production and trade. The socialist,
looking at our tamed and comparatively law-abiding culture, takes the
great achievement of capitalism *for granted,* and concentrates only on
what it has *not* accomplished. He frequently compares capitalism with
the tooth-and-claw struggle in the jungle, without realizing that it is
precisely this form of struggle that capitalism, at least in times of peace,
has succeeded in repressing. He gives capitalism no credit for the great
moral advance it has achieved in persuading man to confine the pursuit
of his selfish interests within channels which serve mankind; he blames
it for the fact that selfishness still exists. He would eradicate the motive
of self-interest, and replace it by the desire to work for the general
good. But it is evident that, if new incentives are to replace the old
selfish motives, then man will respond to them only if his whole moral
nature is changed.
If the socialist revolution is to succeed, then it must be accompanied
by a moral revolution of the most complete and all-embracing kind.

But for the above moral revolution, you need not economic
materialism, whether Marxist or liberal, but ethical idealism. A

conservative (ethics-conserving) socialism — a "Christian socialism" — makes good sense (within limits).[1] Its ideals, even now,
temper America's mixed-economy, which fortunately is not pure
Adam Smith. Democratic capitalism likewise makes good sense, of
course. But Marxist-materialist socialism lacks the moral change
that must accompany an economic change away from profit selfishness. Therefore, Marxist-materialist socialism makes no sense as
a constructive movement, only as nihilism.

America-baiting Europeans, fed on old translations from outdated muckrakers, imagine that American capitalism is still in its
nineteenth-century robber-baron stage. They ignore or minimize
the social co-operativeness and social responsibility subsequently
shouldered by American capitalism.

It is true that many of the responsibilities and restraints were
shouldered by our capitalism involuntarily. Many resulted from
public pressure and from the indispensable counterweight of our
trade-unions. Other restraints were adopted voluntarily by our
capitalism as a result of education in economic statesmanship. "The
old concept that the owner has a right to use his property just the
way he pleases, has evolved into the belief that ownership carries
social obligations, and that a manager is a trustee not only for
the owner but for society as a whole." When recently the president of a great steel corporation said the first question for any decision is what steel capacity would best serve society rather than
private profit, "it was a quiet remark, and neither the speaker nor
his listeners paid any particular attention to it. That fact, perhaps,
is a measure of the social progress American capitalism has been
making."[2]

Whether involuntarily or voluntarily, what counts is that American capitalism recognizes unions and collective bargaining, sometimes even with a sliding scale of wages based on standard-of-
living changes. How widely is this known abroad? Unlike
European capitalism and unlike our own capitalism of the nineteenth century, our mass-production today depends on the principle of extremely high wages and low prices, so as to reach ever

[1] Within the "statist-margin" limits discussed on pages 260-261 and
264-268.
[2] From U.S.A.: The Permanent Revolution, edited by Fortune magazine
and Russell Davenport (New York: Prentice-Hall, 1951).

wider markets. Result: Europe's luxury products are America's mass-products.

Most European businessmen, especially in France, aim at small but expensive sales of goods, based on high prices and low wages. European intellectuals resent this in Europe. Rightly so. But they wrongly and ignorantly, though understandably, have the same resentment and distrust for American capitalism, whose practice is the exact opposite, with everything more imaginative and on a vaster scale of initiative and production than in the war-weakened capitalism of France.

Several years have passed since John Chamberlain got lambasted from all directions for imploring novelists to reconsider their stock portraits of evil American capitalists. His appeal showed a remarkable courage for which I admire him heartily (despite my very basic rejection of his overemphasis on economics). All the Babbitt Juniors turned on him furiously. They did him real injustice by pigeonholing him, in the minds of most readers, as an arch-philistine attacking the integrity of their craft.

This was not his purpose. In many ways it was they who were the philistines, because it was they who wrote with a stock stereotype: the businessman as Simon Legree. That my view of the Old Guard Republican businessman is less rosy by far than Mr. Chamberlain's is another matter. He was right in pleading for open-minded independence of observation instead of prejudiced stereotypes. And he was right in saying that stereotypes don't make good art.

The point is: portray people as they are, and not according to either dark or rosy stereotypes. This applies to businessmen and labor leaders alike. The Marxist outlook, indirectly adopted by so many modern naturalist novelists, is mechanical; it categorizes; it sees men as economic classes, not as individuals. To see humanity only as economic classes creates a fiction as lifeless and dull as the Nazi habit of seeing men in racial categories. As dull and as unfair. Escaping from classes and categories, whether Marxist, Nazi, or Hegelian, let us see all men, even businessmen, even trade-unionists, as individuals first of all.

I would be appalled to see novels or "schools" of thought devoted to nothing but capitalist propaganda. And this for the same reason I am appalled by "proletarian verse." But why should fear of being labeled a Babbitt by Babbitt Junior prevent American intellectuals from striking a fairer balance in portraying "the business crowd"? Aren't we all in the same shaky boat today? Not to mention the same uninhabitable planet.

STOP BAITING CATHOLICS:
PLEA BY A PROTESTANT

> Say, Daddy, won't you tell me of the terrible news I heard?
> I scarcely can believe it, each cold and cruel word.
> They say because I love the Lamb and Catholic doctrines share,
> I never can be President or hope to fill that chair.
> — *From "Why Can't I Fill That Chair?" a bar-room jingle of the 1890's*

Disagree with Catholics? As a Protestant: yes! Criticize Catholics whenever necessary and as strongly (no more, no less) as you would any other group? Yes, of course. Bait them? Go ahead and do so — it is becoming the popular Advanced pastime — but only if you have abandoned all sense of justice and proportion.

The Elders of Zion were used by Father Coughlin's *Social Justice* to frighten reactionaries. Purpose: to distract attention from the real menace. Namely Nazi Germany.

The Elders of the Vatican are being used by the *Nation* to frighten liberal intellectuals. Is this again distracting attention (doubtless unintentionally) from the real menace? Namely the Kremlin.

"But," protested one liberal writer, after reading my arguments against hiring communist professors, "are not Catholic professors incompetent to teach for the same reason? What about Paul Blanshard's book comparing the Vatican and Kremlin party lines? Does not this neat analogy hit the nail right on the head?"

It hits the nail right on the thumb. Papal infallibility, very rarely resorted to, applies only to dogmas proclaimed *ex cathedra* and only within the specialized field of faith and morals. Of these there have only been two since the infallibility decree of 1870. The Kremlin dogmas, constantly resorted to, must be considered infallible in every field of knowledge. This holds true from music to economics, from genetics to politics. A pickaxe in the skull reminded Trotsky of this in Mexico. The corpse of "deviationist" Juliet Poyntz, on that Soviet boat on the Hudson, reminded party heretics of this in New York. Leading Catholics like Maritain and Bernanos, respected by the Church in high diplomatic or literary roles, disagreed publicly with the earlier Pope's support of Franco, a subject on which no Pope would ever speak *ex cathedra*. Is there a single instance of a communist party member deviating unpunished from Stalin on Franco or similar great issues?

When Cardinal Spellman wrote a bad novel, the Catholic weekly *Commonweal* in his own diocese printed a review calling it a bad novel. The point is not that this weekly, like intellectual weeklies of any religion, has a much smaller circulation than its cruder coreligionists. The point is that such independence is inconceivable in any fraction of the communist press. Try to imagine the editor of *Pravda* failing to swoon with ecstasy for a novel by Molotov and then failing to join the icebears next morning.

From my civil-liberties outlook, my complete opposition to censorship by any clerical group is self-evident. For example, the obnoxious campaign against a film like *The Miracle*. But opposition to abuse of Catholic power or to abuse of Protestant power does not make me anti-Catholic or anti-Protestant; it makes me anti-abuse. It makes me distrust all unchecked power anywhere.

Commonweal and the *Catholic Worker* backed the famous gravediggers' strike. By so doing, they defied the strike-breaking efforts of their Cardinal. Yet they were still allowed, as a matter of course, to remain in the church as "good Catholics." Facts like these refute the Blanshard analogy between the church hierarchy and the Soviet hierarchy.

Some liberal circles act as if international Catholicism threatened liberal Protestantism today as much as does international Communism. As Stalin said to Churchill, "How many divisions has the Pope?" Has anyone noticed 225 poised divisions of — Swiss guards? If America should treat Catholicism and Communism as equally our enemies, then we would simply be handing France and Italy over to Stalin. Without the Catholic parties in those countries, the Communist party would win easily. *"Paris vaut une messe."*

This does not mean I am proposing the Machiavellian doctrine of "any means" to the end of stopping Communism. I oppose the Roman Catholic dictator Franco as much as any dictator of any other religion. But the Catholic parties in France and Italy, the MRP and the Christian Democrats, are valiantly democratic and anti-fascist. Their leaders, like De Gasperi, are heroes of the anti-fascist underground of World War II.

In the Italian elections of May, 1952, the Vatican and its press supported the anti-fascist De Gasperi and his Christian Democrats strongly against the neo-fascist parties and not merely against the Communists. The official Catholic trade-unions of Europe (the International Federation of Christian Trade Unions) have urged the removal of Franco. The Pope recently received Don Juan, the anti-Franco claimant to the Spanish crown, while refusing to negotiate a postwar concordat with Franco. Even within Spain, the bishop of Malaga and others are criticizing the regime.

These facts do not change the harm done today by the pro-Franco enthusiasm of so much "political Catholicism." They do not change the initial mistake of the Church in backing Franco in the Civil War instead of seeking a free central coalition to oppose communism and fascism equally in Spain. But what all these facts do show is that today, in those countries where conditions permit a center position, the Church backs the democratic and social-minded kind of Catholic party in preference to fascists and clerical fascists. This is true not only of Italy and France, where the democratic and Catholic De Gasperis are saving the centrist position from fascists and communists alike. It is also true of Holland, Belgium, Austria, and the West German Republic at Bonn, where the Catholic (Christian Democrat) Adenauer is defending democracy and his alliance with America against neo-Nazis and Communists alike.

Here is what an anticlerical liberal, thoroughly antiauthoritarian, thoroughly in favor of separation of church and state, writes about the folly of our trying to stop communism without Catholic aid:

Separation between church and state is a basic tenet of Liberalism. But today Catholicism is possibly the greatest force checking the spread of Communism in the Western world; of the sixty states whose representatives met in Paris [for the United Nations Assembly] at the beginning of November, 1951, thirty are inhabited mostly by Catholics, in another ten the Catholics form large and influential minorities. On the borders of the Communist empire, what holds Western Germans, Italians and Filipinos against Communism is . . . the Catholic Church.

Necessity dictates co-operation between the American nation and the Catholic and other churches. It will be of interest to see to what extent Americans can remain Liberals (Democrats) while compromising on the question of state-church relationship. Personally I believe that *no threat to liberty of conscience* is involved if the compromise is effected by people consciously aware of the necessity of preventing a religious organization from dictating a policy to the state. The present outcry would show that such awareness does exist in the United States.[1]

As a Protestant, I disagree with Catholicism on fundamentals. But the greatest fundamental of all is what all churches of the Christian-Judaic heritage have in common, in contrast with communist-Nazi diabolism. Against the latter, all the diverse servants of the universal civilized values must stand united to survive.

STOP BAITING ONLY YOUR OWN SIDE

"Exit, pursued by a bear."
— Stage direction in Shakespeare's *Winter's Tale*

Suppose you consider, as an important special case, only that form of alienation which is subjectively conditioned and for which objective social programs are merely a facesaving rationalization. These are the temperamental agin'-ers. Potentially they are one of the most artistically creative and socially effective fractions of mankind. Of such inner-directed alienation, roughly the same percentage occurs in any country. The same percentage in Russia as in the West. The difference is: what happens to them?

In Russia they either are under the sod, with lead in the back of the neck, or they are digging gold for sixteen hours a day in Kolyma. In either case, the world never hears them. The world never hears their potential great works of art or of social criticism. But in the West, this same minority of nonconformist introverts holds key posts in the artistic, journalistic, and academic world. Right now, they are helping to mold the fate of the world — today

---

[1] Max Salvadori, in *World Liberalism*, winter, 1951, p. 20.

as in the eighteenth-century salons — through their exciting intellectual contributions.

Whether these contributions are socially good or bad, cannot
be answered sweepingly either way. It depends on whether their
talented sensitivity has been canalized within or without the
Christian-Judaic ethical tradition. If they choose, they have the
opportunity for launching a nihilistic social criticism against all
their own institutions. Their equivalents in Russia have no such
opportunity.

In that sense — hardly the sense intended by Marx — capitalist
democracy does bear within itself the "seeds of its own doom."
By having a higher standard of living and of tolerance than any
communist country, our free system gives critics more leisure and
opportunity, more magazines to criticize in, more civil liberties to
protect their dissidence, and a larger audience to read it and act
upon it. As a result, *small* crimes in a prosperous, *free* capitalist
democracy receive vastly more criticism — and result in a greater
revolutionary resentment among "outside" listeners in China and
India — than *large* crimes in a poor, *unfree* Soviet dictatorship.
The execution of Willie McGee got front-page headlines in even
the most pro-American Paris press. The news of over ten million
slave laborers and thousands of official Soviet lynchings — news
fully confirmed in Paris by the Rousset trial on the very day of
McGee's execution — got a small back-page headline. Such news
is comparatively disregarded by European and Asian intellectuals.

Western intellectuals criticize mainly their own society, where
they can move about relatively freely and can speak up freely.
(Not always freely enough from our own civil-liberties standpoint
but relatively freely.) They criticize the Soviet world less, because
they cannot go to see with their own eyes the current purge of
Jews (as "cosmopolitans"). With their own eyes, they can see
inexcusable discrimination in any American railway car in the
South. Russia, with its big crimes, allows neither inspection nor
criticism from its allies. America, with its small crimes, allows
both. Try to imagine a Soviet purge or lynching being criticized
by a Bulgarian intellectual in the way America is criticized (with
absurd inaccuracy, as it happens) by Sartre's play, *The Respectful
Prostitute!*

Hostile criticism of America, being a source of self-correction and self-improvement, is to the interest of America. As such, it is eagerly welcomed by Americans who not merely defend its free speech but make Broadway hits out of anti-American caricatures like that Sartre play. But, though to the interest of America as anti-smugness insurance, is this propaganda barrage of America-baiting to the interests of France? Does it not endanger the lofty cause of peace by encouraging neutralism? Neutralism endangers peace because it gives Soviet Russia the impression that France and Italy are softened up and can, therefore, be invaded and occupied easily by the Red Army.

These "seeds of doom" are as inherent in our society as Marx said they were. But they inhere not in the many admitted faults in the West; ironically, they inhere in what is best in our democratic capitalism: its prosperity, its free atmosphere, its open com-munications, its responsiveness to public opinion — four qualities unthinkable under communism-fascism. A current illustration of this is the denunciation by almost every Western liberal of French mistreatment of her Tunisian Moslems. The protests of Tunisian nationalists are reprinted on the first page in every paper in the world, including the most conservative press. Their cousins, the Uzbek Moslems, came under Russian rule at the same time that North Africa fell under European influence. Russian education, first tsarist and then Soviet, did not teach its colonials the ideals of anticolonialism. Western education did.

Think of the political books read, as a matter of course, by African students in the Sorbonne, Hindu students in Oxford, Indonesian students in Holland. Unlike the glibly-damned "West-ern imperialists," Russian imperialism never taught its colonials the ideals of democracy, parliamentary opposition, and popular revolu-tion. Consider the case of the Cairo mob that recently lynched innocent British tourists. While tearing them to pieces, it shouted undigested democratic slogans that its leaders had read in British democratic literature — literature brought into Egypt by British capitalism.

Today the Uzbek Moslems are undergoing a terrifying repres-sion, thousands of times worse than Western rule of their Tunisian cousins. Today not one paper in the entire globe headlines the tyranny and purges in Uzbekistan. Why? Simply because no independent antigovernment Uzbek group is allowed to protest to U.N., send demands to the Kremlin, telegraph news releases to the Western press, or be interviewed by sympathetic Western liberals. For twenty years, Western imperialism has been damned more than Soviet imperialism, whether among Chinese or French or even American intellectuals, for one basic reason: Russia's Gandhis (or Neodestour leaders, or Robesons, or pacifists, or neutralists) are giving no interviews these days. They are every single one of them dead.

Two wrongs never make a right. The solution is not the reactionary one of ceasing to support the aspirations of, say, the Tunisians. They have every right to borrow — from their contact with an allegedly "exploiting" capitalism — those rebellious democratic ideals of the West which nobody teaches the Uzbeks. The solution is to continue to rectify the small crimes of the West. But the West must insist that, if U.N. is to investigate the oppression of the Tunisian Moslems, it investigate equally the state of civil liberties, free elections, and free trade-unions among their silenced Uzbek cousins. If that balanced attitude were adopted in every field, by all intellectuals whose function is social criticism, then their function would become a genuinely liberating one, opposing social injustice in all parts of the world and not merely in the freest and justest part. But in that happy event, they would have ceased to be freedom's inner "seeds of doom."

"THE EMPIRE"

"I've tried to make it clear to Winston — and the others — that while we are their allies and in it to victory by their side, they must never get the idea that we're in it to help them hang on to the *archaic, medieval Empire* ideas."
— F. D. ROOSEVELT to his son Elliott

Now that "Rudyards cease from kipling and the Haggards ride no more," it is time to do justice to a maligned past, to even the balance in the other direction, to bait not all empire-baiters but

the more facile kind. It is time to out-kiple any Kipling by a dirge
for a lost greatness, partly a reverent dirge, partly a grateful one,
most of all an ironic nostalgia.

Am asked: "Are you against imperialism in the Egyptian situation of 1952?" Oh yes, I am against imperialism there — against
the only imperialism I can observe in that "situation." Namely,
the imperialism of Egyptian aggressors against the prospering,[1]
pro-British peoples of the Sudan. If imperialism-baiting is *de
rigueur*, why not bait the Egyptian imperialism that is threatening
the Sudanese?

The much-maligned British imperialism was the new Roman
Empire, the cement holding together the entire globe. Its weakening meant not more freedom for the globe but less: conquest by
the Axis and then by the Cominform. Left to themselves, the un-
industrialized colonial peoples are a power vacuum. Today they
are frankly admitting there was more freedom and more humaneness when the vacuum was filled by the British imperialism of
Disraeli and Churchill than by the mass-murdering terror of Nazi,
Japanese, and Soviet conquerors. So, once before in history, did
lawless barbarians on the march destroy the lawful order and unity
of civilization by dissolving the Roman Empire.

Racial discrimination and economic exploitation are admittedly
execrable. Admittedly they have been committed by British and
American imperialism, acting not on principle but in defiance of
our principles. But these were steadily being abolished by the self-
corrective device inherent in Anglo-American imperialism: free
parliamentary criticism of our admitted abuses. This self-cor-
recting device, by which Anglo-American imperialism leads to
dominion status and eventual self-government, is completely lacking
in Soviet, Nazi, and Japanese imperialism. Their lack of the self-
corrective device, and the reign of terror innate in their system,
makes it unjust to equate their imperialism with our Western
imperialism or even to call both by the same name.

---

[1] For the greater medical, educational, and economic welfare and greater
freedom of the Sudan under England than under Egypt, see the article by
A. T. Steele in New York *Herald Tribune,* January 22, 1952, editorial page;
"Britain in the Sudan: Benevolent Administration Prepares Nation for Self-
Government and Self-Determination." Also his subsequent articles.

The British crown is an example of how much more is achieved by the dream-nexus of magic than by the cash-nexus of economics. Economically, politically, and legalistically, the function of the Crown is negligible. Psychologically, it is indispensable as the cementer of ethnic and cultural diversity. Churchill did not hesitate to use the unscientific, unprogressive word "magic" in his public statement of February 2, 1952: "The Crown has become the mysterious — indeed, I may say the magic — link, which unites our loosely-bound but strongly-interwoven Commonwealth of nations, states, and races."

In 1952 a Hindu with an anti-British past published a book dedicated "to the memory of the British Empire in India" which "made, shaped, and quickened" what was "good and living within us."[1] What had happened to cause this change? What made an independent, nonsycophantic, sensitive Hindu realize the greatness of British imperialism? Most dramatically, there were the 1947 partition riots. These killings could never have happened under British rule; they made even its most oppressive qualities seem like pinpricks. Less dramatic but equally undeniable is the fact that India today has more political prisoners in jail, more newspapers censored by the government, less civil liberties, and less economic prosperity than under the "Western exploiter" at his worst.

The cause of world freedom must be considered also, as well as the decline in Indian freedom and well-being. Has at least the cause of world democracy gained from Indian independence? The question is answered by citing the following fact: in World War II, two million British Hindu troops fought heroically — and as *volunteers* — on the side of world democracy against aggression. This will not be the case with any independent India in any World War III. Where, for example, are the two million Hindu volunteer troops today in Korea — or two thousand, or twenty of them — in the new stand of world democracy against aggression?

II

The old fashioned Lenin-Hobson view sees Western imperialism as mainly predatory and as leading to violent capitalist market

---

[1] Nirad Chandhuri, *Autobiography of an Unknown Indian* (New York: Macmillan, 1952).

rivalries and inevitable war. This oversimplified view has been refuted once and for all by the more sober and scholarly researches of men like Joseph Schumpeter and Herbert L. Feis. Before again baiting imperialism in standard liberal-Hobson fashion, take a look at Feis's book, *Europe, The World's Banker*.

Moreover, the *only* expanding imperialism today is the Moscow-Peiping communist empire; and its millions of new colonials are at last learning what real and not alleged "exploitation" means. All the "capitalist imperialists" today are rapidly contracting — a euphemism for "clearing out." What little aptitude England's former colonials have for self-government, they owe to imperialism in large part. Imperialism gave them more educational and economic progress and more training in public affairs than they ever had received under their native potentates. Instead of rioting against the British imperialists, the Iranians (or Egyptians, etc.) should riot for reservoirs of clean water, for the borrowing of D.D.T. from the Wall Street warmonger, and for the return of the British oil companies who paid their Iranian employees higher wages, far higher, than did any of their own fellow-countrymen — plus respecting (lest I seem to overstress material advantages) their human rights better.

The historian D. W. Brogan is no Tory Blimp nor imperialist but a democratic liberal. He now has joined the increasing number of scholars who debunk the notion that colonies get nothing except exploitation from Europe. He points out that British imperialism has brought vast gains in self-rule, education, sanitation, industry, and just administration to its empire — above all India, "the most important imperial experiment in modern history."[1]

For the peoples of Africa and Asia, British imperialism sometimes did include crass economic exploitation as well as economic development (though more of the latter). But this was only the short-run aspect of British imperialism. Its long-run aspect, its most important effect, was not reaction or oppression or prejudice or exploitation but the replacement of frightfully oppressive tribal tyrannies, especially in Africa, with the British rule of law and humanity. Consider only what the introduction of English com-

---

[1] Brogan, *The Price of Revolution* (New York, 1952).

mon law means to people whose only courtroom has been the whims and torture systems of the local Caligula. Today in Asia and in darkest central Africa, tribal chieftains, wearing the same British wig and gown as their colleagues in London, are administering British freedom and British laws to countrymen who would still be slaves of blood sacrifices and caste systems, had imperialism not painted their part of the map pink.

And when British imperialism was (in effect) hounded out by the Boer anti-imperialists, was this exactly a gain for the Brotherhood of Man and the Children of Starvation? Is there anybody in the shamefully-oppressed nonwhite majority of South Africa who does not prefer the Exploiting Englishman back instead? Just ask them.

The British common law is unexcelled as freedom's most fertile soil. It is a law for which the British paid by centuries of "sweat and tears," ever since "castra" became "chester." They paid for it at Hastings and Runnymede, at Naseby and Waterloo and Dunkirk. I say such a precious heritage of centuries as the British common law was cheaply and quickly and easily bought for the price of a mere stamp tax or a tea tax, a throat-clearing arrogance here or a trivial snub there. America's gratitude for the priceless gift of this heritage was — the Boston Tea Party; and Africa and Asia show a similar "gratitude" in their behavior today. For the price of some admittedly annoying tea tax, America has permanently its version of the British Bill of Rights. Indians and Africans have their versions of it. Still other versions of British law and British liberty thrive in Australia and Canada and wherever communism's enslaved third of the globe has not replaced the free fourth of the Commonwealth.

III

What about Egyptian claims to illegal unilateral control of the European-built Suez Canal, a claim that violates the existing bilateral agreements? What about the unilateral abrogation of British oil rights in Iran in 1951 (in violation of international arbitration and international law) by a premier who got his job because his agitation helped cause the assassination of his more moderate predecessor?

These events must be judged in the context of world freedom, desperately resisting communism. Seen in a vacuum, there are many arguments against these remnants of what looks like an exploiting imperialism (an exploitation without which there would never have been any canal or any oil industry, both built entirely by European vision, European techniques, and European money). But see it not in vacuum but in perspective: the survival of world freedom against ruthless and expanding communism has a higher priority than the triumph of local freedom (actually not freedom but nationalism) over some last, unruthless remnant of a contracting imperialism. The need of world freedom for oil and for strategic waterways takes precedence over chauvinistic local needs. The freedom of Egypt and Iran themselves depends on whether world freedom, their only protector, can resist Soviet world conquest.

Were I an Egyptian or an Iranian, I would say: the freedom of my native land (Egypt, Iran) depends on whether the British have the courage to refuse to surrender freedom's Suez; and this in turn depends on whether America and those Egyptians who know their self-interest have the sense to back England to the hilt. Fantastic folly: that our myth about the supposed meaningfulness of colonial "mass ferment," plus our unjustified Western guilt complex about imperialism, should prevent us from fully backing Churchill's reasonable stand at Suez. Allied naval security, of which we are part, depends on this canal, as it does on Gibraltar and Malta, to *prevent war* by restraining Soviet aggression.

Those who by accident control indispensable resources of nature — Iran only one of many — must in a world emergency sacrifice the local part to the world whole. Such resources must be at the disposal of the entire free, noncommunist world. They must not be merely at the disposal of some local gang of hinterland-braggadocios, who use the accidental strategicality of their cabbage patch to blackmail loans out of us by threatening to shoot themselves (in other words, by threatening to call in Russia). Resources like Iranian oil and the Suez Canal will simply have to be put out of the reach of local blackmailers and local suiciders and placed by U.N. under a democratic international committee for the good of all.

It is impertinent for local despots, more oppressive and "exploiting" to their own people than were the ousted British companies, to prate of "freedom from imperialism" and "awakening nationalism." Their spade is a spade; it must be denied its fancy name of "freedom"; it must be called by its rightful name of blackmail. Yet the blackmail succeeds with much of our liberal opinion, which is afraid to condemn anyone who claims, no matter how preposterously, to be victimized by capitalism or imperialism.

A parallel: Hitler at first paralyzed any Western response to his criminal violations of Versailles by playing upon the guilt complexes of decent men about the undoubted past injustices of some aspects of Versailles; local despots in Africa and Asia paralyze any Western response to their irresponsible killings, riotings, and expropriations by playing upon the guilt complexes of decent men about the undoubted past injustices of some aspects of imperialism.

The postwar Indonesian riots massacred in cold blood a vastly larger number of helpless Dutch families than the total number of Indonesians plus Hindus killed by European punitive actions over half a century. But no outcry over these brutal killings of Europeans appeared in the liberal weeklies that helped build up our Western guilt complex about colonials. Neither European imperialism nor colonial revolt but brutality is the enemy here. Needed is a more genuinely liberal sympathy for all victims of European or colonial brutality, equally and regardless of race.

"Millions for defense but not one cent for" — blackmail. I wish America had provided not blackmail but the proverbial marines to stand beside our British allies in Suez today; and in the past to nip Hitler's violations in the bud the instant he remilitarized the Rhineland in 1936; and in the future wherever else our survival against communism requires it, from French Indochina to the Elbe.

IV

"The Empire" (the phrase can mean only one empire), was it a military convenience or a Disraelian political flamboyance or a grubbing economic greed? It was all these things.

But only secondarily. Primarily and beyond all that, the two words "British Empire" meant: a sense of responsibility towards history. To serve your servants; to rule by self-restraint of rule. It was, for example, the proconsular responsibility that a certain thing should not happen, an evil thing that did happen *after* the Empire's end: the mutual butchery of a half million Hindus and Moslems . . . burnt alive in their own homes . . . women and children. Would or could this dark deed have happened under the "foreign imperialists"?

Think of those deaths by fire, concretely and one by one, if you still cheer India's "liberation" — in an un-Romed world, cracking apart at the seams, divvied among barbarians to whom compassion and proconsular moral responsibility are a sign of weakness.[1] Think of these deaths if today you still dare gloat over the decline of what was a blessing to lovers of peace, a blessing to the great and suffering peoples of India, a blessing to all mankind except to those kindly-strong, responsibility-burdened, overburdened islanders who manned it: "The Empire."

STOP BAITING INTELLECTUALS

> "If a poet asked the state for permission to keep a few bourgeois in his stable, everybody would be amazed. But if a bourgeois asked for some roast poet, it would be considered perfectly natural."   — BAUDELAIRE

> "You have business managers. But we have an Orpheus. Unless you also get the immortal soul of a musician, as a governor to rule you, we have put you everlastingly in the wrong."   — VACHEL LINDSAY, 1922

And having stopped baiting businessmen, stop baiting intellectuals. Bad enough that in the past the businessman found professors and literati absent-minded, gaga, or sexually immoral. Today a fourth quality is added. If he is unable to prove them absent-minded, gaga, or immoral, he can always call them "Reds."

---

[1] For the communazi view that compassion, tolerance, and morality are signs of weakness, read the official proclamation of the People's Commissar for Justice in *Izvestia*, No. 37, Feb. 12, 1936: "In the opinion of liberals and opportunists of all kinds — the stronger a country is, the more lenient it can be to its opponents. . . . No, and again no! The stronger the country is, the mightier it is . . . the more justified are we in taking stern measures against those who disturb our socialist construction."

There is an important need for keeping real communists out of our universities, where — as party-disciplined haters of the search for truth — they don't belong. This important need is not helped but discredited when outsiders organize patriotic posses against intellectuals. This kind of thing for a while demoralized the University of California. There the thoroughly anticommunist majority of the faculty, which had voted overwhelmingly against employing communists, was harassed by outside demagogues and unqualified politicians.

The faculty themselves, through committees studying the problem conscientiously, must enforce their own standards, keeping out communists because no communist can meet academic standards of integrity. But there must be no spy system inside the classroom, no system of informers gabbing and blabbing their endless loose rumors of what Professor X supposedly remarked to student Y. This can be as demoralizing as the outside politicians. The American intellectual is simultaneously menaced by the fellow-traveler infiltrations on one front and by such patrioteers on the other front.

Here is another objection to the outside harassers, the yellow journalists and loud sensationalists. Are they not likely to trap the innocent — those ornery enough (would there were more) to talk back on Loyalty Day — and let the guileful and guilty escape? Unlike a serious academic committee, most outside harassers have never in their life studied the problem of communism and the still subtler problem of differentiating between wily fellow-travelers and honest independent radicals. Often the demagogues and harassers don't even know what a communist is. Often they use the word "communist" improperly against intellectuals in general. They do so partly out of a boorish and indiscriminate distrust of all those strange objects known as ideas. Their distrust has nothing to do with "bolshevism." That word they wrongly use as synonymous with social reform and with the fight for civil liberties instead of properly using it as synonymous with Russia's class-line despotism and with her communist suppression of civil liberties.

Often this political distrust of the free mind has nothing to do with any kind of politics. Though sublimated into politics, its root may be physiology and psychology: the endless vendetta of the cerebrotonic introvert versus the extrovert alliance of the endo-morph and the mesomorph. Is not the folksy baiting of literati, as absent-minded, gaga, immoral, or Red, the eternal inferiority-complex-plus-superiority-complex of the Sancho Panzas toward the Don Quixotes?

Some degree of neutralism and of distrust of American Marshall Plan motives is endemic among most liberal intellectuals of Europe and Asia. More surprising: it is also endemic among many American intellectuals. Though they have lost most of their illusions about Russia by now, their first instinctive impulse still is to "bait" their business community, not their Reds. This is because their shortsighted business community grants no status nor self-respect to any nonutilitarian intellect and has scant sympathy for their literary and ethical ideals. Here is the result partly (though only partly) owing to such business-community shortsightedness: "normally" all free intellectuals of the West should rally ardently against the Communist threats to freedom; but abnormally — that is to say, in reality — their rally is lukewarm; their heart just isn't in it.

For the reasons shown at length in Eric Hoffer's book, *The True Believer,* a society which alienates its intellectuals cannot long survive. This holds true no matter how few, helpless, weak, un-influential, and unread they seem to be. From their group and only from their group — the disaffected intellectuals — come the leaders who will win over the masses in some future revolution during some future weak moment (a depression, a lost war) in the status quo. One of the first aspects to examine in any society is whether it has achieved the conservative function of rooting or rerooting its men-of-ideas. Can our industrial society (business plus labor) still give the American or West European intellectual a status inside of the status quo?

Status means a lot more than merely material gain. That would be bribery, prostitution; any intellectual who can be bought ceases to be one. Status means dignity: the acceptance of free, non-utilitarian intellect by the business community. It means acceptance of that bulwark of the Christian-Hellenic heritage: the priority of beauty-seeking and truth-seeking over utility-seeking and over the merely practical, technological, and manipulative aspects of intellect. In short, it means acceptance of the human soul by a seemingly soulless materialism. The mutual baiting of the business world and the intellectual world will have to stop on both sides, or it will stop on neither. Be this an appeal for reconciliation, for old honor, for the West.

Which Kind of Conservatism?

"Democracy is the worst form of government, except all those other forms that have been tried from time to time."
— WINSTON CHURCHILL

"To affirm, as has been done, the indispensable union of moral and economic powers is equivalent to proclaiming, not the submission of the former to the latter, but on the contrary, the hegemony of the moral forces over the economic. . . . *The economic forces must not determine the moral forces,* as happens, for example, when relationships are established between liberty — which is moral life — and certain economic systems, or between liberalism and Manchestrian [capitalist laissez-faire] free competition." — BENEDETTO CROCE, *monarchist, conservative, and anti-fascist, in 1941*

THE NEW CONSERVATISM

"Back out of all this now too much for us . . .
Here are your waters and your watering place.
Drink and be whole again beyond confusion."
— ROBERT FROST

Though diverse subjects have been treated in these pages, their unity is basic because it reflects two underlying themes. The one unifying theme has been negative, the other positive. Negative theme: to examine the ethical, artistic, and political dangers of the new philistinism. Positive: a humanistic conservatism to meet the danger in these three fields.

At its best, the new conservatism may be defined as the rediscovery of values. This is what makes conservatism so fresh and exciting today, unlike the earlier Colonel Blimp, as cartooned by Low. A generation of pompous, Laski-indoctrinated leftists has intervened, a generation of Comrade Blimps, to whom conservatism is a subversive Dirty Word[1] from the wrong side of the intellectual

---

[1] In July, 1950, the *Evening Chronicle* of Newcastle, England, reported that a man was brought before a court charged with creating a public disturbance. One witness accused him with: "He was using abusive and *obscene* language, calling people Conservatives and all that."

railroad tracks. No wonder the British Labor Government was so philistine and boring: on European unity uncreative and without Churchillian vision, in economics more skilled at afflicting the comfortable than comforting the afflicted. Conservatism is the rediscovery of tradition, the daring search for that lost Grail, the value code of Western man.

Society is in a bad way when too many people reject every ancient value in ethics and politics and art because thereby they can show off better at cocktail parties. Civilization is an infinitely fragile bundle of accumulated habits and restraints. The necessary conservative function of any generation is not just to enjoy itself but to pass on this bundle in good condition to the next generation.

Radicalism and revolt are just as valuable as conservatism so long as they really do correct social defects. But not when their insurgency accentuates, instead of corrects, social defects. In the past, when society had too much *laissez faire,* the thunder from the left was a valuable corrective to social defects. Today, when the world is afflicted by too much statism, the left accentuates, rather than corrects, social defects. Because society has changed. Today Bohemia and Left Bank and Left Wing, all the dully "daring" defiance of bourgeois conventions, have become the rheumatic jitterbugging of aging *enfants terribles.*

In the Victorian and Coolidgean ages, civilization was stuffy and stodgy, conservatism at its worst. It was dull to have only law and tradition; it was healthy and useful for obscure and surrealist poems and paintings to stir up placid reality with a nightmare art. It was healthy and useful to have the young rebel poke dull old civilization in its stuffed shirt; the *enfant terrible* served a real purpose.

Today the whole world is *terrible.* The whole world has become a surrealist painting. What was shocking in early surrealist painting was: legs and arms strewn about, buildings torn open. This contrasted with an unstrewn and untorn Victorian and Coolidgean reality. Today, however, reality is strewn all over the place. To us who were soldiers in Italy, strewn limbs and buildings became the norm. If the Babbitt is he who kowtows to fashionable conventions, then it is the wilfully obscure poet and the surrealist artist and the *enfant terrible* Greenwich Village genius who is the philistine; *he* is accentuating society's defects. The traditional moralist, the conservative in politics and in poetry, is correcting the defects. When reality is itself a nightmare, then an art which is lucid and calm and ennobling — an eighteenth-century neo-classical art — is more helpful, more original, and more exciting.

For a generation brought up not under Queen Victoria but under Princess Rita Hayworth, with not Bishop Wilberforce but Dr. Kinsey as Father Confessor, for such a generation Flaming Youth is not exciting but a bore. The only way to shock your reader in a modern non-Victorian novel — if that's what you want to do — would be to use the word "limbs" instead of "legs." That would shock them more than all the boring four-letter words of our war novelists.

But an affectation of archiepiscopal reactionary stodginess would be just as tiresome as the present rebel stodginess. In both art and politics one pendulum extreme is as bad as the other. Why have any affectations, either reactionary or revolutionary? Why not be yourself? Integrity may be the dullest platitude in the preaching of old Polonius, but integrity is the two-plus-two that does make four. A reverence for integrity, not because it's fashionable but because it's true, such a reverence would work a moral revolution deeper and more helpful than all the shallow artistic and political and economic revolts of our panting apostles of progress. It would be a moral revolution against that inner smirk which prefers cleverness to love and prefers statistics to wisdom.

AN UNPOLITICAL START FOR AN AMERICAN CONSERVATISM

"In 14 million homes equipped with radios, *no* magazines are read; families with television sets read fewer magazines than those who do not have them; half the adults in America *never* buy books." — GILBERT SELDES in *The Great Audience*

"To the editor: I am 100 per cent in favor of the curtailment of library service. There are too many interests in the world of entertainment today for people to bother chiefly with books. Especially in this new era of television, who finds much time to read anything but a newspaper? Don't get me wrong. I don't condemn literature entirely. But there is such a thing as over-reading." — Letter in the *Philadelphia Inquirer,* May 21, 1952

"To make a prairie, it takes a clover and one bee, —
And revery.
The revery alone will do
If bees are few."   — EMILY DICKINSON

Unlike the ancient conservatism of Great Britain, the young American conservatism is still primarily a cultural, ethical, and educational movement, not primarily political.

The proper start for a new American conservatism, aiming not at success but at truth, not at activism but at long-range education, is in the world of literature, the arts and sciences, intellectual history, the universities, the humanities. Starting there and slowly osmosing into more "practical" spheres of American life, such a movement will eventually affect politics and economics by raising in both parties the *level of insight* into historical and ethical processes. By being more contemplative than activist, by asking all those basic questions the activists ignore rather than by too glibly answering them, a conservative return to values will transform politics and economics indirectly. If instead it tries to start by being directly and actively political and economic, it will at best fail and transform nothing at all. At worst it will lend itself to unscrupulous material exploitation. The thoughtfulness here recommended to new conservatives is not a flight from practical action but an inner prelude to practical action. The most successful political conservatism in history, the Tory party of Disraeli and Churchill, derived to a surprising extent from sources that were almost entirely literary, like Coleridge.

Our civilization is very old, very broad; we Americans are only a very young, very small part of it. Its essentials, its truth and its beauty, together with a deep understanding of human nature, are transmitted more through the humanities than through that up-to-date journalism of the academic world, the courses in current politics, economics, and other uselessly "useful" techniques. Not that the latter are unworthy — call them the Good Housekeeping of American education — but they happen not to be the main value transmitters and insight transmitters. Values and insights are transmitted by saturating yourself in the Elizabethan and Greek plays, the Aeneid and the Song of Roland, the poetry of Dante and Hölderlin, the psychological insight of Augustine, Pascal and the nineteenth-century Russian novelists.

The American conservative can transform his country more by teaching these value transmitters, and by raising their status above the media of mass-entertainment in public esteem, than by any directly political action. (It should be evident that courses in practical technical training and in the humanities can both be happily combined, wherever economic need so dictates.)

Saturation in the value transmitters of literature is an intimately personal part of every free citizen's growth. It is achieved not by streamlined public lectures on Great Books Predigested but by lonely reverie. It is aided not at all by our mechanized and progressive "teaching aids," replete with loud-speakers, with tape-recorders, and even with thinking-brain machines for grading multiple-choice questions. There is no substitute for the traditional, even sentimental Abraham Lincoln picture of the young boy brooding alone by candlelight over the dog-eared open book. Only such daily individual reverie can think through — to its future implications — every exciting idea of the past. This does more than inane loyalty oaths and patriotic propaganda to prevent two kinds of disloyalty:

1. The constant unconscious echoing of fellow-traveler clichés in intellectual circles.

2. On a more frivolous plane, the daily cultural betrayal of our past in the mass-entertainment — the Don't Think Clubs — of the air waves and the celluloid.

Neither form of value betrayal can be compromised with even slightly. It is not enough to apologize, "I only tune in on the better programs." It is true that already today a television set can serve what its ads call "your beautiful American way of life." But only when chopped up into firewood and blazing merrily.

The new conservatism — meaning: a fresh and creative traditionalism — never admires the past passively in sterile escapism. It must daily and actively re-experience, as if for the first time, the aspirations of the past — and then fulfil them in the future.

Here is another unpolitical, cultural field in which the conserva-

tive is more valuable than if he takes sides in mere party politics —
the need for "liberal intellectuals" to re-assess their cult of progressive education; no sweeping indictment but an honest weighing
of pros and cons. The value-conserver criticizes the progressive
program of books like *The New Leaven* (by the founder of the
Progressive Education Association) not for the anti-freedom mob
reasons of the disgraceful Pasadena incident but because progressivism does not really lead to the freedom it rightly seeks. At best
it leads to shallowness and "Whiggery," the glib two-dimensionality
of herd animals, never tragic, always well "adjusted." At worst it
leads to the tyranny of blueprinters and total planners over the
stubborn human spark that resists becoming a wholesome and happy
robot. The "liberal intellectual" reader rightly accepts the familiar
positive achievements of progressive education in furthering self-
expression. I wish he would also accept this admonition by Professor J. Glenn Gray against imposing social engineering on the
unmechanized and unsocial inwardness of man:

The modernist educator . . . has too often conceived the personality of students as utterly plastic, for educational engineering to make
of them what it will. Given time and the application of the newest
methods, he has believed all problems are solvable, everyone is "ad-
justable," all tastes can be socialized. Planning is all. Such a faith,
implicit on nearly every page of *The New Leaven* and other progressiv-
ist writings, seems naive in underestimating the recalcitrance, the com-
plexities, and the unpredictable creativity of human nature. It is also
dangerous. For it does not allow the *deeper* reaches of personality to
evolve of themselves, in solitude and silence. The faith in total rationality, in "human engineering," leads to the manipulation of persons in
total disregard for the element of sanctity essential to the full human
being. Although the visions of George Orwell in *Nineteen Eighty-Four*
seem a little fantastic, we may yet one day need to be saved from facile,
transparent individuals for whom the world is nothing but surface. . . .
   To live together co-operatively and sympathetically! Who can deny
in today's world the nobility of this aim? But the process of social
adjustment and socialization of taste can hardly put one on the high
road to free individuality. Nor can adjustment and socialization com-
pensate for the sterner demands of mastering subject matter and the
slowly acquired discipline necessary to achieve distinction in any
sphere. It is not surprising that progressive schools are accused of creating, in someone's phrase, "thousands of individualists all exactly
alike."

TAKE CONSERVATISM AWAY FROM THE CONSERVATIVES

"Allow me to furnish the interior of my head as I please,
and I shall put up with a hat like everybody else's."
— HENRI BERGSON

In the 1930's Edmund Wilson, agonizing over the contrast between radical ideals and Soviet realities, implored intellectuals to "take communism away from the communists." And, indeed, one of the finest achievements of the New Deal era, now drawing to a close, is that it achieved many humanitarian ideals of the so-called left without the murderous police-state practices of the far left. In the 1950's, to reverse the slogan of the 1930's, our more responsible leaders ought to take anticommunism away from the anticommunists. And to take conservatism away from the wrong — the solely economics-minded — conservatives. It will be as important to keep the present era of *pause* under humane conservatives as it was to keep the past era of *change* out of the hands of the leftist version of terrorists and thought controllers.

Youth has been called too wonderful a thing to waste on the young. Conservatism, which ought to mean the freshness and zest of rediscovery, is too wonderful to waste on the old-in-spirit.

Diction is revealing. He who says "goodbye now," instead of "goodbye," is also likely to be he who, when declining a cigarette, uses the verb "use": "No thanks, I don't use them"; and there you have the personality that wishes Taft had got the nomination in 1948 or 1952. Exception: if this personality happens also to be a YMCA secretary with rimless octagonal spectacles, then he'll timidly prefer a Truman, strictly for Uplift reasons — the reason he prefers a plain-spoken jug of milk to liqueurs with insinuating accents. Bourbon drinkers — a Truman, a regular feller — are still not beyond the pale of Wholesomeness for milk-drinkers. But cocktail drinkers — a Governor Dewey, say, or the folklore concept of New York city slickers — are definitely out; that's only one step from a demitasse, the next thing to a demimonde.

The typical Taft worshiper is not a plutocrat. Instead, some of our richest plutocrats are more likely to be do-gooder angels to a fellow-traveler magazine or to some bogus, trashy, and fashionable art gallery. The Taft worshiper is not plutocratic, but would-be plutocratic. He is that kind of American failure known as "a success in life." He is that suburban commuter who swore by the stock market until October, 1929, who on his Long Island expresses read the New York *Sun* before it failed, and who sympathized with "America First" before it dissolved. Everything he touches fails or dissolves. For his is the Midas touch in reverse; even such true gold nuggets as the Constitution, free enterprise, and patriotism change into baser metals at his touch.

A conservative sympathizes with aristocracy, never plutocracy. *"Ich dien'."* Aristocracy serves; plutocracy grasps. The distinction has been basic to freedom ever since Plato's *Republic* defined at length the distinction between aristocracy and oligarchy. The aristocratic spirit sustaining our democracy is whatever conserves not real-estate values but real values, not gold standards but cultural standards.

The Eisenhower case — the case for defending his great NATO achievement against isolationism and Asia-firstism on the right and against appeasement on the left — is so familiar by now that it needs no repetition here. The real question — for which not 1952 but 1956 and 1960 will be decisive — is whether the case for the Republican party is as excellent as the case for Eisenhower. The Republicans must still choose — have not yet chosen with finality — between evolving Eisenhowerwards (less isolationist than Taft in foreign policy and less statist than the New Deal at home) and evolving Taftwards. Their final choice has not yet been made, despite their sane 1952 nomination; for this nomination reflected not a final change of heart but merely a desire for office.

The Republican party of the future will either be (as in the nursery rhyme) "very, very good or horrid." It will either be much better or much worse than the so-so Democratic party, which is likely to remain in between these extremes in 1956 and 1960. Of long-run interest is not the untypical melodrama of 1952 but whether by 1960 the Republicans will have become the liberators or the neo-isolationist annihilators of the rest of mankind.

There is no American conservative party — in the sense that

Churchill is conservative. The Republicans are Manchester liberals, the New Dealers are Social Democrats.

From the standpoint of a nonpartisan conservative, equally detached from both parties, the long-run historical alternatives are:

1. Let the Republicans evolve a real aristocracy, with real patrician virtues, including that sense of magnanimity, responsibility, and international vision which Eisenhower, Cabot Lodge, Jr., and the Vandenberg school might give them and which the semi-isolationist xenophobes cannot give.

2. Acceptable alternative: if our men "in trade" and their Taftian Old Guard are simply unable to evolve a mature and ennobling vision of humanity and a patrician, Hamiltonian restraint and responsibility, then let us under the Democrats continue to grope toward the Jeffersonian ideals in America's fruitful democratic experiment.

"My medieval knees lack health unless they bend" — but not before an élite of mere money and mere physical power, without adequate restraints or codes. Without the *savoir vivre* that the Renaissance called "virtù" and that America calls "style." Without the ripeness needed to relax the countinghouse into the drawing room instead of merely into the parlor. And with oceanless, isolationist resentment of what Europe can teach them.

One basic contradiction in the election campaign of 1952 was this: esthetically (if prosaic politics may be so considered) and in temperament and background, Stevenson has more in common than Eisenhower with those aristocratic, "eastern-internationalist" Republicans (the Lodges, the Saltonstalls) who had originally nominated Eisenhower. Mr. Adlai Stevenson, America's most civilized candidate since Hughes in 1916, has more in common with that special kind of Republican than he or they have with either of the two unaristocratic, west-of-center rivals: the folksy Truman Democrats and the commercial Taft Republicans. In regard to this civilized, anti-shopkeeper, and social-reform wing of the Republicans, the New Deal Democrats are the imitative me-too-ers (since that wing goes back to Teddy Roosevelt and 1912) rather than the other way around; but try explaining *that* either to the Old Guard wing of Republicans or to the New Dealers!

Taft is wiser and more attractive and less important than the movement behind him, which will continue as a major force despite its defeat at the Republican convention of 1952. Taft's high I.Q., his stubborn outspokenness, his brilliant record as head of his class in law school, are one thing. Another thing are the Babbitt Seniors and Jefferson Sellecks whose imagined self-interest sums up the Republican Old Guard. These are not the great world-minded statesmen of capitalism (who prefer a Vandenberg or Eisenhower). Rather, they typify the narrower variety of businessman described in 1912 by Charles Francis Adams, brother of Henry Adams and former president of Union Pacific:

Indeed, as I approach the end, I am more than a little puzzled to account for the instances I have seen of business success — money-getting. It comes from a rather low instinct . . . rarely met with in combination with the finer or more interesting traits of character. I have known, and known tolerably well, a good many "successful" men — "big" financially — men famous during the last half-century; and a less interesting crowd I do not care to encounter. Not one that I have ever known would I care to meet again, either in this world or the next; nor is one of them associated in my mind with the idea of humor, thought, or refinement. A set of mere money-getters and traders, they were essentially unattractive and uninteresting . . . a coarse, realistic, bargaining crowd.

No, the McKinley-style pseudo élite of Taft Republicanism — the Old Guard — can hardly be called aristocratic or conservative. It has more nouveau-riche cash than *noblesse oblige*. It links individuals by the cash-nexus: inadequate, disenchanting, a nexus psychologically unsatisfying. A genuine, organic, society-binding conservatism links individuals by shared passions, not by cash alone. It links them by lofty aspirations, ripened by common experiences, by a long history of shared grandeurs and miseries. Savior of the West against Hitler, and Cassandra against communism, the truly conservative and aristocratic Churchill drew on such passions and aspirations to bind British society together during the Battle of Britain.

The "Old" Guard élite is not exactly "old" either, in the sense that oldness means mellowness and traditions. It has no traditional roots deeper than the Gilded Age that followed the Civil War, the get-rich-quick age of robber barons. The Jeffersonian philosophers of the Democratic party can at least go further back than that in their roots. This partly atones for their inacceptable limitations: their top-of-the-brain shallowness when confronted by the profounder terror and beauty of history; their overoptimistic, eighteenth-century notions of inevitable progress.

Conservative political theory is almost never developed by the rich (or by their sycophants). If sensitive, the rich intellectual is likely to become super-"progressive" to salve his conscience. (Frederick Vanderbilt Field, the communist millionaire, is only the most extreme of countless familiar examples.) If insensitive, the rich man is likely to espouse a politics that puts preservation of his private profits before preservation of traditional institutions and ethics; and this, being merely a decadent version of Adam Smith's more high-minded economic liberalism, is not conservatism either.

Perhaps conservatism is a luxury so expensive humanly that it can only be afforded by the poor. Conservative, classical, and aristocratic in his tastes and standards (his motto: "not innovating wilfulness but reverence for the archetype"), Herman Melville wrote in 1849:

The class of wealthy people are in the aggregate such a mob of gilded dunces, that not to be wealthy carries with it a certain distinction and *nobility*.

BRITISH VERSUS AMERICAN CONSERVATISM

As meat requires salt but never much salt, so democratic capitalism, to be rooted solidly in the entire nation, requires occasional doses of Disraeli's "Tory socialism."[1] This was a lesson that both Churchills never forgot and that Baldwin, Chamberlain, and most American Republican "conservatives" never learnt. Disraeli:

Instead of falling under . . . the thraldom of capital — under those who, while they boast of their intelligence, are more proud of their

[1] For the American general reader, the best available presentation of British conservatism is the anthology, *The Conservative Tradition* (London: Nicholas Kaye, 1950). Brilliantly edited by Professor R. J. White of Cambridge University and with the passages from Burke and Disraeli particularly well selected, this instructive anthology deserves — has not yet found — an American publisher and a wider American audience.

wealth — if we must find a *new* force to maintain the *ancient* throne and monarchy of England, I, for one, hope that we may find that novel power in the invigorating energies of an educated and enfranchised people.

The British Conservative party temporarily lost its soul when that great conservative might-have-been, Winston's father Lord Randolph Churchill, resigned from Salisbury's Tory cabinet on December 22, 1886. His advice to continue the Disraeli tradition of allying aristocrats and industrial workers within the ancient framework of throne and altar was fatally ignored by Salisbury and later by the big-business governments of Baldwin and Neville Chamberlain. It took Lord Randolph's son Winston to revitalize the British conservative tradition. Churchill's democratic record of humane labor and housing laws, blindly ignored by his American Republican admirers, proves that his conservatism is not limited to property but serves the organic unity of all classes. At the same time, his warnings against hasty nationalization of steel and against the dangerous police-system needed to enforce the excessive statism of the Laborites, differentiate his viewpoint from the Labor party and raise the unending, perhaps unsolvable issue of liberty versus security. His spirit, the spirit of freedom-loving Tory democracy, was earlier proclaimed by that nineteenth-century parliamentarian, Richard Oastler:

A Tory is one who, believing that the institutions of this country are calculated, as they were indeed, to secure the prosperity and happiness of every class of society, wishes to maintain them in their original beauty, simplicity and integrity. He is tenacious of the rights of all, but *most* of the poor and needy, because they require the shelter of the constitution and the laws more than the other classes. A Tory is the staunch friend of Order for the sake of Liberty.

In this spirit, Disraeli "dished the Whigs" by extending the right to vote to the working classes in 1867, after the Whig reform bill of 1832 was turning England into a narrow capitalist oligarchy by giving the suffrage to the richer middle classes. In this spirit, Disraeli's farsighted labor laws of 1875-1878, against the opposition of Gladstone's laissez-faire Liberal party, made possible an effective use of the right to strike and picket, codified minimum-wage laws, and became a charter of trade-union liberties for the rest of the century, so that a Labor member of Parliament, Alexander Macdonald, was able to say:

> The Conservative party have done more for the working classes in five years than the Liberals have done in fifty.

After 1906, too much of this tradition was abandoned by the Conservative party, first to the reforming Liberals of 1906-1914 and then to the statist and class-war Labor party. This departure from conservative principles and from Shaftesbury, Coleridge, Disraeli, and Randolph Churchill was the party's greatest single mistake. This accounted for its long eclipse (as it did for the American Republican eclipse of 1933-52). But at the same time, the worst enemy of the freedom and economic security of the industrial worker is a bureaucracy that creates a slave state in the name of his economic security. Of this the Soviet Union is a fantastically extreme example. But the statism of even the well-meaning, sincerely democratic Labor party and the more radical wing of our milder Fair Deal, was refuted in advance by the last sentence of the following conservative credo of Lord Hugh Cecil. It occurs in his prophetic book *Conservatism;* written in 1912, it is full of warnings to both laissez-faire Republicans and statist New Dealers in the 1950's:

> Conservative social reform need not proceed on purely individualist lines. There is no antithesis between Conservatism and Socialism. . . . The point which principally distinguishes their attitude . . . is a rigorous adherence to justice. It is in insisting that injustice [bad means to good ends] shall not stain national help to the afflicted that Conservatism finds in respect to social reform its peculiar and distinctive task. . . .
> The State as a trustee acting for others may, and indeed must, prefer the good of the community to the good of any individual or minority. . . . Quite recently measures have been taken to protect miners, although adult men, from what are thought to be excessive hours of labour, and to require, in respect to certain sweated trades, that the wages paid should be subject to the control of a wages board. . . . These reasons seem sound. . . . [But] it may often happen that, by combination or otherwise, workmen may find their own way out of an inequality in bargaining, and may be able to do *without* the help of the State. It is far better if such a way can be found, because the State in the end depends on the vigour of the character of the individuals which make it up. . . . A trade union is in the workmen's

own control and is a flexible organisation which can be adapted from time to time as need requires. The State is controlled by a complexity of forces certainly not identical with the desires of a workman in a particular trade. And *the State is a clumsy, rigid instrument,* difficult to handle and operating heavily and unexpectedly. It might easily have happened that workmen would have found themselves in a position unpleasantly approximating to *State slavery,* governed at every turn by bureaucratic regulations and, worst of all, enervated by having all the conditions of their industry ordered for them and nothing left to their own initiative and resolution.

In conclusion, here are four debatable questions for the American reader:

1. Is any universally valid definition of conservatism possible? (For example, Prince Metternich wrote in 1847 to Premier Guizot: "The Conservative principles are applicable to the most diverse situations; their worship is not enclosed within narrow bounds; they are enemies of anarchy, moral and material. . . . I made myself a conservative socialist.") Or is this not too abstract and doctrinaire, too French and un-Burkean an approach? Are there many different conservatisms, each defined separately according to local time and country?

2. How and why does British conservatism differ so deeply from what is loosely and popularly called "conservatism" in America? Is not the laissez-faire capitalism and ca'canny commercial outlook of Senator Taft and Old Guard Republicans better characterized as Whiggism, or even as Jacobinism and (economic) anarchism, than as Toryism? Is theirs not the program of Gladstone's Liberal party? — but without his freshness, humaneness, and generosity of soul; for what was fresh and inspiring in nineteenth-century Liberalism becomes petrified when parroted across the Atlantic in a new, more complex situation a century later.

3. Is or is not British conservatism, owing to the heritage of 1688, Burke's sympathy with the American Revolution, Shaftesbury's and Disraeli's "Tory socialism" and humanitarian sympathies, and Winston Churchill's anti-Nazi heroism, *inherently* more enlightened than American conservatism?

4. To what extent is British conservatism merely a rationalization of vested material interests (such as empire, landed gentry, established church, etc.)? And if, like most of its rival *isms,* it

partly is a rationalization, does this necessarily invalidate what contemporary Americans can learn from its leadership, its accumulated historical experience, and its social and psychological insights?

OUR JACOBINS *ENDIMANCHÉS*

In America a fascinating confusion has resulted from the fact that journalists unhistorically apply the term "conservative" to the laissez-faire economics which our Old Guard Republicans and N.A.M. have indirectly derived from Gladstonian liberalism and French Jacobinism. Wherever the armies of the anti-conservative French Revolution went, one of their first thoughts was to abolish the allegedly "outworn" guilds and establish laissez faire. This was their means of establishing the middle class in power. It was one of their means, more effective than their guillotine, of overcoming the anti-bourgeois workers, artistocrats, peasants, and kings, with their system of the just price, medieval guilds, or modern trade-unions.

The liberation of capitalist energies and the strict legal ban on trade-unions was one of the few consistent aspects of the French Revolution, from Jacobins and Girondists through the Directorate. Every one knows the guillotine devoured aristocrats, espousing monarchy, and priests, espousing ultramontanism. It is often forgotten today that the Jacobin guillotine of Robespierre and the rest was likewise devouring countless workingmen espousing trade-unions. (Cf. the researches of Professor R. R. Palmer of Princeton on Jacobin laissez-faire capitalism and Jacobin execution of worker representatives.) Taft is Robespierre *endimanché*. Our Old Guard (or right-wing) Jacobins are a French Revolution gone respectable and kid-glove after becoming a well-fed top dog instead of the lean, sans-culotte underdog of 1789.

Neither then nor today has the middle-class businessman succeeded in convincing either workers, farmers, priests, or aristocrats of the mystical, self-regulating perfection of laissez faire. Laissez faire has had to give way to social reform and to restraints on an anarchic capitalism whenever workers and aristocrats have joined forces. Examples are the "Tory socialism" of Disraeli, the antifascist democratic Conservatism of Churchill, certain phases of the mellow Hapsburg monarchy, and the New Deal of that fabulous character straight from Disraeli's *Coningsby*: the aristocratic Squire of Hyde Park. Far from being Marxist or revolutionary or leftist or a monopoly of liberals, a compassionate and humane approach to economic suffering is the logical outgrowth of the oldest Christian, Jewish, and Hellenic ethics. This holds true from the reforms of the democratic aristocrat, Pericles, in free Athens right through the encyclical *De Rerum Novarum* of Pope Leo XIII on working conditions in 1891 and through such Protestant theologians as Reinhold Niebuhr.

This is not a criticism of the middle class as a whole, nor an admission that human beings should be thought of as classes rather than individuals, nor a sop to the too easy Bohemian pose of safely "defying" your middle class while owing almost everything to it. Rather, this is a criticism of the unrepresentative, extremist elements of the commercial interests in Europe and America. Those elements represent merely a bourgeois version of "the dictatorship of the proletariat"; both versions are rejected by the majority of so-called bourgeois and so-called proletarians, who rightly see the folly of a dictatorship by either "class." To stress the superiority or inferiority of either class, as if it were a Chosen People of history, is exactly as silly as racism, which also has its gaga "historic destinies."

Social reforms do indeed become perniciously Marxoid, collectivist, totalitarian, or in the narrow sense "socialist," when they threaten civil liberties and a responsible individualism with the curse of statism. With its dangerous and economically needless nationalizing of steel, the British Labor Government crossed the statist margin. That margin may be defined as the line beyond which liberty is sacrificed to security. The Fair Deal and New Deal have crossed it only partly, far less than alleged by the Old Guard but still unduly far. It was part of Stevenson's unique honesty and vision to admit this (unlike Truman). Just as economists have to rely on the margin of diminishing utility, so I have recently suggested (in *Conservatism Revisited*) coining for politicians the phrase "the statist margin" as the margin of diminishing returns for humanitarianism. Beyond it, the gain in local working conditions — though in itself obviously desirable — is less than the loss in liberty, so that the balance sheet holds a net loss for society as a whole.

A post-1952 Republican reaction against state blueprinters can be indispensable as the watchdog of antistatism, growling warningly at leftist or rightest prowlers who cross the statist margin. Indispensable — provided the watchdog of free enterprise takes more precautions against degenerating into the lapdog of big business.

WILL AMERICA PROVE MARX RIGHT?

> Not magnitude, not lavishness,
> But Form — the site;
> Not innovating wilfulness,
> But reverence for the Archetype. . . .
>
> The spider in the laurel spins,
> The weed exiles the flower;
> And, flung to kiln, Apollo's bust
> Makes lime for Mammon's tower.

— HERMAN MELVILLE, *great American conservative, on tradditional values versus the nihilistic materialism of Economic Man*

I

The discrediting of the Soviet fraud has made it a lot easier for intellectuals to become American traditionalists without being howled down as "reactionaries," "flag wavers," or "fascists." Recognition of the blood-stained nature of the Soviet banner makes it seem less deliciously clever to trample on the American banner at every possible occasion. This swing from the outworn poses of revolt is releasing a burst of creative new thinking.

But the same change brings new dangers as well as new blessings. In time the new traditionalism may degenerate into a new whitewash of pretentious philosophy for what has always been unpretentious: the old robber baronism of public-be-damned. At least those endearingly unshaved and candid old pirates did not try to be smoothie "philosophers" of "conservatism." Genuine giants of our dinosaur era of chaotic expansion, like crusty Commodore Vanderbilt, swashbuckling Dan Drew carelessly trailing seminaries and suicides, or old J. P. Morgan, would have puffed their black cigars scornfully at such fancy nonsense. If this whitewash takes place, then the American flag, rightly saved from the muddy boots of fellow-traveler liberals, would be saved in vain. Or is it a patriotic triumph if the dawn's early glare reveals our flag progressing from being a door mat to being a fig leaf?

Such patriots, reaping unjustified fruits from our justified revulsion against communism, now have their grand opportunity. They can now suddenly seem the Great Oaks of the American Dream instead of the parasitic vines. History itself seems beckoning us toward their comforting shade, those stalwart "uncommunistic" pillars both of profit system and of God-fearingness.

But what if there be a contradiction between these two supposedly equal pillars? What if the essence of the patriotic American tradition, along with the tradition of the whole Christian-Hellenic-Judaic world, is an awareness of this contradiction between our profits and our prophets?

Lay not up for yourselves treasures upon earth . . . for where your treasure is, there will your heart be also. . . . No man can serve two masters . . . ye cannot serve God and mammon.[1]

I have faith in American capitalism because I believe its profit system has been sufficiently modified by ethics — and because I believe it can continue to be revised peacefully, without need of socialism, when it does violate the demands of humanity. Defending it on this basis, we can create faith in our system in Europe, in India, and at home. But if we adopt the un-American principle of putting profits above humanity and ethics, we shall discredit American capitalism and aid Moscow. This will have two results, the first abroad and the second at home:

1. Abroad we will find ourselves fatally without allies, a fate not displeasing to some of the "go it alone" isolationists. In that case, the American Adam Smith will produce Cain and Abel Smith in Europe, a fratricidal destruction of the free world for Stalin's benefit.

2. More ironically, we will at home be *behaving exactly as*

---
[1] Matthew 6:19-24 (Sermon on the Mount).

Marxism says we behave: namely, putting our capitalist profit motive over all religious, ethical, and cultural ties. By combating Marxism in the wrong way, we would for the first time in our history become Marxist economic determinists in our behavior.

Can anything happen that would prove Marx right? Though he was steeped in enough Western humanism to make him preferable to the Soviet terror, yet his doctrinaire Hegelianism and Prussian statism produced a dogma seemingly impossible to justify. Here is the achievement of our Old Guarders: their triumph would accomplish the dazzling feat of justifying the following passage of Marx and Engels, which our past history had gloriously disproved:

> The bourgeoisie has played an extremely revolutionary role. . . . It has destroyed all feudal, patriarchal, and idyllic relationships. It has ruthlessly torn asunder the motley feudal ties that bound men to their "natural superiors;" it has left no other bond betwixt man and man but crude self-interest and unfeeling "cash payment." It has drowned religious ecstasy, chivalrous enthusiasm, and humdrum sentimentalism in the ice-water of selfish calculation. It has degraded personal dignity to the level of exchange value; and in place of countless dearly-bought chartered freedoms, it has set up one solitary unscrupulous freedom — freedom of trade.

Capitalism has many other merits but happens not to be a sacred religion. The current ambitious attempt to make it one in our textbooks is being incorrectly denounced as "fascism" by New Deal liberals and incorrectly hailed as "free individualism" by Republican conservatives. It is neither. It is a return to that Sahara of inhuman aridity: the belief in Economic Man. It is a return to the incomplete liberties — merely top-of-the-iceberg — of private economic liberty. It ignores the nine-tenths of human liberties beneath the top of the brain: the nine-tenths of imagination and art and religion.

Fortunately American capitalism and American capitalists — for example, their promising "Committee for Economic Development" — are a lot better than that. It is a slander to indict the Double-Breasted Business Suit by equating it with the fascist or imperialist uniform, as do so many distrustful leftist intellectuals. The man in the business suit is indispensable to freedom. He was indispensable in the war against fascism and is again indispensable in the cold war against communism. Both are also production wars. In World War II fascism was defeated partly by the industrial production-miracles of that capitalism which, according to the Marxists, fights on fascism's side.

THE PECULIAR FEEBLENESS OF SOCIAL DEMOCRATS

> "To bring about government by *oligarchy*, masquerading as democracy, it is fundamentally essential that practically all authority and control be *centralized* in our Federal government. . . ." — F. D. ROOSEVELT, *radio address, March 2, 1930, while governor of New York State*

The cause of democratic socialism, opposing both fascism and communism, contains more good will than most -isms of our time. Why is most of that good will squandered without producing more than High-minded Editorials? Why, to put it cruelly, is democratic socialism ultimately a failure?

Social democracy has an attractive social program for both the masses and the intellectuals. Then why has it so frequently failed to stop either communism or fascism in Europe? Why has it failed to summon forth the energy and enthusiasm to keep itself in power firmly and long? The Weimar Republic is a classic case of such failure.

The answer is not only economic but psychological. Surely it is an obvious answer, though perhaps not normally stated in just that way. The answer is simply that an inherent inner conflict condemns all social democrats to be Hamlets. An innate schizophrenia paralyzes — (with great but rare exceptions like Reuter) — their ability to *take action* in any crisis or to stay firmly in power against aggressive enemies who know what they want.

The source of their paralyzing inner conflict is that they want incompatibles. They want economic collectivism and political individual rights at the same time. With what consequences? Their *economic* wish for collectivism requires *political* dictatorship to enforce. Their sincere *political* wish for individual liberty requires some individualism also in all the nonpolitical fields, *economics* not excluded.

But the very phrase "free enterprise" — here their conditioning makes them inflexible — the very phrase "free enterprise" horrifies all socialists and also the less moderate wing of New Dealers. Their conditioned response is to dismiss it as some Wall Street plot, some insincere propaganda slogan for selfish undemocratic interests. This it is — sometimes and superficially. But not always and not basically. Nobody is speaking of total laisser faire nor of materialistic profit worship; but basically the economy healthiest for democracy is most certainly the free market and free consumer choice, that encourager of individual diversities.

The humiliating failure of Weimar and the social democrats to prevent Germans from voting Nazi tempts one to misquote Churchill: never has so little been achieved with so much effort by so many. "But what about Scandinavia?" a socialist asks. The success of Scandinavian social democrats, insofar as it is really a success, proves my point. Where they do well, they are not democrats-plus-socialists but democrats-period. Being democratic includes social reform; "democrat" by itself already means "social-reform democrat." But social reform — Christian humanitarianism or nineteenth-century "Tory socialism" — does not at all mean the statist "socialism" of present American and European socialists.

Here I am using "socialism" not in any watered-down sense. I use it to mean a statism that socializes the economic and industrial life of the country. Socialism is a statism that nationalizes not merely a post office here, a public utility there, but the main means of production.

Full socialist control of press and radio by the government, even if indirectly via newsprint, control of most economic power by government and lack of economic power by any kind of opposition, will make democracy impossible. Impossible not in theory but in actual practice, even if sincerely maintaining every one of the outward democratic forms in theory. After becoming emperor, Augustus maintained the sovereignty of the Roman Senate in theory; did that mean Rome was still a republic?

But though democratic socialism is a contradiction, it is not one that necessarily leads to ruin. That depends on which half of the contradiction your social democrat stresses. In Europe, America can and should work with democratic socialists against communism wherever they are democrats first, as they are in the case of Reuter, Attlee, and most French and Scandinavian socialists. Europe's unsocialist socialism and America's classless, democratized capitalism are both in practice — never in theory — living in a thoroughly mixed-up economy, flexible and undoctrinaire, and doing very well, thank you.

All this does not change the fact that, in the long run, the Hamlet wavering between freedom and statism will continue to enfeeble the socialists themselves. It will also enfeeble and demoralize any country under them. In the long run they will have to face the need of shifting their position: from the outward leftist fringe of society toward the more conservative center. They will have to say quite brutally to themselves, "Come, come, no nonsense now!" and throw out their "revolutionary" dogmas. Those dogmas are a hang-over from an earlier century, before history established beyond challenge the unrevolutionary nature of freedom.

Then overboard with such dogmas as class war. (What is a class in America anyway? Have you ever seen one in the flesh?) Overboard, and good riddance, with the Hobson-Lenin misinterpretation of capitalism as an inevitable imperialist war. And finally overboard, bag and baggage, with the delusion that fascism is the creation of capitalism, its shield against the working class. Ask the ghost of Thyssen and other German millionaires; they know better now.

Fascism is not capitalism or any other economics, but a state of mind. It is a surrender of the soul to evil, to the temptation of power, to the particularly murderous brand of evil that results when you substitute egotistic domineering for Christian self-restraint and when you substitute hate for mutual sympathy and substitute pre-Christian, tribal loyalties of blood for post-Christian brotherhood.[1]

Nazism set its rigid state control over more German capitalists than did all German socialist and communist parties put together under Weimar. Nazism—and Mussolini's increasingly anticapitalist

---

[1] No space here for evidence; for detailed documentation of this hypothesis about fascism, cf. P. Viereck, *Metapolitics: From the Romantics to Hitler* (New York, 1941).

"Social Republic" of 1944 — would have gone still further in this direction if the Axis had won the war. The very few revolutions that did take place against Hitler inside Germany came from the high aristocracy, not from the docile, duped, and cheering masses in the factories. Some foolish and desperate capitalists may in the future finance some fascist movements as once a Thyssen or a Schacht did; the future will soon teach them the same lesson as the past: an armed praetorian guard eventually takes over the real power from its emperor, its economic paymaster.

But our socialist allies must move to all these centrist, anti-revolutionary conclusions by their own concrete experience and by their own free choice. American busybodies must never try to bully them into it. That would only make them react chauvinistically to the opposite extreme.

Lamenting, "Protect us from our friends who embarrass us," such socialists will denounce and repudiate my praise of their unsocialistic practice. They will play again the cracked phonograph record of their hymn to revolution. Partly they will do so for fear of giving one more excuse to the communists to "expose" social democrats as "selling out to Wall Street." That this accusation is a lie, is realized both by the communist accusers and by that old, toothless, moth-eaten lion of Wall Street, who after twenty caged years can roar forth no more than an astonished squeak on being told he "dominates" the anticommunist world.

Not communism, not Wall Street, but only the socialist Hamlets themselves worry — as vacillators always do — about the absurd "sell out" accusation. They should stop worrying about it and stop denying it. Nothing they can do — they can brush the inch of dust from their old Jacobin caps and drink bourgeois blood by the bucketful — nothing they can do will make the communists stop calling them capitalist tools. Nothing will ever change this because communist accusations are not aiming at truth and hence not amenable to evidence. The one way to cope with communist accusations is to go about your business unswervingly, looking straight ahead and disregarding the snappings at your heels.

Not yet daring to breathe aloud the heresy of sobriety, some socialists tacitly have reached these centrist, mixed-economy conclusions already. Still a minority, these more reasonable souls are found with increasing frequency in England and Scandinavia; perhaps by the time of his death the wise French socialist Léon Blum had also evolved to this stage. At this stage, the ambiguous word "socialist" becomes — like Disraeli's Tory socialism or maybe Niebuhr's Christian synthesis — a sound sense of the organic ties between free individuals. It becomes a sound rebuke to the laisserfaire atomism and anarchism of the more doctrinaire capitalists, yet without crossing the fatal statist line.

But while many social democrats are democrats first, let us not optimistically overlook the fact that many others still are socialists first. The Marxists, the Bevanites, and the Schumacher wing of German socialists really "mean business" with their socialism. This does credit to their sincerity.

It does not do credit to their capacity for preserving liberties. The Achilles heel of even the wisest democratic socialists is that they recognize no statist margin, limiting the usefulness of even the wisest social legislation beyond a certain point. Instead they put their faith (that same old Rousseauistic faith) in counterbalancing the superstate by the mass-electorate, via its theoretical "democratic controls." The "natural goodness" of the Ortegan mass-man is somehow to prevent an all-powerful bureaucracy from abusing politically its excessive economic power. Well, it can't be done.

THE "NEW DEAL" MYSTERY:
CRYPTO-RED OR CRYPTO-CONSERVATIVE?

"The more we condemn unadulterated Marxian socialism,
the stouter should be our insistence on thoroughgoing social
reforms."   — THEODORE ROOSEVELT

I

What about it, was it crypto-Red? This question, though mainly I'd answer it in the negative, is not merely a crackpot or "smear" question that ought to be hush-hushed. It is a legitimate question that deserves to be raised in public after books like *Witness* by Whittaker Chambers, after the confessions of men like Wadleigh at the Hiss trial, after the evidence about Harry Dexter White (assistant secretary of the Treasury), the Silvermaster ring, the temporary communist penetration of NLRB in 1939, and so on (by now a familiar list). The mystery or apparent contradiction is this: the New Deal, at one and the same time, did most to smash communism in America — by removing the grievances it feeds on — and yet was partly infiltrated by it. This contradiction requires an unprejudiced reassessment of the New Deal.

Can the New Deal be defined? Hardly. It was a debauch of empiricism, an orgy of hit-or-miss. None of the -isms applies to it because it was never consistent enough, except in being diverse and improvised. Sometimes it was trust-breaking, sometimes it was trust-making; it prided itself on its anti-fascism, yet its NRA — its most unworkable blunder and its furthest venture in statism — resembled nothing so much as the corporate state of Mussolini. Meanwhile it saved the shirts of those small businessmen who most denounced it; it insulted bankers and saved and reopened their closed banks. Herbert Hoover at its very beginning called it a "bastard Soviet"; General MacArthur twenty years later still saw it as allegedly tending to "socialism or even communism." The *Daily Worker* alternately denounced it as "fascist reactionary" (before the Popular Front, when communists called the Blue Eagle of NRA "the blue buzzard") and hailed it as mildly and incipiently "progressive." Amid these contradictory definitions, the one thing the New Deal can definitely not be called is old-fashioned liberalism, in the sense of Bentham, Sumner, Gladstone's Liberal party, and the antistatist Manchester school of liberals.

As for the enshrining of the industrial worker by the New Deal laureates and literati: this recalls the sentimentalizing of the Noble Savage by all the eighteenth-century French sophisticates who had never seen one; it recalls the fact that all contemporary fallacies of progressives seem to lead back to Rousseau; only now it is the Noble Savage of the industrial jungle whose supposed unspoiltness and vox-Deism attracts the New York or Parisian intellectual. Obviously the industrial worker in reality is no better nor worse than any other guy. To treat him as inherently nobler (or viler) than capitalists is an economic version of the racist fallacy, the fallacy of judging men by group labels and group determinism instead of as individuals with a partly (not wholly) free will.

No American who cherishes his individuality will let himself be stampeded into choosing either one of the two bullies: Big Labor or Big Capital (or, for that matter, Big Brass and Big Government). Solution: play economics by ear, with deliberate amateurishness, by distrusting both forms of overcentralized power, and play 'em both off against each other. Only thus can you keep free some small clearing for unstandardized individuality within our dense jungle of economic Bigness.

Humanitarian reforms, though at first they may be loosely denounced as "socialistic," often prevent class war and real statist socialism by making capitalism more stable and more popular. Many once-challenged New Dealiana — not the dictatorial, statist NRA and not the infamous radical Court-packing attempt but SEC, federal deposit insurance, and countless laws like the Fair Labor Standards Act — are of this stabilizing, crypto-conservative category. These reforms are bound to be maintained also (though with less fanfare) by any Republican administration, regardless of "campaign oratory" by the lunatic fringes of both parties.

These two fringes exaggerate party differences. They pretend that some vast gulf of ideology separates our two rather similar parties. The attempt to exaggerate the gulf between both our parties by oversimplified slogans like "liberty versus socialism" will please some unrepresentative editorial writers, will misrepresent the rank-and-file Republicans, and will repel the decisive independent voter by its crude demagogy.

Is there really anything so "new" about these New Deal reforms? They recall Disraeli's philosophy — reread his novels *Coningsby* and *Sybil* — of wooing the workers from radicalism to traditionalist solidarity by giving them a just stake in the status quo; they recall Randolph Churchill, that indispensable connecting link between Disraeli and Winston Churchill; they recall Winston Churchill's introduction before 1914 of minimum-wage and social-security laws and of a thirty-years-earlier version of the Wagner Act. The New Deal was really an Overdue Deal, blending statist mistakes with brilliant social gains.

On the other hand, New Dealers should no longer deny the very existence of their Red infiltrations, as if such accusations were always "wild and reckless" instead of often sober and documented.

Chambers' book names names in the Departments of Agriculture, Treasury, State, and NLRB. Independent sources (Hede Massing, the sworn confession of Lee Pressman, Nathan Weyl, Julian Wadleigh, etc.) substantiate much of Chambers; the evidence is overwhelming — and appalling. Do these infiltrations contradict the crypto-conservative nature of the Overdue Deal? No, they were an attempt — sometimes successful, sometimes not — to pervert its anti-class-war nature into class-war radicalism. They are one more example of how closely the good and bad halves of the New Deal are interwoven and why one must refuse to oversimplify this process into any final verdict, such as: "The New Deal was the savior of mankind" or "The New Deal was a fellow-traveler plot," neither of which statements is true.

If you choose to put main stress on the mistakes of the Roosevelt era, its statism and its infiltrations, have you a right to say that the alternative at hand would have been better? What had the opposition to offer? If only the Republicans could have produced in 1936 a Hamilton, a Calhoun, a Randolph of Roanoke, in short a statesman-like conservative! Nobody was holding out for another Washington or Lincoln; we would have settled for one of the second-string Adamses or even a frayed Clay. But, no, no, no, the Republican alternative to Roosevelt was — Landon!

II

When demonstrating communist infiltrations of the New Deal, the danger that this may play into the hands of Old Guard enemies of the New Deal social reforms is very easily averted so long as the following qualifications are kept in mind. The chief susceptibility to communist fronts — The League of American Writers, for example — was not among the New Dealers in the narrow, less intellectual sense of the word (the economists devising concrete reform programs, thereby preventing communism) but among the New Deal sympathizers in the literary world, the world of the liberal weeklies, the abstract "bloody-minded professors" discussed earlier. The former group was often trying to make capitalism work better, the latter to bury it.

Logically, two groups so opposite in aim should have been

hostile or at least neutrally aloof from each other. Psychologically, the fact is they were inextricably mixed-up together, whether as personal friends or as public associates, serving on the same committees, magazines, and government organizations (Office of War Information, Board of Economic Warfare, Department of Agriculture, etc.). In those days, though not now, the partial overlapping of these two groups existed in their own minds and not merely in the minds of their anti-New Deal slanderers. Therefore, this partial overlapping — now denied with such understandable touchiness by anticommunist New Dealers — must reflect not merely coincidence and the communist espionage normal in all governments but some profounder affinity.

The affinity was not political since politically the groups had opposite aims and loyalties. It must have been psychological, the kind of rapport that enable strangers with different long-range aims to strike up a congenial friendship and to cooperate closely and trustingly on short-range aims. Among other things, this affinity between the anticommunist New Dealers and the Popular Front fellow-travelers included an exaggerated faith in economics (or even economic determinism) as solving human problems and an infinite capacity for getting intoxicated over blueprints, manipulating and planning and sculpturing society, as if human individuals were so much clay in the hands of the godlike Prometheuses on the swivel chairs of NRA or NLRB.

The gap between these groups, though today more apparent than in 1942, was always basic. Otherwise it would not have been necessary for the Hisses and the Ware cells constantly to disguise their identity. Disguise would not have been needed if there had been an objective logical affinity and not only the subjective psychological one. That need for concealment refutes the cheap partisan attempt to equate Roosevelt with Stalin. Such attempts are as absurd — and no more so — as attempts on the left to equate the Republican party with fascism.

Consider also the inner moral confusion behind the crusades (Abraham Lincoln Brigade and all that) of the 1930's. It combined unattainably high ideals with an all too attainable expediency, combining the worst caricatures of our transcendentalist and our pragmatist traditions. This moral confusion encouraged most

Popular Front liberals and some, though fewer, New Deal liberals to combine an excessive idealism about ends with an equally excessive toughness about means. It made them rashly, self-destructively indifferent to the tough, unidealistic company their idealism got them into. Such confusion among New Deal idealists gave the open Popular Frontists — not to mention the concealed communists — their opportunity for honeycombing and corrupting American liberalism. This fact no more discredits the New Deal as a whole than the very similar fascist infiltration of 1939, in France's "two hundred families," discredits capitalism as a whole.

A curious fact, which nobody seems to have pointed out, is the similarity between Republican and fellow-traveler views of Roosevelt. Both a Hoover and a Hiss, with opposite motives, saw Roosevelt as a Kerensky interlude, easily manipulated in order some day to lead America on to total collectivism and revolution; neither saw Roosevelt as really a crypto-conservative, the hero of one of Disraeli's romances. I suggest that in part Roosevelt was fulfilling the aristocratic British Tory ideal of the highborn nobleman joining with his yeomen of factory and farm — in defiance of laisser-faire shopkeeper commercialism — in order to give them a stake in our traditional status quo, the American equivalent of throne and altar.

In contrast, the 1930's also saw the Red agents Pressman, Abt, Hiss, Harry Dexter White, Wadleigh, Weyl, and all the other infiltrators working to push the New Deal toward Marxist radicalism, as a prelude to communism. The Republicans tended to accept this fellow-traveler view of the New Deal. The fellow-travelers exaggerated the potential radicalism of the New Deal in order to infiltrate it; the Republicans exaggerated its actual radicalism in order to oust it.

There are many grains of truth in this curious leftist-rightist agreement about the New Deal, in view of the Chambers revelations. But there are far more grains of truth in the opposite view: the world depression of 1929-32 turned the masses of Europe towards revolutionary extremism and would have done so in America also, under another Harding-Coolidge-Hoover administration; instead, the crypto-conservative Roosevelt won the worker, the farmer, the Negro, and the "underprivileged minorities" away from revolutionary extremism by giving them a stake in America. As a result they feel at last that America is also *their* country.

On many specific points, by all means let's be beastly to the New Dealers: the Court-packing at home, Yalta abroad. I find it excruciating to listen to the progressive cliché-talk of professional New Dealers (for the same reason that the jargonized platitudes of sociology professors are unbearable). Still, the debit side of Roosevelt's improvisings are presumably a price worth paying for our social peace and social justice and for America's comparative unity in resisting Soviet aggression today, in contrast with the disunity of Europe and Asia.

Roosevelt's foreign policy is another matter, rightly firm against fascism, wrongly faltering against communism, never a disloyal sell-out in motive, yet — for all its honorable intentions — tending at Yalta toward an unjustified trust in Soviet co-operation and an unjustified distrust of Churchill's conservatism and imperialism. But in domestic policy, the viability of the American economy today and the restoration of faith in it among those who once stood in breadlines are the answer to the question: crypto-Red or crypto-conserving? In five successive elections, the New Deal, despite all its inexcusable Red infiltrations, achieved the stabilizing, antiradical miracle of convincing the potentially radical masses that American capitalism was not killed by 1929 but could be made to work better than ever, with higher living standards, workers' wages, and business profits than ever before. Would that the radical workers of France and Italy had been won over to a similar faith in the viability, through reform, of the free-market economy and the traditional parliamentary system.

Now that this restoration of faith has been achieved, it can be continued and will be continued by the moderate majority of either American party (though not by the extremists of either party). Candid and grateful admission of this New Deal historical achievement does not prevent those of us who have mixed feelings about the New Deal and Fair Deal from continuing to resist their ventures past the statist margin and from continuing to work for clipping the wings of Big Government, Big Labor, and Big Business. That balanced role ought to become the historic mission of Eisenhower Republicanism — but only if it can still muster the boldness to break with the creeping anarchism of the Old Guard Jacobins of laisser-faire just as much as with the much-exorcised "creeping socialism" of the neo-New Dealers and the blueprint-intoxicated statists.

THE AMERICAN EXPERIMENT IN VOLUNTARY CO-OPERATION

"Instead of noblemen, let us have noble villages of men."
— THOREAU

The fresh breeze overcoming nationwide despair in 1933 was Trumanized into a "big business" of its own, the uplift equivalent of "Wall Street"; it became just as "vested" an interest as those it drove from the temples. What, then, is needed to replace it? No return to a pre-1929 era of cutthroat competition. The only movement of the future which can command the quixotic loyalty of youth as once FDR did will be a noneconomic stress on a closer co-operation between independent individualists united not by state compulsion and endless new social legislation but voluntarily by common cultural, ethical, and religious ideals.

The distinction between coercive and voluntary co-operation reflects the innermost nature of man, his individualism; a collectivism that does violence to it is poison from the start, no matter how many grandiose Five Year Plans it flogs out of its violated souls. We are the descendants of apes, not ants; fifty men, Rotarianizing or trade-unionizing together, still don't make a centipede; even in the most organically unified society, that innate individualism is easier killed than caged.

Our counter-1929 reforms have proved — not only narrowly through the New Deal but broadly through the good sense of Americans of most groups and ideologies — that the American kind of capitalism brings more prosperity and more liberty than any socialists have ever achieved, provided it gets "mixed-up" with social reforms short of socialism and thereby achieves a flexible balance between the powers of private business and those of the state. By haughtily dismissing as "socialistic" this united American effort to save capitalism from socialist class war, the Old Guard caused the great Republican party to lose five presidential elections in succession, and even in 1952 to trail in votes far, far behind the nonpartisan magic symbol of "Ike."

No way of life is a hero to its valets. Living in the midst of it, most of its beneficiaries take the American way of life as a matter of course or even deprecate it. But look at it from the perspective of history: it is an almost miraculous achievement; it alone has raised its standards of welfare ceaselessly while at the same time, Atlas-like, it supports half the globe, the entire free world, through two wars and two post-war depressions. America's cultural lag of know-why behind know-how means that this economic prowess is not enough for a balanced civilization and is consequently no pretext for smugness or boasting. Nevertheless, justice must be rendered where justice is due; and the American achievement in democratic welfare for all is conceded silently even by the Soviets.

Significantly, even this material achievement would be impossible without a spiritual base. Ultimately the base of America's economic prowess is neither unlimited competition (the laisser-faire fallacy) nor a state-coerced co-operation (the socialist fallacy) but a voluntary co-operation. America's basic voluntary co-operation depends on the spiritual qualities of trust, common goals, and social responsibility. For example, the voluntary co-operation of blood donors or of town-hall forums, of our public libraries or our volunteer fire brigades, or of a civic music auditorium like that open-air one at Denver, Colorado. Are all these private competition, or are they government socialism? Neither, of course; yet something very real in the American spirit. *"Hier oder nirgends ist Amerika."* These typical examples of American co-operativeness have nothing to do either with state control or with profits; they are far removed from either socialism or a ruthless capitalist competition. Socialist statism and ruthless private rivalry are two sets of hollow verbalisms, irrelevant to the reality of our spiritually-based mixed economy. The results of that co-operative reality are enough to pop the ideological balloons of any Karl Marx or Adam Smith.

Like many indispensable cranks, Vachel Lindsay in certain inspired moments understood the United States better than the more "accurate," more "sound" observers. The spiritual basis for the still unfinished American experiment is not our deceptive appearance of pragmatism and utility. It is not our seeming "romance with practicality" nor with any uninspired cash-society. Not always but in our highest moments, it is that enthusiastic, uncoerced, and *nonstatist* co-operation between individualists which Lindsay called "civic ecstasy":

> And I say: change not the mass, but change the fabric of your own soul and your own visions, and you change all. . . . Civic ecstasy can be so splendid, so unutterably afire, continuing and increasing with such apocalyptic zeal, that the whole visible fabric of the world can be changed.

AN APPEAL TO EISENHOWER: WHICH KIND OF CONSERVATISM?

In 1952, Stevenson was not running for President in the first place; he was running for Prime Minister. Let us hope that our young country soon grows up to appreciate the exciting integrity of mature and aristocratic understatement (as first perfected by the parliamentary debates of the British Conservative party). Meanwhile, America did appreciate something equally needed: the very real unity value of that trusted symbol, "Ike."

Note the Eisenhower-Stevenson identity of views on the two main issues: maintenance of NATO, Marshall Plan, and collective security abroad; maintenance of our revolution-preventing social gains and civil liberties at home. On these two issues, on which our very survival depends, no political leaders disagree with Eisenhower-Stevenson except certain Republican right-wing radicals, who are the real enemies of Eisenhower and Stevenson alike. Therefore, the moderate "Ike" Republicans and the moderate Stevenson Democrats ought to unite unofficially against the rightist isolationists and leftist appeasers (the ostriches and the Yaltizers) in their respective parties, exactly as Roosevelt and Willkie did in a curiously similar war crisis.

The names of the Eisenhower appointees of 1953 imply that at last America has an FEPC even for capitalists — a defiance of the prejudice often found against them in the Fair Deal version of bigotry. Foes of bigotry should rejoice if at last it is possible to appoint even a banker from that leper-outcast, "Wall Street," on the basis of his personal qualifications, instead of unfairly pre-judging him by one's prejudices pro or con his profession as a whole. If intellectuals now learn to judge businessmen as in-dividuals rather than as a collective "race" and if businessmen similarly individualize intellectuals, then the tension between them will ebb. That tension, with the resultant moral weakening of re-sistance to communism, is a central concern of this book. Since the "egghead" will never lie down with the tycoon (each deeming the other the lion and himself the lamb), their needed armistice requires that two such respected leaders as Eisenhower and Stevenson move closer toward a common center and move away from the Old Guard and Fair Deal peripheries in their own parties. But in the '52 campaign both at times lost control of their parties to the Taft Old Guard and the Truman Fair Deal statists; so America should be skeptical, not optimistic, until both apron strings are truly cut.

Before the defeated Fair Dealers flee in panic from America to New Zealand as the last unsullied refuge for the welfare state, let them speculate about the following unexpected but possible future at home. Our country's fashionable pace-setters have be-come so apologetic about the privileges of business, and moderate Republicans are so terrified of being again voted out as "tools" of a semi-mythical Wall Street, that they may lean so far away from Wall Street as to hit the floor. This would cause a lovely confusion among New Deal Democrats and Old Guard Republicans alike. Equally far from a balanced center would be a surrender to the Taft wing instead. The title of this entire section — "WHICH kind of conservatism?" — is a question addressed di-rectly to Dwight Eisenhower. Addressed by millions of inde-pendent voters, corruption-weary Democrats, and Vandenberg Republicans. They elected him not *because* of his party's cash-nexus Old Guard and isolationists but *in spite* of these discredited extremists, and in order to let him reorganize his divided party into the more responsible, world-minded, and Churchillian kind of conservatism.

The almost providential emergence of just one particular human being — Adlai Stevenson — is rehabilitating the good name and self-confidence of American intellectuals at the very moment when they most needed rehabilitation against their own small but pestiferous Lumpen fringe. To indict the latter is not enough; remember equally the long list of liberal and even radical intellectuals who were never once fooled by communism but fought it from the start. The Stevenson miracle tacitly reminds America of that honorable list; it refutes those who see only the opportunistic and herd-minded intellectual (Babbitt Junior) and not this ethically-dedicated and independent-souled intellectual now re-emerging at last (as embodied even for his enemies by Stevenson). "Challenged" (in Toynbee fashion) by the Soviet crisis, America's free culture "responds" superbly by producing simultaneously the maturer new intellectual (the Stevenson speeches) and the maturer new businessman (the original Eisenhower movement). This dual response is the first step out of that unspiritual "Crowd Culture" indicted so movingly and so intelligently by Bernard I. Bell's new book of that title.

The mature kind of businessman has learnt the lesson of 1929 and won't let it be repeated. His organs are, for example, the New England, world-minded Republicans or the Committee for Economic Development. The existence of any such statesman of business is still ignored by those liberals whose only knowledge of business is from the crumbling satiric novels of the 1920's. Admittedly he is far from controlling his party; all the more reason, then, for supporting him. At the price of being demoted still another notch in the Latin Quarter, here is one egghead who affirms that this new (non-Taft) kind of Republican businessman and banker deserves the same unprejudiced confidence or benefit of the doubt, until proved otherwise, that so many intellectuals lavish on labor leaders or on themselves. Meanwhile, those of us who have tried to "keep our own house clean" by attacking the business-smearing and leftist sins of our fellow intellectuals have a right to expect our Republican friends to be equally self-critical in the new Republican era ahead. "Watching like hawks," we expect them to be equally unsparing of personal friendships in trying to clean the Republican domicile of trade-union-smearing, anti-intellectualism, chauvinism, soulless hucksterism, dissolute misuse of the word "Red," and other Old Guard (that is, moneyed-plebeian) sins. Gaylord Babbitt must be superseded in art, in academe, and in politics. But not, heaven forbid, by exhuming Babbitt Senior!

Will Eisenhower lead us *forward* beyond Babbitt Junior: to more individual freedom at home and closer moral integration abroad with all genuinely free societies? Or will Eisenhower lead us *backward* to Babbitt Senior all over again? If the backward alternative, then the Mardi Gras of the electoral Tuesday will lead a confetti-strewing America straight to some heart-breaking Ash Wednesday, just as surely as Babbitt Senior once resulted in 1929 and in the Babbitt Junior era. But if instead Eisenhower heeds the appeal of millions of us nonpartisan independents, he may lead us forward inspiringly into history's greatest experiment in voluntary co-operation.

SECTION TEN

Free Dissent Versus Conspiratorial
Dissent: Some Further Distinctions

"The United States has been greatly maligned as a war-nervous, witch-hunting nation. I failed to find the tension, hysteria, or warmongering about which one hears such a lot abroad."

— *The democratic Hindu liberal*, M. R. MASANI, *parliamentary representative of the Indian Congress party, in December, 1951, after a nationwide tour of America, returning to India to warn his fellow Hindu liberals against the widespread myth that democratic anticommunism is a threat to civil liberties*

"It will always remain the best joke made by the democratic system that it provided its deadly enemies with the means of destroying it." — GOEBBELS

CALL THEM "REALLY-THE-SAME-THINGERS"

"Foolish curs that run winking into the mouth of the Russian bear, and have their heads crushed like rotten apples."
— SHAKESPEARE

If it is a bad thing to tell lies, then it is not a good thing to encourage lies by an evasive, tactful silence merely because they occur in your personal friends and professional colleagues. Therefore —

A maxim for fellow professors: never to associate or shake hands with that kind of "anticommunist" who mildly (for the record) deplores the physical torture of innocent millions in Stalin's witch-hunt and then asks you:

"But naturally this new American spirit of orthodoxy, America's smearing of the Hisses and nonconformists, the medieval inquisition against The Eleven, the ordeal of the Hollywood martyrs, the absolutely unbearable torture of having to take a teacher's loyalty oath, isn't all that — come to think of it — really the same thing?"

"ARMED OPINION": PITT VERSUS STALIN

This and the later chapters of this section are written in the confident faith that civil liberties and academic freedom will be strengthened, nor weakened by this kind of open-forum discussion of their ambiguities. The purpose here is not to try to answer the following two questions (except perhaps tentatively) but to shove them forward for free debate: (1) in this chapter and *passim*, the question of communist and fascist misuse of our devotion to civil liberties; (2) in the later chapter on "Academic Freedom," the plutocratic and communist threats to free universities.

On a few specific details, such as whether the communist "right" to teach is a civil-liberties issue, I disagree with the American Civil Liberties Union; but in general and on most things, I agree enthusiastically with the principles of this indispensable group — indispensable for a "ceaseless vigilance" against the opening wedge of tyranny. The Civil Liberties Union is farsighted in defending the rights guaranteed by the Constitution to communists and other minorities (insofar and only insofar as free opinion and not armed conspiracy is involved); the Union is likewise farsighted in not admitting communists to membership in its board of directors, for communism means anti-civil-liberties. On some points its directors disagree with each other. Those who don't accept the semi-closed nature of freedom and who deem it a wholly open society get more distressed about current threats to American liberties than the facts warrant; yet I'd rather see them erring in the direction of overexcitement against thought control than in the direction of sluggishness.

The Civil Liberties Union should be encouraged to combat this sluggishness among the nonacademic mass of Americans; among academic and literary circles, it is vastly less necessary, relatively speaking. As on so many other issues, here, too, America breaks apart into two worlds: (1) the nonintellectual and business world;

this world is not yet converted nearly enough to the need of defending the civil liberties of one's opponents; (2) the intellectuals; they are not only converted to this need already but are almost lemming-like in their obsession with it. Result: professors worry almost exclusively about the less-than-world-shattering piffle of accusations "against our fellow professors" by the usual half-witted, loose-mouthed windbags of the backwoods, instead of worrying also about the truly world-shattering atomic treason of certain other fellow professors, named Fuchs, May, and the rest. The former overpublicized worry has no armies behind it; it can and ought to be removed by ballots; so much the worse for the American voter if he fails to remove it. The latter worry has over two hundred armed divisions behind it and is more likely to remove America than be removed by America if we ignore it.

By now, most politically active intellectuals have recognized the need for our fighting the McCarran Act's racial and visa restrictions. The author has joined with groups fighting discrimination against Negroes or against noncommunist dissenters and has, as a matter of course, like any other citizen with a normal interest in cultural freedom, signed protests against teachers' oaths and against the McCarran Act's exclusion of liberals (specifically and most recently, Milosz and Moravia). These are the kind of obvious, unheroic activities for human rights that any informed intellectual does as a matter of course; it is an indecency — like conspicuously wearing a Phi Beta Kappa key or, analogously, a football sweater — when some liberals and their periodicals boast at great length of such activities, as if they were heroically facing death (instead of performing routine duties) in defying the thunder of some McCarthy. The false pathos of this hero-martyr pose is especially tasteless at a time when truly heroic martyrs of civil liberties are being literally butchered for defending civil liberties in the anticommunist undergrounds of Eastern Europe.

Americans must remain free to express their opinions, whether communist or any other, in the press. This principle should be assumed throughout the discussion that follows. On this, liberals and conservatives and capitalists and socialists may all agree. Not the Civil Liberties Union but a Tory Prime Minister said in July 1952 about the pro-communist Dean of Canterbury:

Free speech carries with it the evil of all foolish, unpleasant, and venomous things that are said; but on the whole we would rather lump them than do away with it.

If no more than this principle were involved, nothing would remain to discuss.

Unfortunately, owing to the very special concealment methods of the communist armed conspiracy, the problem is not always so simple as the Red Dean's undoubted right to free speech. For not only free opinion is involved. There is also something for which Pitt the Younger (Prime Minister 1784-1801) coined the phrase "armed opinion." This may be defined as violent revolutionary military conspiracy disguising itself as free opinion in order to win gullible liberal support. One and a half centuries ago, when Fox (the leading British "appeaser" of the aggressions of the French Revolution) protested that Prime Minister Pitt was "making war on opinion" in resisting the French Revolution, Pitt replied:

> It is not so. We are not in arms against the opinions of the closet nor the speculations of the schools. We are at war with *armed* opinions. . . . They will not accept under the name of Liberty any model of government but that which is conformable to their own opinions and ideas; and all must learn from the mouth of their *cannon* the propagation of their system in every part of the world. . . . It is a species of tyranny which adds insult to the wretchedness of its subjects by styling its own arbitrary decrees the voice of the people.

"It is not so"! Every word of Pitt's reply might be repeated today by an anticommunist to reply to the very same liberal protest.

Today the Trojan dove is cooing not only for so-called "peace" abroad. It is also cooing for so-called "civil liberties" and "parliamentary rights" for its communist spies and saboteurs inside democratic countries. Just as the West champions peace against "peace," so must it champion civil liberties against "civil liberties." After Czechoslovakia, how can any American liberal still believe that Communist "parties" are really parliamentary parties or that they use their "civil liberties" for words and social reforms instead of for crimes? Listen to that authoritative source, Stalin himself: [1]

---

[1] Stalin, *Foundations of Leninism* (New York: International Publishers, 1949), pp. 53, 56, 104, 115, 120, 121. Italics mine.

The scientific definition of communism is the dictatorship of one class, alone unto itself, based on power, *absolute* power, and not on any laws and regulations. . . . The dictatorship of the proletariat is the rule . . . *unrestricted by law and based on force* . . . of the proletariat. . . . In other words, the law of violent proletarian revolution . . . is an inevitable law of the revolutionary movement. Lenin is right in saying: "The proletarian revolution is impossible without the *forcible* destruction of the . . . state machine and substitution for it of a new one. . . ."

To a reformist, reforms are everything. . . . To a revolutionary, on the contrary, the main thing is revolutionary work and *not reform;* to him reforms are by-products of the revolution. The revolutionary will accept a reform in order to use it as an aid in combining legal work with illegal work, to intensify *under its cover* the illegal work for the preparation of the masses for the overthrow of the bourgeoisie. . . . The parties of the Communist International, which base their activities on the task of achieving and consolidating the dictatorship of the proletariat, cannot afford to be "liberal" or to permit freedom of factions. . . . The existence of factions is incompatible either with the Party's unity or with its iron discipline.

Our democratic creed need not fear communism as an ideology; if that were the only threat, then the "free debate" with Russia, of which some liberals still dream, would indeed suffice. Never once in history has the communist ideology won a majority in any country. Never once in history has any communist party won an election where other parties could also run freely. The highest popular vote it ever had in any country was perhaps one-third: in the Russian elections of 1918, in Czechoslovakia before the coup, and in postwar Italy. With those three exceptions, no communist party ever received even so much as a third. By its own electoral figures (Lenin, for example, accepted those of January 1918), communism has been opposed by at least two-thirds of the masses of every country that ever voted on it. Usually, as in the postwar Hungarian and Austrian elections, the figures average about nine-tenths against communism, not to mention the still smaller figures in America and England.

This means: only by violence, against the majority will, can communism ever come to power. Though we may be ideology-proof to communist economic theories, to which we should certainly never deny free speech, we are not bulletproof to communist saboteurs, insurrectionists, or invaders. Therefore, the free nations have every right to act in self-defense by democratically passing laws to arrest or expel their communists as the "invading army of a foreign nation." This apt phrase for them comes not from any capitalist but from the French socialist leader Léon Blum. He ought to know, having tried to "coexist" with them in a Front Populaire.

To avoid misunderstanding by those who are eager to misunderstand, it must still be repeated repeatedly: this analysis is not an attack on civil liberties — no communist in America has lost habeas corpus, trial by jury, and the rest — but an attack on the confusion between civil liberties and conspiracy. Here is a concrete example of this confusion. A leading fellow-traveler scientist wrote an article in *The Nation* in 1952 explaining trials of communist scientists as persecutions secretly motivated by the fact that "they are internationalistic rather than chauvinistic in outlook." The article implied that Fuchs and Allan Nunn May were tried in order to persecute their internationalism and civil liberties rather than to stop their spying for Russia. This implication is nothing less than enraging in its dishonesty, especially as the price of such confusion may be the atom bombing of the United States. Indeed, Fuchs is estimated to have speeded up Soviet atomic research by two whole years, bringing that much nearer a possible Soviet surprise attack on our cities.

At gatherings of literary intellectuals in New York or at many of our universities, someone usually bursts out — not a communist sympathizer but an honest, confused man of good will — saying: "Aren't those frame-ups of Hiss, Fuchs, and I.P.R. really an attempt to intimidate free speech and civil liberties? Isn't it McCarthyism to believe they were guilty?" The memory of countless such conversations rings through my ears as I write, somehow linked with two lines from some nineteenth-century sonnet:

> The blessèd part has not been given to me
> Calmly to suffer fools.

Another confusion: those civil libertarians who quite properly defend the constitutional rights of communists sometimes forget that the Constitution and Bill of Rights don't list as a civil liberty the communist right to teach or to hold a government job. Neither does any other law of the land. Therefore, this is not a civil liberties issue; let us not be duped into making it one. My particular state has a Fair Employment Practices Commission to prevent the injustice of racial discrimination in jobs. But no state or federal law gives communists or fascists an FEPC of their own for employment, whether in colleges or in movies or in atomic labs.

I am assuming that the overriding purpose of the American Communist "party" is to be a recruiting ring for spies. (Only secondarily is its purpose its undoubted right of free speech for communist ideas.) For documentation of this assumption, see such books as Oliver Pilat's *The Atom Spies* on the actual workings of the party as a recruiting agency for Soviet spies and couriers and on the constant osmosis to and fro between being an open, "legal" party member and an illegal underground spy or trainer of saboteurs.

Everything said in this civil-liberties discussion about communists also holds true of fascists, and vice versa. Here, for example, is a revealing boast by Hitler's wily Minister of Propaganda. For "we National Socialists," substitute "we Communists" or "we flag-waving American fascists, anti-Semites, and nationalists." Then take this Goebbels boast to heart when discussing anybody's "right" to indoctrinate schoolchildren:

We National Socialists have never maintained that we were representatives of a democratic viewpoint, but we have openly declared that we only made use of democratic means in order to gain power, and that after the seizure of power we would ruthlessly deny to our opponents all those means which they had granted to us during the time of our opposition.

Take equally to heart the boast of Hungary's wily dictator, Matyas Rakosi, of how he tricked Hungarian liberals and noncommunists in order to use their democratic ideals as a means for destroying them. Writing for fellow-communists in the party magazine *Social Review* in Spring 1952, Rakosi outlines his formula for taking over noncommunist liberals by pretending to join a parliamentary coalition with them:

Join with noncommunists in a coalition and then proceed, by various methods, to take over . . . demanding a little more each day, like cutting up a salami, thin slice after thin slice. . . . We held [the secret police] completely in our hands. . . . Soviet "interferences" in internal affairs . . . were of great value in strengthening our party. . . . After the liberation [from Germany], we did not clarify this problem [of the communist goal of dictatorship] before wide masses of the party but only in limited audiences. Any discussion of the dictatorship of the proletariat as our final aim would have caused great alarm among our coalition partners and hindered our efforts to win over a majority of the petty bourgeoisie — even of the working masses. . . . Our party demanded the leadership and tolerated no respecting of coalition-proportion whatsoever.

Thus do Nazis and communists gloat — in these words of Goebbels and Rakosi — about tricking democracy into giving them the means to kill democracy.

In view of his deserved eminence, Justice William O. Douglas has a particular responsibility to the free institutions of the democracy that has brought him so high. He should be doubly careful not to lend his influential name — here mentioned only with deep respect — to a new kind of witch-hunt. By denouncing mainly the right-wing witch-hunt instead of both kinds, these good men are encouraging what I would call the McCarthyism of the left. From that atmosphere of confused idealists spring the Hisses, Fuchses, and Allan Nunn Mays who may yet destroy us. No wonder many young idealists confuse communist military treason (Pitt's "armed opinion") with the honorable right of intellectual nonconformism when they hear our necessary attempts to expose communism denounced as "the black silence of fear," "the new orthodoxy," and "the witch-hunt."[1] The conservative Pitt would have answered Douglas' panicky anti-anticommunist "warnings" as coolly as Fox's anti-anti-Jacobinism: "It is not so."

---

[1] It is interesting to study how Soviet Russia, against Douglas's sincerely anticommunist intentions, is using his New York *Times* article about this as effective propaganda. Albert Parry, in his article "The Kremlin Eyes U. S. Elections" on editorial page of New York *Herald Tribune,* June 18, 1952, summarizes the Kremlin attitude toward the Douglas-for-President movement: "A yet clearer indication of the Kremlin's favor can be seen in the case of Supreme Court Justice William O. Douglas. The Soviet press (read, for example, *Literaturnaya Gazeta* of April 22) has referred sympathetically to his much-discussed magazine article "The Black Silence

II

The most impressive thing about American parliamentary democracy is its self-corrective capacities. Impressive is not that
the Soviet threat to America's very existence has inevitably produced, after an excess of apathy, an excess of wild charges and bad
nerves. Impressive and unusual is that we have far less excesses
today than in our two earlier outbursts of antisubversive emotionalism: the 1920's and the late eighteenth century. Such emotionalism
is being discredited more rapidly than in the two earlier crises.
The reversal of the California Teachers Oath by the courts is a
typical reassuring straw in the wind. So is the fair, long, thorough
trial accorded to the eleven communists, Judith Coplon, Remington, Hiss, etc. Contrast these trials with the unfair Sacco-Vanzetti
trial and the illegal raids and arrests made by Attorney General
Palmer in the 1920's.

Suppression of unorthodox ideas and of lawful radicalism is
blind emotionalism. It threatens the freedom of every single one
of us. I admit its evil spirit dominates some quarters (just as
the equally evil spirit of apathy about communism still dominates
other quarters). I admit I may be too confident — time will tell —
about finding so much less of it than in the 1920's. Nevertheless,
lawful resistance to violent communist conspiracies, sabotage and
espionage is not emotionalism but reason, not thought control but
thought defense.

Such self-defense — freedom's will-to-survive — should have
been adopted much earlier, in view of the Fuchs spy case and
also in view of the fate of Czechoslovakia. Freedom's self-defense
is no threat to ideas, no threat to free intellectual dissent. It is a
threat only to crimes of violence and conspiracy, such as the Nazis
and Communists were allowed to plot successfully in the Weimar
Republic, in Prague, in half of Europe. Those who want to turn

---

of Fear" as proof enough that fascism is engulfing the United States. The
Communist party in the United States has been plugging, surely without
Justice Douglas' permission, five-cent reprints of the article. But it is being
done by the American comrades with full awareness of the fruitlessness of
any Communist effort to force the Democrats to nominate Justice Douglas.
The booklet is being used only as aid to Communist propaganda on the
theme of 'black reaction' allegedly descending upon America."

every democracy into a suicidal Czechoslovakia and Weimar Republic find it to their interest to denounce such self-defense. Here is their strategy, and it is brilliantly successful among intellectuals: denounce America's defense against totalitarian *acts* of conspiracy as if it were suppression of *ideas* and hence of freedom.

Except in the anarchic dream of "infantile leftists" and adolescent bohemians, freedom never means the absence of all restrictions. On the contrary, freedom is a very special and restricted type of value-framework. For example, its values of racial tolerance and of class tolerance ought to restrict from the classroom — and also from parliamentary elections — the fascist or communist preaching and practice of bloody civil war between races or classes.

In the past it was definitely unjustified and unnecessary to pass laws defending democracy against internal subversion. The communist fifth column has now made such laws necessary (even though some — like the Smith Act — are loosely drawn and may need revision to prevent their abuse). For the first time, we must draw a line between where lawful advocacy of ideas ends and where lawless conspiracy begins. This sane distinction will prove all to the good. When fairly applied, it will not take away civil liberties; it will prevent their Czech-style subversion from within. Of course, we must maintain the distinction. We must never prosecute noncommunists and nonconspiratorial radicals for their unpopular ideas. But has not freedom always depended on whether or not people really practice its distinctions?

ART VERSUS PROPAGANDA

"Patriotism is not enough." — NURSE EDITH CAVELL

A false choice for writers, poets, and artists: either to strike the anti-value pose of indiscriminate radicalism or to become patrioteers for the status quo. Many writers have tried both: the former in 1932, the latter in 1952. Both sides of this false choice result in bad art and bad politics. "Patriotism is the last refuge of" the ex-communist.

James Thurber, one of the most honest and attractive literary figures of our time, illustrates unintentionally the fallacy of the false choice when, in defending liberal writers from being falsely called Reds, he carries his defense too far in the other direction and practically makes 1952 boosters out of the 1932 rebels:

> The simple fact is that writers and entertainers have made an enormous contribution to *patriotic propaganda* on behalf of the security of the nation. Nobody has yet turned up sound evidence that any writer has seriously tried to overthrow the Government.[1]

Two comments on this. First of all: governments come and go; their overthrow, though justly prohibited by laws under which eleven communist conspirators have recently been justly convicted, is ephemeral and infinitely less important than the overthrow of our lasting Christian-Judaic value-framework; and the assault on this by "bloody-minded professors" has (in the proper economic context) helped cause all the bloody-minded dictatorships from the French Revolution through the current Soviet ones: this is "sound evidence" and is cause for serious, though sober, alarm. Second comment: the alternative to this value-devaluation by writers is not "patriotic propaganda"; the alternative is to tell the truth. A "patriotic propagandist" has ceased to be an artist or serious writer; he has become a hack.

By its hollowness and by harnessing Pegasus to some ephemeral government status quo instead of eternal values of the spirit, "patriotic propaganda" can be nearly as subversive of values as fellow-traveler propaganda. Mr. Thurber himself fully realizes this, as the rest of his article and his other articles show. For him this lapse into right-wing, Babbitt Senior cant is merely accidental. It is far from accidental for others. What happens is: intellectuals, wrongly accused of communist sympathies today for having joined communist-front letterheads in the past, get stampeded into appeasing precisely the wrong — the conformist — kind of anticommunist by making needless patrioteering gestures. So does a left-hand folly produce a right-hand folly.

The genuine value-conserving intellectual opposes not only an anti-value radicalism but also a "patriotic" fawning upon some momentary secular government. Antisecular means: "I die the

---

[1] James Thurber in Section 2, New York *Times*, July 27, 1952; italics mine.

king's good servant" (to quote again More's words on the scaffold) "but God's first." I am not using "secular" from any sectarian or clerical viewpoint. I am using it to describe all of "vanitas vanitatum," the "short-haired mad executives," the pushers and rushers, the obscenely wholesome ones, the loathsomely well-adjusted ones, all those go-getters who never once in their whole lives glimpsed the Virgilian "lacrimae rerum" behind whatever "vanitas" they are go-getting.

The same Thurber article in the *Times* protests against

defamation of liberals with talent who joined various political organizations to find out what communism is. . . . They get into things, but this can be defended on the sound ground that nothing can be intelligently accepted or rejected unless it has been examined and understood.

Insofar as he protests against defamation, McCarthyism, etc., Mr. Thurber is magnificently right and on the side of the angels; so are countless other writers who have been publishing the same sound old truth in newspapers and magazines so prominent in prestige and circulation that these writers cannot possibly be considered suppressed, martyred, or thought-controlled. But it is the second point of the above-quoted sentence that has an implication more newfangled than that. On the same "sound ground," would Mr. Thurber urge writers to join the Ku Klux Klan or the Gestapo in order to "get into things" and "find out what fascism is"? If the answer to this admittedly rhetorical question is no, then are we being told to set up a new moral code of double bookkeeping, making us more mellowly indulgent toward Stalinist fascists and "progressive" mass-murderers than toward other kinds of fascists and more humdrum murderers?

But most writers, poets, and artists, including Mr. Thurber and his present friendly critic, are — quite properly — far more interested in art than politics. Let us, therefore, turn back to the vistas opened earlier by his phrase "patriotic propaganda" and explore them one step further. Between long intervals of dormancy, like seventeen-year locusts, American writers suddenly buzz into the market place in loud droves, proclaiming: "Look, everybody;

we've stopped being Irresponsibles!" The apt Carlylian rejoinder to this is: "Egad, you'd better!" — inasmuch as ivory towers are no longer bomb-proof. Yet being "responsible" will dry up the creative imagination if it merely means the respectable kind of responsibility. Responsibility, yes (in view of the Soviet threat); but responsible to the universal laws of ethics and to the individual laws of integrity, not to the book sellers; not to that entertainment market known as "the public"; not to the all-too-solid tastes of the "solid, taxpaying citizen."

That is why I feel as uncomfortable with the new "responsibility" of the *engagé* artist and poet as with the old, bohemian irresponsibility pose. The uncomfortable feeling increases when "patriotic propaganda" is brought in, which surely the artist can normally leave to others, not because patriotism is unneeded but because he can serve it more permanently by deepening his insight and broadening his sensibility in his works of art. Like every other citizen, the artist must be willing to "lay down his life for his country" when freedom is at stake, as it is today. But let him refuse as savagely as possible to lay down — in the name of "responsibility" — his dream life for his country.

ACADEMIC FREEDOM
VERSUS PLUTOCRACY AND COMMUNISM

I

Efforts to glamorize plutocracy as antistatism and to make mammon an educational arbiter have caused as much confusion about academic freedom on the right as the defenders of "communist civil liberties" have caused on the left. Let us consider the fellow-traveler version and the plutocratic version of what I allege to be confusion. Representative examples of the leftist confusion are already familiar from the well-intentioned attempts of the liberal weeklies to turn our anticommunism into a civil-liberties issue. Not for its own sake but as the most representative example of a nationwide plutocratic campaign against our academic freedom, let us examine once again *God and Man at Yale* by the intelligent, sincere, and wrongheaded William H. Buckley, Jr.[1]

Buckley exalts laisser faire in economics as conservative and true-blue. He denounces laisser faire in ideas and in academic freedom as subversive and pink. Actually both forms of laisser faire, in economics and in ideas, are neither conservative nor radical. They are the twin components of nineteenth-century liberalism. It is inconsistent, and likewise inimical to freedom, to keep your Adam Smith without keeping your John Stuart Mill. Buckley's young "conservatism" is an old free-enterprise liberalism, permanently abandoned by the Republican party platforms (not only the Democrats) after 1929. Buckley is inconsistently reviving only half of that old liberalism, its free enterprise in economics, without its historical and logical counterpart: free enterprise in thought and teaching.

Academic freedom is as fragile as it is indispensable. Hands off! Standards of scholarship and integrity are best enforced by qualified academic colleagues. Excited bludgeonings by unqualified outsiders usually smash the innocent and miss the guilty. This has been proved by the experience of centuries which counts for more than a mere twenty years of admitted laxness toward the anti-integrity of fellow-travelers. For centuries, even through the unliberal Middle Ages, universities have functioned best as self-governing communities of scholars. Buckley's radical revolutionary innovation of stirring up so unqualified a hornet's nest as the alumni to enforce standards, would only create chaos and demoralization.

Buckley calls the alumni "the paying consumers." I thought the parents and students were that. Actually the biggest "paying consumer" in Yale history was the federal government, which financed thousands of veterans under the G.I. Bill of Rights. By his "logic" of consumer choice, Buckley should have urged the Fair Deal government to dictate Fair Deal courses in economics.

---

[1] In following Stendhal's advice to "enter society with a duel," this still young and still (let us hope) changeable, still evolving new writer has been smearingly sinned against as well as sinning. Some reviewers dragged in his private religion insinuatingly. Others misrepresented him as "a fascist" when actually fascist statism is incompatible with his extreme antistatism.

In any case, nothing will irritate students quicker into the arms of communism and atheism than to mobilize those Elder Statesmen of educational omniscience, the alumni, against economic and religious deviation. Just picture their scholarly Feasts of Reason in the football stadium, debating the nuances of Keynes-versus-Hayek between waves of the pennant and swigs of the bottle.

The Buckley book seeks to find a legal and moral basis for firing alleged noncapitalists. By noncapitalists, he means not merely communists but Keynesians. Rightly or wrongly, Keynesians are sure capitalism would be saved and strengthened by their reforms. The basis he offers for firing them, or not hiring them, is this: the majority of alumni supposedly believe in an unreformed laisser-faire capitalism; they contribute funds without which the private universities would collapse; therefore, they are "consumers"; therefore, they are entitled to "choose the product" to consume.

Any analogy between the free spiritual realm of ideas and the material realm of purchasable commodities is in itself disturbing, even hair-raising. But let us pursue this consumer train of thought still further. It leads us to a logical conclusion that would make Buckley's hair stand on end also. The alumnus-consumer names the idea-product. He wants the mind-factories to "produce." Very well. Suppose the alumni-consumers lose their faith in God and capitalism at Yale and become converts to atheism and communism. As consumers and as the fat moneybags of the institution, they could still name their product. Thereupon Buckley would have to join the alumni in merrily plunking atheists and communists into the shuddering chairs of learning. "If the alumni wish secular and collectivist influences to prevail at Yale," he writes at page 114, "that is their privilege."

"Their privilege" is a curious criterion for right and wrong. Here is relativism with a vengeance. Obviously the evil of communism (or nazism) is absolute, no matter what a majority of alumni may happen to decide. This burst of potentially atheist and potentially communist relativism comes from the same book that elsewhere damns the teachings of Dewey and of religious agnostics for their relativism.

The Buckley school would subject intellect to money. This is implied by his appeal to the alumni. Their intellectual "qualification," their ultimate weapon, is their control of university purse strings. He exhorts them to enforce a sectarian party line upon education, and this in the wholly open, unresolved, and debatable field of economics. Not a socialist or New Dealer but the father of the Republican party, Abraham Lincoln, had a nasty word for this un-American outlook: plutocracy. Has plutocracy the right to enforce, by money pressure, the views it cannot propagate by the fair methods of reason, argument, and ethics? The answer to this question is remarkably easy. The answer is: no!

II

God and Man at Yale asks good questions and gives bad answers. It muffs a great opportunity for capitalistically challenging our economic statists *within* the framework of academic freedom and free debate. I believe democratic capitalism and conservatism can stand up well in free debate. They need not admit defeat by resorting to the outrageous technique of suppressing debate. In the intellectual world left-wing views do or did dominate many influential circles in sharp contrast with the larger "outside" world of American life. The rational remedy is a fairer hearing for right-wing and even reactionary views in intellectual, literary, and academic circles so that both sides may be heard. Analogously, there should be a fairer representation of social-reform views in business circles, so that both sides may be heard there also.

The remedy in the universities is to appoint more representatives of the Hayek school of economics, alongside any predominance of New Dealers. Then let them fight it out freely. By hearing the ablest scholars from both camps, students would learn to think for themselves about such wholly open (being nonspiritual) issues as economics. But this is not the remedy suggested by Buckley's best seller. He would fire or restrict the anti-Adam-Smith professors. He would replace a partly one-sided New Dealer monopoly with an even more onesided anti-New-Dealer monopoly. In some crucial areas, American thought was unofficially suppressed from the left, especially in the Popular Front 30's and 40's. Instead of restoring freedom by a fair balance between left and right, this neo-plutocratic movement would suppress it still further. Only this time from the right.

The result would be "denominational colleges" not only in religion but in economics. Each denominational college would teach only its own dogmatic version of economics! By quoting selected Sacred Texts from the Founding Fathers, you can prove "the American value-system" to be either individualistic or social-reformist, either laisser-faire or New Deal, whichever you wish — or, in actual practice, a play-by-ear synthesis of both. Americans of highest intellect and religion are fairly evenly divided between many shades of both schools. Neither has a right to claim a monopoly on "the American tradition."

Let us distinguish between real and fake threats to academic freedom and fight the former. There is no excuse for harassing the self-governing academic community by inciting unqualified alumni against it. As for anticommunist Loyalty Oaths, is it not naive to think that murderers cannot also be liars?

At the same time, a university would be crazy to hire a slavish member of the Communist party as a professor for, say, genetics. Party discipline, by definition, disqualifies him from following the aim of scholarship, the search for truth. He would be compelled to genuflect before every shift and reversal of the Lysenko line. The same holds true of the rigid party discipline in most other fields of knowledge. American universities have every right and duty to refuse to hire these communist foes of the whole university spirit. That no more violates academic freedom than refusing to hire a Nazi to teach a course on race relations. The American value-system allows free play in the arena of discussion to all ideologies, capitalist, socialist, monarchist, feudal, or philosophical anarchist. In turn, they must accept as prerequisite the restraints as well as privileges of that arena and that value-system. They must accord to others the same liberties they demand for themselves. Otherwise, they are ethically unfit to teach; they are unfit to preserve academic freedom.

Unlike democratic socialism, communism is not primarily a program of ideas nor a parliamentary discussion. Communist party membership is *an act,* a military deed. It is a conspiratorial program (as the Canadian and American spy trials clearly showed) for sabotage, for espionage, and for murderous insurrection.

Never punish a man for his ideas, no matter how fatheaded. They are his own business. Even if communist ideas. The Bill of Rights gives him that right.

But the law is entitled to punish a man for his acts. Civil liberties do not protect all actions. Certain acts, for example murder, are barred. Membership in the Communist party is morally an act comparable to murder. Mass-murder, in fact. Morally every Communist or Nazi party member is up to his elbows in the blood of his party's victims (Belsen, Dachau, Katyn, Korea), provided he has joined that party voluntarily, not under duress. By following its line 100 per cent and supporting its crimes and directives 100 per cent, he deliberately accepts responsibility for the acts of his party. This is not true of any other party: Democratic, Republican, Socialist, Conservative, or Laborite. Such parties do not demand 100 per cent discipline. Nor is theirs a party line of mass-murder. You can freely disapprove the acts of such parties, even while a member. In contrast, here is the official Resolution of the Ninth Convention of the American Communist party:

All Communists must at all times take a position on every question that is in line with the policies of the party. . . .

Note "all times" and "every question." With all parties except Stalinist and Hitlerite fascism, you need merely agree most times and on most questions. The above official declaration is echoed in all communist instructions to their members. Communist instructions to teachers insist especially on indoctrination of students. Not to mention espionage and sabotage, in case of scientific researchers. Then why not freely and democratically pass a law recognizing that active Communist party membership is what it is — a serious criminal conspiracy?

An *independent* Communist party member would be fit to teach. But no such case exists. Discipline is the first rule of the Kremlin-ruled party. In case any communist did have the ideals qualifying him to teach in America, the ideals of free research and academic freedom, then he would automatically get expelled from the party if in America; liquidated if in Russia.

Readers will be familiar with the countless quotations from top Communists and Nazis despising "bourgeois prejudices" like truth and stressing the need for exploiting the classroom to propagandize their shifting party line. Except for these two termite groups, it is not to be countenanced that other sects be excluded from teaching, whether democratic socialists, capitalists, or monarchists. No other groups, except those two, enforce in practice such party discipline in *all* fields, though certain groups may have such discipline in certain individual, specialized fields.

Being a matter of faith, not scholarly research, religion is a matter apart from this. Denominational colleges are, and ought to be, readily available for those who choose them. Yale happens not to be a denominational college.

Regardless of differences over economics and material rivalries, the West is united on the dignity of the individual and his moral responsibility. These values underlie our varying religions and philosophies and reflect our common Hellenic-Roman-Judaic-Christian heritage. These values, even more than force of arms, saved the West from nazism and are saving it from communism. Both forms of totalitarianism butcher the individual for the state. Both replace his moral responsibility with slavish subservience to the arbitrary commands of a Fuehrer or Politburo. Can you conceive of any kind of freedom, including academic freedom, without these universal values? Disagreeing with the materialist and relativist liberals as well as with Buckley, I say: inconceivable! The universal value-framework of the West is as indispensable for supporting personal freedom as the trellis is for supporting its grapevine.

Not the least precious of these values is academic freedom itself. Communists and Nazis hate it fanatically and invoke it hypocritically. Superficial or false conservatives would suppress it for the sake of rigidly enforcing their particular pseudotraditionalist version of the American capitalist system. But the virtue of American capitalism is not at all its nostalgia for laissez faire. Its virtue is its flexibility, its adaptability. This virtue is precisely what the rigid socialist bureaucracies lack. This is what enables it successfully to harmonize free enterprise with our social security laws.

By suppressing the academic freedom of those who, unlike the communazis, share our ethical truths and who deviate on mere economic opinions, the false conservative creates a cultural sterility. He fosters that indiscriminate (rather than sanely discriminate) distrust of intellectuals which is the folly of the United States of America. A distrust of fellow-travelers and Lumpen-intellectuals is something else; today at long last, this is being settled by intellectuals *"within* the family." But a vengeful posse of Healthy Extroverts from "the outside" against intellectuals-in-general would kill the goose that lays eggs richer than mere gold.

III

What Buckley and his growing school lack psychologically is not sincerity but sensitive human experience; life as it is really lived; life below the top of the brain, below the top of the iceberg. Not head but heart is lacking in that famous Gobi Desert of spiritual and cultural dessication: the cash-nexus of laissez faire. Not head but heart is lacking in the incomplete freedoms of "free enterprise." The experience most needed here is participation in the sacrament of the brotherhood of all suffering. This universal brotherhood, of which Baudelaire said, *"Je sais que la douleur est l'unique noblesse,"* sweeps aside all distinctions of economic classes and of nation or race. This Christian experience is what turns a dry doctrinaire into a human being. A complete human being is also a humane being, with sensibility and sensitivity.

It is beguiling to imagine what would happen at Yale after our author abolishes there "the myth of academic freedom" and begins purging alleged welfare statists. Presumably Pope Leo XIII himself, enthroned over urb and orb in all his resplendent tiaras, would be booted out of the Yale economics department onto the sidewalk by Buckley Junior: — as a "pinko." For like all conservatives, from Metternich (that *socialiste conservateur*) through Churchill, this greatest of nineteenth-century popes denounced the drab and unimaginative laisser faire of Adam Smith.

Several reviewers attacked Buckley most unfairly for concealing a Catholic bias. The trouble is that in economics he is not Catholic enough. His is the Calvinist profit-thrift-prudence economy, which has partly led to an anti-Christian capitalist materialism. In our Protestant "bourgeois democracy," a healthy function of challenge is served by a book that is aristocratic, Catholic, and conservative. Brilliantly such is Erik von Kuehnelt-Leddihn's newly-published *Liberty or Equality*. But *God and Man at Yale* is neither aristocratic nor Catholic nor conservative. It is plutocratic, Calvinist, and Manchester-liberal.

INVESTIGATE THE INVESTIGATIONS

> "The fire alarm bell at Camp Drake rang so vigorously, summoning U.S. soldiers to a routine fire drill today, that it resulted in an electrical overload and caused a fire."
> — *News item of March 21, 1947*

The sensible key questions for smoking out a fellow-traveler have by now become fairly standardized. Here are three such smoke-out questions (incidentally, Owen Lattimore was guilty — *not* of communism nor of McCarthy's recklessly alleged "espionage" but of persistent fellow-traveling — on all three of these test questions): 1. Does he swallow the Moscow frame-up trials? 2. Does he praise (or deny the existence of) the slave-labor camps? 3. Did he zigzag docilely from "anti-fascist war" to "imperialist war" after the Hitler-Stalin pact?

But if the communist line is usually identifiable by such questions, then so are those who travel with it. This means: there is no excuse for confusing a truly democratic socialist or a truly independent radical, who follows no foreign dictator's line, with *the most shifty, slippery, devious dishonesty of our time*. By the latter, I mean the gifted noncommunist intellectual (writer, educator, pillar of society, molder of youth) who fellow-travels with the Kremlin line on essentials, luxuriates in deviating on nonessentials, and then protests his noncommunist, liberty-loving virtue — while the corpse of Liberty spins in her grave.

For this familiar public character, as prominent today in Paris, Rome, and London as he once was in 1946 in New York, let us use a good old phrase from Dickens: "the artful dodger." His artful goal is nothing so crude as pro-communism. Rather, it is

a general cultural climate, among literati, book reviewers, and educators (eventually filtering through to a wider public), a climate
that would view never enthusiastically but with complacency and
mild regret the loss of Asia to that "grass-roots populist" Mao and
of Europe to that "anti-fascist" Stalin. The partial success of this
goal during 1944-47 was aided mainly by the apathy of most
Americans of all outlooks, New Dealers and capitalist Republicans
alike; it cannot be blamed mainly on Red infiltrations or (out of
mere partisan politics) on the Administration that happened to be
in power. Pollyanna was even more dangerous than Hiss; the
American Milquetoast has helped Stalin more than has the
Progressive party.

The distinction between the artful dodger and the genuine radical
dissenter is stressed again and again in this book, with every bit of
intensity I can command, because the freedom of all Americans
and the purity of our anticommunist sacrifice depends on this distinction. It is disillusioning to see this distinction ignored at some
of our Congressional investigations. There are times when the
investigator seems bent on confusing fellow-traveling with whatever innocent phenomenon he happens to dislike at the moment,
such as: whoever is the opposing candidate, or some witness whose
personality he finds too intellectual or too courteous to stomach,
or some sincere New-Dealish social reformer. Fellow-traveling,
being a serious sin against the spirit of intellectual integrity, should
never be lightly attributed.

The investigations into communist espionage and fellow-traveler
infiltration must continue, lest the caterpillar be destroyed from
within by the egg the wasp concealed in it. But I further suggest
that these be accompanied, when abused, by a thorough investigation of investigations, in order to prevent loose use of the word
"Red" and to protect more fully the right of the accused. New
procedures must be devised to protect the accused against premature newspaper publicity of charges not yet proved, which raise
the problem of denials not catching up with slanders. We are
fighting communism partly in order to protect the rights of the
individual from Vishinsky-style trials; that is, from arbitrary
bullying by the insolence of office. Therefore, those of us who are
totally-committed anticommunists feel a particularly strong sense

of outrage every time some demagogue stains this crusade by himself Vishinskyizing.

Fairer methods of investigation, sounder loyalty procedures, even such details as shorter and less cumbersome questionnaires must be, can be, and will be devised. To deny the possibility of this (as do some liberals without faith in the democratic nature of anticommunism) is quite simply to deny that democracy can stay alive. To live means to protect yourself against your potential murderers. American democracy managed to outlive a war against Hitler's kind of totalitarianism; it has just as good a chance of fighting back, without any "inevitable" loss of civil liberties, against Stalin's kind.

THE SUBVERSIVENESS OF BLANDNESS

There is no more communist menace in most American colleges today. There is something more insidious, the anti-anticommunists. This is too subtle and elusive a specter for the unrapier-like thrusts of loyalty oaths, tabloid press exposés, committees of local politicos, and other sledge hammers. Instead, the intellectuals themselves must fight out on the free arena of their campuses the issue of the anti-antis.

The anti-anti has lost faith in communism. But out of fear of seeming inelegantly *engagé* or of being called a witch-hunter by his fancier friends, he is scared to buckle down and fight Stalin's fellow-travelers exactly as aggressively as he once (rightly) fought Hitler's and as he now (rightly) fights our thought-control demagogues. The anti-anti's evasiveness about standing up for liberty applies even more when confronted with Mao's apologists — because there has been less time to get disillusioned about that latest great Experiment in Social Engineering. But no matter how the anti-anti exasperates you, remember: he is no communist, he is violating no law, and he can be — if you bespeak him softly — sometimes converted. At least temporarily, whether out of sincere disillusionment or tactics or both, the all-out pro-communist — that familiar campus character of the 1930's — disappeared sometime around 1950.

Hence, the folly of looking for threats only on one front. American education faces many fronts, many dangers. Those from communism and those from plutocratic pressure on the teaching of economics have both been discussed. But it is poppycock to consider any kind of threat to academic freedom, whether communist or plutocratic, the present main danger to education. The main danger is unimaginative mediocrity. This has plenty of academic freedom all right. But what does it use it for? Don't ask its students for the answer; they were snoring at the time.

The fact that I consider communists unqualified to teach (in view of freedom being a semi-closed society) does not mean I want deadwood mediocrities instead of them. Today in most colleges a finishing-school urbanity — offending nobody and playing it safe — is a greater threat to education than the now diminishing one of communism. In America, even under perfect free speech, a respectability complex among students and teachers can subvert the scholarly ideal of free inquiry more than any leftist or rightist encroachment on academic freedom.

The danger to students of being branded for life by a socialist is less than that of being blanded for life by a socialite.

SYMBOLS: HISS AND POUND

"Long ago my life was a banquet at which all hearts opened, at which all wines flowed. . . . I fled. O witches, O misery, O hatred, it is to you that my treasure was entrusted."
— RIMBAUD, *A Season in Hell*

"True genius without heart cannot exist — for neither high intelligence, nor imagination, nor both together make genius. Love! love! love! that is the soul of genius." — Words written by GOTTFRIED VON JACQUIN in Mozart's album when Mozart was a very small child

I

Alger Hiss and Ezra Pound are the two ghosts at the happy feast of Babbitt Junior. They are the ghosts whose implication Babbitt Junior evades with concealed panic. Yet the implication is plain. It knocks at every locked door of the mind. It knocks too loudly to be evaded too long. For years these two brilliant careers were the heroes of progressivism in politics and literature respectively. That both heroes ended as they did is partly coincidence. Not wholly.

What is the lesson when progressivism, after sincerely setting out to liberate literature and politics, ends by flirting with treason? Avant-garde and liberalism, the two halves of Babbitt Junior in culture and politics, won't face the lesson. But more detached minds must insist on its being faced. They must insist on "vulgarly" and tactlessly rubbing the face of American progressivism in Ezra Pound and Alger Hiss.

Whenever conversing with the robot tribes of Babbitt Junior, you must steer the conversation toward Hiss and Pound with the seeming obsessiveness of a dentist drilling near an exposed nerve. This is hardly the road to popularity — every gadfly-Socrates is likely to end up with hemlock in his cocktail — but it is the road to truthful understanding.

Toward Hiss and Pound personally, the only decent reaction is not vindictiveness but compassionate human sympathy; "judge not that ye be not judged." Nor is there danger that the familiar esthetic contribution of a *miglior fabbro* will ever be bilked of its admirers and endless commentators. But personal considerations and esthetic considerations are at least partly irrelevant to assessing the role of both men as impersonal moral symbols. They were the dominant prestige-symbols of the two alternative poses adopted by Babbitt Junior in the Thirties and Forties. Either "social significance" or else literary mandarinism: these were the two club-handshakes needed (what, you suddenly don't remember?) for admission into the Rotarian-baiting Rotaria of intellectual chic.

Two ironies cut across both cases and distract the unwary from the moral symbolism:

1. Neither man is confined for his real crime. Like Capone, who could only be confined for income-tax evasion, Hiss could only be confined for perjury. The statute of limitations prevents his treason trial. Pound likewise had no treason trial for his pro-Axis broadcasts to American soldiers during the war in Italy. His hospital confinement prevented it.

2. As a further irony, there are some who exploit both cases

undisinterestedly. They exploit our distress over Hiss by turning it indiscriminately not merely against fellow-travelers but as a cheap smear against all liberalism, against all mild social reform, against that entire complex mixture of good and bad known as the New Deal. Others exploit our distress over Pound by turning it indiscriminately not merely against fascism but against all modern art and all experimental poetry, likewise a complex mixture of good and bad.

Those who attack Hiss and Pound for unscrupulous reasons cause both to be far more widely defended than would otherwise be the case. Result: a few honest anti-communazis defend both crimes, against their better judgment, lest they allegedly "play into the hands" of reaction and philistia. Fortunately the sound larger part of the reforms of modern poetry (post-1912), and likewise of the New Deal, are rooted too solidly now to be discredited. The bogus lesser part of both ought indeed to be re-assessed far more critically by American intellectuals; it is high time!

I said "by American intellectuals." I did not say "by anti-intellectual Americans in general." "Far more critically" is not the re-assessment needed in those more general quarters; for many of them, it is "high time" to re-assess more positively, or even to have heard of, the best new experimental thought about art and about society.

Justice will be done; art outlasts politics. But only if truly art and not fashion, not coterie. In case Pound has truly made the artistic contribution his admirers believe he has made, then I hope the future will reward him by remembering only his poems and not his ephemeral rantings against "Jew York" and "President Rosenfelt."

II

To whitewash Hiss has become a compulsive defense-mechanism for those fellow-travelers who (unlike many candid men of integrity) don't admit they ever fellow-traveled for Communism. During 1930-47, they befriended its fronts, parroted its poppycock, but lacked Hiss's guts for logically translating a criminal ideology into criminal action. Today every word against Hiss awakens unwanted, half-conscious memories. It awakens their long-suppressed, semi-treasonable, semi-idealistic day-dreams about Russia in that early era of Writers Congresses and Leagues against War and Fascism. Where they merely strip-teased with revolution for the thrill of feeling progressive and unbourgeois, Hiss is the intellectual who really meant business and eloped. Those passionate but unconsummated flirtations of the Thirties, once so dashing, are no longer fashionable memories after Korea. The Hiss case is the bad conscience of all America's political *demi-vierges*.

In future decades, Hiss may become an "epic figure," the mythic national symbol of the whole guilty 1930's. The guilt is "tragic," in the true sense of the word, by being intermingled with the noble social idealism of the 1930's, which inspired the heroes of the anti-fascist resistance movements and some parts of the New Deal. Here are the five Freudian slips, already standardized reflexes and all around you, by which the bad consciences of the Thirties reveal themselves in casual conversation in the Fifties:

(1) belittling the importance or influence[1] of Hiss's high posts;

(2) finding excuses or doubts on his behalf which the excusers would not raise in the parallel cases of a Fritz Kuhn or a Vidkung Quisling;

(3) alleging that the verdict "reflects war hysteria, not objective evidence," though not alleging the same about the verdict against Laval;

(4) being the life of the party by spreading scandalous rumors against Mr. Chambers and his act of public service and moral atonement;

---

[1] From the Congressional hearings: "MR. MUNDT: Did you draft or participate in the drafting of parts of the Yalta Agreement? MR. HISS: I think it is accurate and not an immodest statement to say that I did to some extent, yes." Nor is this merely his own immodest estimate. The published memoirs of Secretary of State Stettinius stress Hiss's "help" in preparing the Yalta agenda. Comment becomes superfluous when to this you add Hiss's job as none other than "special assistant to the director of the Office of Far Eastern Affairs." If so much influence in high places could be potentially exerted by merely one bourgeois-baiting "bourgeois intellectual" in his alienation, then what damage is being done at this very moment by perhaps many others not yet detected?

(5) worst of all, simply refusing to *see* the broader implications of the case, like a shell-shock victim suffering from hysterical blindness. Simply refusing to see that the exaggerated myth of the intellectual as "the traitor within the gate" is reborn, despite the obvious ethical decency of most intellectuals, every time some new duped liberal sallies forth to impede America's self-defense against some new communist treason, as if such self-defense were normally (rather than exceptionally) a "witch-hunt against civil liberties."

The mistake of the 1930's: to justify any means, or any associations, by your "worthy" end. Most liberals are guilty of looking with indulgence during the Thirties on Popular-Fronting under Stalinist murderers ("justified" by anti-fascism). Most reactionaries are guilty of looking with indulgence during the Thirties on appeasement of Nazi murderers ("justified" by anti-communism). The last point requires particular emphasis because the lunatic-fringe (or thought-controlling) would-be "anti-communist" indicts solely the communists, forgetting that the eternal enemy is neither communism alone nor nazism alone but communazism, eternally protean.

Past guilt need not hang like an albatross around the present; nobody should be persecuted for honest past mistakes. But the only way to slough off past mistakes is to admit them. The only way to regain your inner freedom from guilt is to recognize it, both left and right. Take a good long look, without downcast or shifty eyes: Hiss's lies, thefts, and espionage for the murderer Stalin; Pound's pro-Nazi, Jew-baiting broadcasts for the murderer Mussolini.

To face the guilt of Hiss and Pound, to accept it in a "change of heart," is the magic by which Babbitt Junior can exorcise his own Babbittry. It is the only magic to make him the independent mind he sincerely wants to be. To rejuvenate his progressivism and make it valid and honest.

The lesson of Pound and Hiss is not, as literary and political reactionaries may claim: "Stop being avant-garde, stop being liberal." The lesson is: "Don't stop, but — watch your step!" The lesson is: "Become genuine apostles of literary and political progress by watching the moral correlative of progress more sensitively in the future."

Pound and Hiss do not invalidate experimental avant-garde. They do not invalidate liberalism. They do not even invalidate honest revolutionary radicalism. What they do invalidate — no more, no less than that — is a hermetic, narcissistic progressivism, so self-absorbed in artistic or political progress that it neglects the inexorable moral framework into which all progress must fit.

Some day Babbitt Junior may stand in front of his mirror, saying of Pound in bedlam and Hiss in prison, "There but for the grace of God go I. For the sake of their misapplied courage and their misapplied idealism, may God have mercy on two miserable sinners! And likewise on the luckier and less courageous human frailty of all the rest of us, who happen not to end in bedlam or in prison."

When that day comes, the spell will snap; the invisible albatross will fall from his neck; he will cease to be Babbitt, whether Junior or Senior. Instead, the matured human being will step from the cocoon of self-deception. It is the step from affectation to ethics; from clever ingenuity to classic pattern; from bohemian artiness to inspired art, "purifying the diction of the tribe"; from an accidental alienation that is resentful and sterile to a necessary alienation that is overcompensating and fruitful. It is the step from "bloody-minded professors" to love: love of the faintest flicker of human dignity wheresoever it may be glimpsed (love, therefore, even of philistia; perhaps — with a tender kind of irony — especially of philistia). This step over a razor-thin, almost imperceptible threshold is, in short, the step from the shame of lumpen-intellectualism into the glory of intelligence. Upon that single step depends nothing less than the soul of the uprooted intellectuals of all the West.

Index

Proper names only, no "ism" words: they would be *passim*. Thus, Communist Party or Conservative Party but not Communism or Conservatism are included. For general subjects and topics other than proper names, see table of contents in front of book — *P.V.*

Soviet Union, 13, 24, 25, 31, 41, 51, 63, 69, 90, 91, 93, 94, 96-99, 101-105, 107, 109, 110, 117-120, 123, 125, 127, 130, 131, 133, 134, 137, 139, 140, 142-144, 146-156, 158, 162-165, 168, 169n, 170-174, 176, 179-181, 195, 203, 205, 207, 209, 210, 212, 213, 216, 229, 231, 232, 233, 235, 239, 242, 257, 261, 269, 274, 284, 285, 288n, 289, 298, 307. *See also* Bolsheviks; Russia

Spain, 25, 90, 168, 179, 217, 230; Loyalist, 31, 40, 94, 178

Spanish: Civil War, 179; Republic, 179

Sparta, 199

Spectator Papers, 66

Spellman, Francis Cardinal, 49, 229

Spengler, Oswald, 187

Spinoza, Baruch, 75

Stalin, Joseph, 3, 8, 26, 27, 49, 51, 52, 78, 82, 93-95, 97, 98, 101, 103, 105, 106, 111, 112, 118, 121, 124, 125, 128, 129, 130, 132, 137, 139, 140, 141, 147, 162, 163, 164, 167, 171, 179, 186, 207, 209, 212, 216, 219, 229, 262, 272, 284, 292, 298, 302, 303, 308; *Foundations of Leninism,* 281n; *Marxism,* 161

Stalingrad, 90, 97

State Department, 25, 108, 119, 271

Steele, A. T., 235n

Steffens, Lincoln, 111

Steinberg, Julien, 120n

Stendhal, 112, 115, 294

Stettinius, Edward, 119, 207

Stevenson, Adlai E., 10, 253, 260, 277, 278, 279

St. Exupéry, Antoine, 190

Stockholm "peace" pledges, 52, 130, 140, 154

Stoics, 81

Streicher, Julius, 54

Strout, Richard, 169n, 171, 172

Sudan, 235

Sudetenland, 171

Suez Canal, 238-240

Sumner, W. G., 224, 269

Supreme Court, U. S., 218, 219

Sweden, 89

Swift, Jonathan, 55, 62n

Swinburne, Charles, 22

Syria, 212

Taegliche Rundschau (Berlin), 96

Taft, Robert A., 18, 105, 109, 154, 251-254, 258, 278, 279

Talleyrand, Charles Maurice de, 55, 222

Tammany Hall, 217

Tannu Tuva, 155

Tartar Crimean Republic, 140

Tashkent, 99

Temple, Shirley, 26

Tennyson, Alfred, Baron, 114

Teutoburg Forest, 77

Thirty Years' War, 89, 93; of communazism, 91-105, 153, 154

Thoreau, Henry David, 8, 191, 201, 275

Thucydides, 200

Thurber, James, 290-292; *The Male Animal,* 60, 61

Thyssen, Fritz, 266

Tibet, 25

Tito, Josip Broz, 130

Tocqueville, Alexis de, 216

Toklas, Alice B., 21

Tolstoi, Leo, 9

Tory Party, 248. *See also* Conservative Party

Toynbee, Arnold, 48n

Treasury, Department of, 271

Treblinka, 99

Trotsky, Leon, 94, 98, 120, 141n, 163, 229

Truman, Harry S., 108, 168, 179, 224n, 228, 251, 253, 278

Truman Doctrine, 108, 124

Tryon Park, 67

Tunisia, 233, 234

Turkey, 213

Turner, Frederick Jackson, 219, 220

Twentieth Century, The, 94n

Ukraine, 94, 95, 140

United Nations, 130, 164, 171, 230, 234; Economic and Social Council, 131

Utley, Freda, 143n

Uzbekistan, 141, 146, 234